An Understanding

of Jane Austen's Novels

John Odmark

An Understanding
of Jane Austen's Novels

Character, Value and
Ironic Perspective

BASIL BLACKWELL · OXFORD

© The estate of John Odmark 1981

First published in 1981 by
Basil Blackwell Publisher
108 Cowley Road
Oxford OX4 1JF
England

British Library Cataloguing in Publication Data

Odmark, John
  An understanding of Jane Austen's novels.
  1. Austen, Jane—Criticism and interpretation
  I. Title
  823′.9   PR4037
  ISBN 0-631-12494-2

Endpapers: *Duck Shooting*, 1790
by G. Morland, reproduced by
permission of the Cooper-Bridgeman Library.

Filmset in Monophoto Plantin by
Latimer Trend & Company Ltd, Plymouth
Printed in Great Britain by Ebenezer Baylis & Son Ltd.,
The Trinity Press, Worcester, and London
Bound by Kemp Hall Bindery, Oxford.

Contents

Preface

This book has grown considerably in purpose and scope since its conception. Motivated in part by Karl Kroeber's *Styles in Fictional Structure*, I originally intended an analysis of Jane Austen's style. It gradually became apparent, however, that this approach would lead to an emphasis on particular features of the texts at the expense of other features which are at least as important for an understanding of Jane Austen's artistic development and achievement.

The main problem is implicit in the concept of style itself. As is well known, this concept has proved notoriously difficult to define, so that it is hardly surprising to discover wide divergencies in its usage among critics of Jane Austen. Although nearly everyone who has written on Jane Austen 'admires' her 'style', it would be very wide of the mark to suggest that they are all talking about the same thing. Since not all of these critics state how 'style' is to be understood, it is rather difficult to determine what the different usages have in common. Presumably, most of them would agree that what they admire is Jane Austen's handling of language, which has been variously interpreted as referring to the selection and combination of lexical items ('proper words in proper places'), the technical means employed to structure the narrative, the expression of the author's personality, and so on.

Oversimplifying to make a point, and ignoring—for the moment—the valuable research which has been done, definitions of style such as these are of limited use to the critic. They point out directions an analysis might follow, but they fail to provide the critic with the theoretical apparatus needed to get beyond his own subjective interpretation. Put somewhat less abstractly, these definitions fail to suggest criteria for differentiating stylistic phenomena from other textual phenomena, which raises the question as to how much gain there is in introducing the concept of style into an analysis at all. If with this concept we are simply assuming that literature is mediated through language and that the object of a stylistic analysis is the verbal work of art in its totality, then we might just as well dispense with the concept.

The second problem is closely related to the first. Even the most cursory review of the research on Jane Austen's fiction reveals that many critics interested in her style tend to treat the novels in isolation and to ignore the contexts in which they were created and in which they are read. Beginning in the 1960s—most notably in the work of Wayne C. Booth, David Lodge and A. Walton Litz—there has been a gradual shift away from this immanent approach to Jane Austen's novels; however, it has only been in the last decade that research in literary theory—in particular, in the aesthetics of reception— has underlined the importance of going beyond the recognition of the literary work of art as an entity with its own mode of being and its own set of rules. Such a view has to be extended to take into account the fact that the literary text is always directed at a reader. Stylistic phenomena cannot be dealt with adequately without regard to their function in the act of communication. Consequently, an analysis of style or language use has to be integrated into an examination of the dynamic process of communication defined by the coordinates: author–text–reader.

Jane Austen is not our contemporary. There is a great distance separating the world in which her characters act out their parts and our own experience of the modern world; nevertheless, the continuing appeal of her novels could hardly be explained as a purely historical interest in the life of a country village during the Regency period. I hope that the notes and references sufficiently indicate my awareness of the important research in language and novel theory relevant to the present study, as well as my indebtedness to the research on Jane Austen, which has contributed significantly to our knowledge of the author and her art of fiction. This study departs most markedly from previous work in its theoretical orientation. The nature of Jane Austen's artistic achievement —and hence the reasons for her continuing popularity— becomes most apparent if we examine the ways in which her novels bridge the distance between the author and her readers; therefore, this study is based on the view of literature as communication. It investigates the means employed by the author to guide the reader in his perceptions of character and conduct.

This study was originally submitted as a dissertation at the University of Regensburg, and I would like to take this opportunity to express my very special gratitude to Professors Karl-Heinz Göller and Herbert E. Brekle without whose continuing assistance, advice and encouragement this study might still fall into the category of 'work-in-progress'. I would also like to acknowledge the numerous useful comments, suggestions and criticisms provided by my colleagues and students at the Universities of Regensburg and Hamburg. This book is dedicated to my grandfather Luther Owen, who has always thought I should have become a lawyer, and to my wife Helga, who suspects I would have had more time if I had.

Hamburg   *November 1980*

The publishers would like to record their gratitude to Dr Neal R. Norrick for helping to see this book through the final stages of production, following the tragic death of the author at the end of 1980.

Introduction

Virginia Woolf once wrote that of all great writers Jane Austen 'is the most difficult to catch in the act of greatness'.[1] In the twentieth century Jane Austen's 'greatness' has seldom been challenged, though, as Virginia Woolf's comment anticipates, there has been considerable disagreement as to the precise nature of Jane Austen's artistic achievement. F. R. Leavis avoids the problem by ranking Jane Austen as one of the four great English novelists and then going on to discuss the other three.[2] Henry James acknowledges Jane Austen's major significance, but, at the same time, he suggests that she is frequently not fully aware of how she achieves it:

The key to Jane Austen's fortune with posterity has been in part the extraordinary grace of her facility, in fact of her un-consciousness: as if, at the most, for difficulty, for embarrassment, she sometimes, over her work basket, her tapestry flowers, in the spare, cool drawing-room of other days, fell a-musing, lapsed too metaphorically, as one may say, into wool gathering, and her dropped stitches, of these pardonable, of these precious moments, were afterwards picked up as little touches of human truth, little glimpses of steady vision, little master-strokes of imagination.[3]

A large body of criticism has accumulated which implicitly—and sometimes explicitly—opposes this view of Jane Austen as the unconscious artist.[4] Her novels have been repeatedly subjected to close textual analysis and have been considered in their literary, sociological, historical and ideological con-texts as well.[5] The present study does not derive from any one of the recent trends in Jane Austen scholarship, but it is related to two or three of them. It involves an examination of the novels in their historical context with an emphasis on the moral assumptions underlying the author's fictional world. This book aims to increase our understanding of Jane Austen's characters and their values by analysing, on the one hand, the relationship between the author and her texts and, on the other, the relationship between the novels and the reader. The investigation is carried out within the conceptual frame of a theory of reception or, if it is broadly defined, a theory of point of view.[6]

The theory of reception concerns the act of reading, more specifically, the relations among the component factors of the reading process: the *author*, the *text* and the *reader*. These three terms require some clarification. The term *author* has three interrelated meanings important to the present study. The word may denote the historical figure who wrote the text, the function or role the writer creates for himself in the text, or the set of values and assumptions which are manifest in the text and which reflect the writer's attitude towards his fictional world. The term *reader* is similarly complex. It may designate a composite or ideal reader, that is, a theoretical construct to account for the range of possible responses to the text;[7] it may refer to the audience envisaged by the writer—the 'implied reader';[8] or it may denote the inter-action with the text of any individual. In what follows the context should make clear in which sense *author* or *reader* is being used. The term *text* is less problematical; for, unlike the terms *author* and *reader*, whether *text* is defined as a product of the creative process or as an object which takes on an aesthetic function in the act of reading, the reference of the term is the same.[9] These two definitions take into account the fact that the text has both a communicative and an autonomous character. It is an entity with its own mode of being, but, at the same time, it is a material artefact which has the potential of becoming an aesthetic object.[10] In other words, there are two alternative perspectives from which the text may be viewed.[11]

Every text is directed at a reader. It mediates between the author and the reader as an aesthetic object. The relation between the author and the reader is asymmetrical, for to a large extent the author determines the reader's relation to the text. But of course the reverse is not the case. The reader may interpret the author's relation to the text, but he does not determine it. The reader comes to know the author— the historical figure—only indirectly through the text, that is, through the image the author consciously projects of himself in the text and through additional objective information present in the text which is not a component of the author's effort at self-expression. In other words, the author actually known to the reader is the *author* in the second and third senses given above. It is on the basis of this knowledge that the reader forms an opinion of the historical author and arrives at a perception of the author's attitude towards his fictional world. As will be shown below, a failure to differentiate between the historical figure Jane Austen and the author as she is known to us through her texts has led to some highly questionable interpretations of her work. The author makes certain assumptions about the reader which influence his choice of subject matter and his means of presenting it. The interpretation given the text by a particular reader may depart, however, in some important respects from what the author has anticipated or, in some instances, could have anticipated. Consequently, a text delimits but it does not determine interpretation.[12] It always contains open spaces or places of indeterminacy, which the reader fills out in the light of his own experience of the world and his knowledge of literary convention, that is, the reader interprets the text in terms of his own linguistic, literary and cultural codes. The codes of the reader and the author must of course coincide to some extent, otherwise no communication would take place; but a complete knowledge of the author's codes may be acquired only through a reading of the entire text.[13] Thus, the reader becomes actively involved in the reconstitution of these codes and the processes of meaning-formation represented by the text. Virginia Woolf makes this point in reference to Jane Austen:

Jane Austen is thus a mistress of much deeper emotion than appears on the surface. She stimulates us to supply what is not there. What she offers is, apparently, a trifle, yet is composed of something that expands in the reader's mind and endows with the most enduring form of life scenes which are outwardly trivial. Always the stress is laid upon character. . . . The turns and twists of the dialogue keep us on the tenterhooks of suspense. Our attention is half upon the present moment, half upon the future. . . . Here, indeed, in this unfinished and in the main inferior story, are all the elements of Jane Austen's greatness.[14]

Jane Austen achieves an illusion of concreteness, while, at the same time, leaving much up to the reader's imagination. As with all authors, Jane Austen's choice of subject matter and her means of organizing her material determine the range of possible interpretations, that is, they determine the 'structure conditioning the reception of the work'.[15] In other words, the author's choices constitute the text's potential and fix the relations between the author, the text, and the reader. This book examines these choices within the frame of a theory of point of view.

Various bases for a definition of *point of view* have been proposed: 'the relation in which the narrator stands to his story',[16] 'the relation of the author to his work'[17] the reader's perspective,[18] or the author's 'only means . . . of discovering, exploring, developing his subject'[19]—to cite just some of the best known approaches to *point of view*. Apart from a lack of specificity, these approaches have little in common.[20] The first of these suggests such categories as 'first-person narrator', 'omniscient narrator', etc. The second fails to indicate where we are supposed to discover the 'author's relation'—in the role of the narrator, or in the technical means of presentation, or somewhere else. The third approach, which comes from Henry James, anticipates what is now termed the 'implied reader'.[21] And the final one focuses attention on the formal properties of the text. All four of these approaches appear to touch on important aspects of *point of view* without, however, offering a satisfactory basis for analysis. A more satisfactory approach to *point of view* has been developed by Robert Weimann. He differentiates between what he terms 'the real point of view' and 'the technical point of view'.[22]

The *real point of view* may be defined as the author's norms and values as well as his assumptions about his reading public as these norms, values and assumptions are manifest in the text; in other words, it is the author's attitude towards or opinion about his subject matter. No narrative is neutral or objective in the sense that it is free of such attitudes.[23] There is always a 'teller' in the tale even if his presence is not made explicit.[24] This implied author may appear to coalesce with the narrator if there is a dramatized narrator in the text;[25] however, they are not the same. The former refers to the historical, psychological, sociological and linguistic context in which the text is created, and the latter concerns the angle of vision from which the story is related. The *technical point of view* denotes the formal means used by the author to structure the reader's experience. These means include the relation in which the narrator stands to the story; the arrangement and sequence of events, that is, the plot; and the strategies of presentation used in individual scenes and inside views. These means all represent commitments on the part of the author and reflect his apprehension, comprehension and interpretation of his imaginative world. Moreover, the language in which the text is written already necessitates a certain degree of commitment.[26] It serves as a complex link between the author's world and the fictional world he creates. The author is situated by the text, that is, the language as well as the formal means employed place the author in relation to his imaginative world. In other words, the *real* and the *technical points of view* are interrelated. The former is dependent on the context of the text and the latter on the formal relations within the text itself. The *real point of view* is manifest in part in the *technical point of view*, but it is also manifest in the language and in the text considered as a whole.

This study of the *real* and the *technical points of view* in Jane Austen's fiction is divided into five chapters. The first two chapters focus on some significant aspects of the *technical point of view*, examining in detail the formal organization of the reader's experience. Chapter I investigates how the reader is situated in relation to the patterns of irony and the plot structures. Chapter II analyses the strategies of presentation in individual scenes and in inside views of the heroines' mental life. In the next two chapters, attention is turned to an analysis of the *real point of view*. Chapter III deals with the author's handling of the conclusion to each of the novels for the light it throws on Jane Austen's attitude towards her subject matter. Chapter IV examines three groups of words that signify the system of norms and values according to which character and behaviour are delineated, discriminated and judged. Finally, Chapter V considers in what respects the interrelations of the *real* and the *technical points of view* constitute a challenge to the reader.

I

Irony and the Shaping of the Novel

This chapter is a consideration of the relationship between the text and the reader—more specifically, an examination of the plot structures as they relate to the role of the reader and the patterns of irony in each of the novels. The basis of Jane Austen's irony is usually shown to be the conflicting systems of norms and values in the world portrayed, the contrast between the author's values and those in the little country village of her setting, or a combination of these possibilities.[1] D. W. Harding and Marvin Mudrick locate the conflict in the author herself, pointing out that the objects of her irony are the same values she intends to uphold.[2] As a rule *irony* in Jane Austen's fiction has been defined primarily in terms of content. What I want to draw attention to is the fact that *irony* is above all a structuring principle that determines the shape of all the novels.[3] Wayne C. Booth, among others, has in part anticipated this position in his study of *Emma*, in which he suggests that the source of Jane Austen's irony is her manipulation of the point of view.[4] Although Booth does not explicitly distinguish between the *real* and *technical points of view*, he deals primarily with the latter.[5] However, it is arguable that such a distinction is necessary in order to determine the place and function of irony in the novels.

In the present and following chapters a distinction is made between what I term 'local' irony and 'structural' irony. The first refers to those ironies readily perceived by the reader from his perspective of superior knowledge. Usually, these isolated ironies are associated with the attempts on the part of various characters to influence one another, with their successes and failures, and with their awareness or lack of awareness of these successes and failures. Such ironies are fixed and even in retrospect unchanging. By contrast, those ironies that are central to the plot—the 'structural ironies'—are dependent on the reader's changing perceptions of character and situation. The limits of change occur at that point in the narrative where the reader's knowledge finally approaches that of the omniscient narrator. The present chapter is primarily concerned with the structural ironies in Jane Austen's novels; in the next chapter the focus shifts to an analysis of the local ironies.

Although there is some uncertainty concerning the chronology of Jane Austen's first three novels, *Northanger Abbey* seems to be an essentially early work.[6] It stands somewhat apart from the other novels in terms of conception and execution. The subject matter has an element of parody more characteristic of the *Juvenilia* than the later novels. Similarly, the problems in the novel's plot structure suggest an early date. In none of the other novels does Jane Austen have such difficulties in working out the action of her story. The reader's role appears to be redefined halfway through the narrative. His position relative to that of narrator as well as to the characters in the novel unexpectedly changes, and these unexpected shifts undermine the unity of the work as a whole. The author seems not to have finished her apprenticeship; nevertheless, *Northanger Abbey* is a good place to begin an analysis of Jane Austen's methods, for already in this novel—although she is working with rather broad strokes and strong contrasts—she employs narrative techniques that anticipate her mature style.

In *Northanger Abbey* the fundamental problem in the novel's plot structure initially appears not to be a problem at all, for the reader's role is clearly defined. He follows the events mainly through Catherine's 'eyes and ears and head and heart', because she is present in all of the scenes;[7] however, there is little of the psychological closeness characteristic of the later novels. In part this is due to the heroine's lack of experience and her naiveté, which necessitate the additional perspective afforded by implicit and explicit commentary. In part it is due to the burlesque tone of the beginning, which makes it impossible to take the heroine very seriously. The ironic distance established between the heroine and the reader in the opening paragraphs is maintained up to the departure for Northanger Abbey.

> No one who had ever seen Catherine Morland in her infancy, would have supposed her born to be a heroine. Her situation in life, the character of her father and mother, her own person and disposition, were all equally against her. Her father was a clergyman, without being neglected, or poor, and a very respectable man, though his name was Richard—and he had never been handsome. He had a considerable independence, besides two good livings—and he was not in the least addicted to locking up his daughters. Her mother was a woman of useful plain sense, with a good temper, and, what is more remarkable, with a good constitution. She had three sons before Catherine was born; and instead of dying in bringing the latter into the world, as any body might expect, she still lived on—lived to have six children more—to see them growing up around her, and to enjoy excellent health herself. A family of ten children will always be called a fine family, where there are heads and arms and legs enough for the number; but the Morlands had little other right to the word, for they were in general very plain, and Catherine, for many years of her life, as plain as any. She had a thin awkward figure, a sallow skin without colour, dark lank hair, and strong features;—so much for her person;—and not less unpropitious for heroism seemed her mind. (*NA* 37)[8]

This opening establishes the ideal reader's role as one of superiority: he is superior both to those readers who come to a novel with the conventional expectations which are being mocked and to those who would take the story of Catherine's initiation into the world too seriously. He shares with the narrator an awareness that this is a burlesque. Throughout most of Volume I the reader is not given much cause to reconsider his attitude towards Catherine or the novel's main themes. The broad parody of the opening pages wanes, but the object of Jane Austen's satire remains the same, namely, the burlesque of the conventions of Sentimental and Gothic fiction.[9] Catherine is less interesting as

an individual than as a participant in conversations about
fiction and as a naïve observer of the behaviour of others.
Her concerns are never serious; they are limited to such
matters as whether or not she has offended Henry Tilney
and his sister or her disappointment in not being able to
visit Blaise Castle. On the basis of the opening chapters the
reader forms the impression that Catherine has a role to
play in a burlesque. She is a parody of such stock figures as
the heroine of Charlotte Smith's *Emmeline, The Orphan of
the Castle* (1788).[10] Emmeline manages to develop every
possible talent such as a correct literary taste, a mastery of the
harp, and a facility in drawing with little or no assistance
from anyone. Catherine is her opposite, for she could never
'learn or understand anything before she was taught, and
sometimes not even then, for she was often inattentive, and
occasionally stupid' (*NA* 37).

The problem in the novel's construction becomes most
apparent when the action switches to Northanger Abbey.
The antiheroine becomes a kind of female Quixote. In the
Bath chapters it is the narrator who points out the disparities
between literature and life; at Northanger Abbey it is Catherine herself who illustrates these disparities 'by trying to find
Gothic romance in the Midlands.'[11] This shift in the focus of
the narrative results in changes in the method of presentation.
Catherine's mental life becomes the center of the reader's
attention. Her thoughts, her feelings, and her reactions take
on an importance that they have not had in the earlier chapters. The reader has not been properly prepared for this
departure from the earlier angle of vision. The dialogues in
the first volume serve to enlighten the reader, but there is
little evidence that Catherine also profits from them. By contrast, in the second volume Catherine as well as the reader
learns from the comparatively small number of conversations
that are included in the narrative. Catherine's reactions to
these conversations and to her situation in general are recorded in inside views which are much more detailed than
previous descriptions of her thoughts and feelings. From
Volume I to Volume II the general emphasis changes from
dramatic scene to narration. The distance between the reader

and the heroine is reduced. In a manner similar to the method used in *Emma*, much of the second part of the story is related more or less from the heroine's point of view. This change in the method of presentation brings the novel's main themes into conflict with one another. On the one hand the inside views of Catherine's mental life while she is pursuing her foolish fantasies parody the experiences of such heroines as Mrs Radcliffe's Adeline of *Romance of the Forest* (1792);[12] however, the object of Jane Austen's satire is no longer primarily the excesses of such fiction but Catherine herself. In other words, Catherine's foolishness at the Abbey is a continuation of the parody of Volume I, though in a different key. On the other hand, the detailed analyses of Catherine's thoughts in the second part lead the reader to conclude that the novel is also about Catherine's education. The problem inherent in this change in the method of presentation is evident in the following passage, which records the final turn of events in Catherine's adventures at the Abbey.

Catherine was too wretched to be fearful. The journey in itself had no terrors for her; and she began it without either dreading its length, or feeling its solitariness. Leaning back in one corner of the carriage, in a violent burst of tears, she was conveyed some miles beyond the walls of the Abbey before she raised her head; and the highest point of ground within the park was almost closed from her view before she was capable of turning her eyes towards it. Unfortunately, the road she now travelled was the same which only ten days ago she had so happily passed along in going to and from Woodston; and, for fourteen miles, every bitter feeling was rendered more severe by the review of objects on which she had first looked under impressions so different. Every mile, as it brought her nearer Woodston, added to her sufferings, and within the distance of five, she passed the turning which led to it, and thought of Henry so near, yet so unconscious, her grief and agitation were excessive. (*NA* 228)

Catherine's mistreatment and her grief seem out of place. Her concerns up to this time have been on an entirely different plane. The passage seems to be neither a continuation of the exposure of Catherine's foolishness, nor a return to a parody of the Sentimental novel, though such phrases as 'a violent burst of tears' and 'her grief and agitation were excessive' might be consistent with either of these objectives. Considered as a whole, however, the passage is problematical. It has been argued that General Tilney's treatment is the final ironic turn in the course of the action.[13] The real world becomes at least as inexplicable and frightening as the fictional. If this interpretation is accepted, then *Northanger Abbey* may be viewed not only as a story on the pattern of Fanny Burney's *Evelina* (1778) of a young girl's initiation into the world, but also as a novel that involves the reader's education as well.[14] Such an interpretation, however, still does not eliminate the weaknesses in the structure of the novel as a whole. The shifts in the point of view including the change of emphasis from dramatic scene to narrative are difficult to justify in terms of the novel's main themes. These shifts are not governed by a clearly defined overall conception. The local ironies are achieved at the expense of unity.

With *Sense and Sensibility* Jane Austen moves away from burlesque to a serious treatment of moral and social themes. Such themes are not absent from *Northanger Abbey*, but they are not central to the development of the plot. *Sense and Sensibility* is quite different and more ambitious. It is a contrast novel, didactic in intent. As the title suggests, two alternatives to similar situations are presented. One of them is shown to be prudent and correct, the other a violation of what is socially and morally acceptable, and, in addition, inherently dangerous to the well-being of the individual who chooses it. In some respects Jane Austen's technique represents an advance over *Northanger Abbey*. There are no awkward shifts in the point of view, and some of her scenes are developed in a more complex and subtle manner. Nevertheless, *Sense and Sensibility* has been generally acknowledged to be the least satisfactory of all the novels.[15] Probably, the weaknesses are due in part to the novel's origin as a novel in letters, and in part to the author's commitment to relating two parallel stories. This commitment leads to a lack of economy in the narration. Moreover, it encourages a schematic presentation of character. There is a tendency for characters to be categorized according to an absolute set of moral values, and to act predictably thereafter. Finally, much of the story is told from Elinor's point of view. This angle of vision reduces the possibilities for irony, since Elinor's views are essentially the same as the narrator's.

It would be an oversimplification to suggest that Elinor embodies *sense* and Marianne *sensibility,* for Marianne is also capable of rational judgement just as her sister is capable of responding emotionally;[16] nevertheless, throughout most of the novel the sisters are diametrically opposed to one another—Marianne allowing her feelings to govern her behaviour, and Elinor refusing to give in to such impulses.[17] The reader is never left in any doubt as to how he should judge their behaviour. They are introduced as follows:

Elinor, this eldest daughter whose advice was so effectual, possessed a strength of understanding and coolness of judgment, which qualified her, though only nineteen, to be the counsellor of her mother, and enabled her frequently to counteract, to the advantage of them all, that eagerness of mind in Mrs Dashwood which must generally have led to imprudence. She had an excellent heart;—her disposition was affectionate, and her feelings were strong; but she knew how to govern them: it was a knowledge which her mother had yet to learn, and which one of her sisters had resolved never to be taught.

Marianne's abilities were, in many respects, quite equal to Elinor's. She was sensible and clever; but eager in every thing; her sorrows, her joys, could have no moderation. She was generous, amiable, interesting: she was every thing but prudent. The resemblance between her and her mother was strikingly great. (*SS* 42)[18]

This introductory description places the sisters for the reader, and in the course of the narrative he is never given any reason to doubt the objective validity of these characterizations. The introduction of all the characters who are not immediately given the opportunity to reveal themselves through their behaviour and conversation is similar.[19] The introduction of a new character is one of the few instances in which it is necessary for the narrator to intrude into the novel.

For the most part past events are related from Elinor's

point of view. There is little reason for the additional perspective of a reliable narrator, for Elinor does not allow her
emotions to distort her judgement of characters and situations. Her values are the narrator's. Her judgements and
actions are based on the assumption that the conventional
rules of propriety are identical with the external manifestation of true propriety. The organization of the plot and the
means employed to render character suggest that the author
shares Elinor's understanding of propriety and its implications. It is therefore hardly surprising that irony is seldom
directed at Elinor, and that it is only directed at her sister
before the effects of Marianne's foolish behaviour become
known. [20] Elinor is placed in an ironic light only on those
few occasions when the course of events takes a turn that she
is unaware of. Even in such instances, however, the irony
does not affect Elinor's image as an individual who is always
conscious of what conduct is proper under any given circumstances. Nevertheless, it would be an oversimplification to
suggest that, whenever alternatives are presented, Elinor's
choice is inevitably correct and Marianne's wrong. In the
long run, Elinor's alternatives prove to be the better means
for maintaining the social order and surviving within it;
but at times Marianne's choices seem more acceptable even
though they threaten the social order, for they are motivated
by deeply felt emotions, which should not at all costs be
suppressed completely.[21]

The conflicts in *Sense and Sensibility* do not exist in the
consciousness of one individual as they do, for example, in
Elizabeth Bennet or Emma Woodhouse. In part the conflicts
arise from the differences of opinion between the sisters,
and in part from external circumstances over which they
have little or no control. The secret agreement between
Lucy Steele and Edward Ferrars, for instance, appears
until the next to the last chapter an insurmountable obstacle
to Elinor's happiness. She knows her own feelings, but her
actions are governed by reason. When Colonel Brandon
asks her to inform Edward that he will be given a living,
Elinor assumes this will be very welcome news, for it will
finally make it possible for Edward and Lucy to marry.

Despite this knowledge or, more likely, because of it, Elinor sees it as her duty to carry out this task and accept what she assumes will be the consequences. Such behaviour leaves little room for irony. Elinor seems at times more like a principle than an individual. Her speeches tend to be long and didactic even at moments of stress, which suggests that they are remnants of letters dating from an earlier version of the novel.[22] Marianne is more clearly individualized, but her thoughts and feelings are viewed for the most part from Elinor's perspective, so that even in those situations where Marianne has a viable alternative to one of her sister's proposals, it is presented in an unfavourable light. The reader has no alternative to Elinor's clear-sighted and rational observations, though in retrospect he may feel that she was not always as clear-sighted as she assumes.[23] Because of the reader's closeness to Elinor's perspective, he is led to accept Marianne's decision to marry Colonel Brandon, although the Colonel embodies those social and moral values for which Marianne has had little use. The reader is informed at the beginning that Marianne has her portion of *sense* as well as *sensibility*, but her decision to marry Colonel Brandon remains unconvincing.[24] It is unconvincing because the reader has experienced so little of Marianne's mental life and has therefore little cause to think she has changed so fundamentally in her attitudes as to be willing to accept this boring, colourless alternative. Like the other contrived developments in the plot, it corresponds to the author's didactic intent and Elinor's sense of what is correct, but it seems inconsistent with Marianne's character.[25]

To summarize, Jane Austen's handling of point of view in *Sense and Sensibility* is once again problematical. The views of the narrator, Elinor and presumably the author coalesce to such an extent that it is difficult for the reader to find the basis for an opinion which differs from Elinor's. His knowledge is only incidentally and not consistently superior to Elinor's. Earlier I suggested that irony is the structuring principle of all Jane Austen's novels.[26] In respect to *Sense and Sensibility*, however, this observation must be qualified.[27] The overall conception of the novel is clearly defined; however, it is not based on an ironic view of Elinor or Marianne. It is based on Elinor's concept of proper moral and social behaviour, and presented from her point of view. As a result, the reader has little opportunity to weigh her opinions against those of others. The exigencies of the plot require a broader perspective. The development of the plot, and above all the revolution, seem forced.

Pride and Prejudice has always been Jane Austen's most widely-read novel, and popular notions of her style have tended to be based on it together with *Emma*. This tendency does not take into account the fact that *Pride and Prejudice* is in some respects atypical. It differs from *Northanger Abbey* and *Sense and Sensibility* in the increasing skill the author demonstrates in handling her narrative, and it lacks the psychological depth and moral seriousness of the novels that were to follow. It is more dramatic than any of the other novels. Jane Austen relies heavily on dialogue for characterization, making use of narration and description largely to place conversation in its setting and to summarize characters' thoughts and feelings. The reader is less an objective observer than an active participant required along with the heroine to reconsider much of what he has experienced. The narrator is employed not so much to clarify ambiguities as to reinforce them.

None of the characters is left untouched by the irony that infuses the novel. The plot structure is obviously ironic, particularly the development of the relationship between Elizabeth and Darcy, which holds center stage most of the time. When Darcy is ready to marry Elizabeth, she is not interested; when she thinks better of the idea, he appears to have lost interest. Mrs Bennet's ambition expressed in the opening scene to marry off her daughters well is ironically fulfilled as far as Elizabeth and Jane are concerned, although Mrs Bennet has hardly been a positive factor in this success.

In *Pride and Prejudice* irony is also used to delineate character. There are two related systems of values by which characters are judged: social conventions and moral virtues. There is, however, no Henry Tilney, Elinor Dashwood or Mr Knightley to serve as mentor or spokesman for the implied standard of conduct. Beginning with Chapter 10, much of the story is related from Elizabeth's perspective, but she is just as capable of erring in her judgement as are the other characters in the novel. But there is one kind of error she does not make. Unlike several of the other characters, Elizabeth never fails to distinguish between a social and an ethical mistake. This moral blindness on the part of some individuals is brought out, for example, in the scene where Elizabeth decides to visit her sister who has fallen ill. Most of those who take cognizance of Elizabeth's action are quite appalled by her disregard of what is considered proper social conduct; however, Elizabeth cannot be condemned on moral grounds for this breach of decorum—a point her critics completely overlook. And, to cite a second example, Wickham's forced marriage to Lydia may satisfy social convention and overjoy Mrs Bennet, but the moral issue is not so easily done away with.

In rendering character Jane Austen often uses manners to mirror morals; however, the correspondences are not always immediately as recognizable as the employment of this literary convention might lead us to expect. The portrayal of Mr Collins is an exception. His obsequiousness is unmistakable, and it reflects his total lack of a sense of what is correct and proper. But the portrayal of the other characters is less obvious. For example, Wickham deceives Elizabeth with his ability to assume good manners and an air of integrity. Here her error of judgement points up the fundamental problem with which she and the reader are confronted: the accurate evaluation of an individual's manners as a means of discovering his moral character.[28] In fact much of the irony in this novel derives from the mistaken judgements made in evaluating the significance of an individual's conduct; and more generally, it derives from the characters frequent inability to communicate effectively with one another. Nowhere is this more evident than in the scenes with Elizabeth and Darcy together and in the assessment each makes of the other's character.

The action in fact turns on the misunderstandings that exist not only for the characters involved but also in some instances for the reader as well. Although the reader retains an ironic perspective throughout the course of the narrative, the ironic implications of a number of scenes become clear to him only in retrospect. The main reason for this is the reader's closeness to Elizabeth. Most of the story is presented from her angle of vision. This encourages a tendency to accept her judgements uncritically, in much the same manner that Elinor's judgements are accepted, though as the plot unfolds it becomes evident that Elizabeth has been much less clear-sighted than she has supposed. A second reason is the fact that although much of the story is related from Elizabeth's perspective, her own mental life is kept at some distance from the reader. He gets to know her thoughts and feelings primarily through her conversations with others, in particular those with her sister Jane, rather than through extended inside views, as in *Emma*. There is even more distance between Darcy and the reader, since Darcy is seen for the most part from Elizabeth's point of view. This distancing enables the author to keep the reader in suspense about Elizabeth and Darcy's changing attitudes in regard to one another. For the first time, in *Pride and Prejudice*, Jane Austen succeeds in coordinating the local and the structural ironies: the ironies governing the organization of the plot derive from the ironies developed in the rendering of individual scenes and characters.

In his well-known essay on *Mansfield Park*, Lionel Trilling suggests that this novel may appear to be a contradiction of its predecessor,[29] and it does in fact represent a departure—if not a rejection—in terms of content and technique. *Mansfield Park* is the first novel conceived and completed in maturity; the three novels already discussed originated in Jane Austen's youth (1795–1799). The author does not reject the subject matter or the method of the earlier novels, but she gives her subject more dimension and develops further techniques of presentation that she has employed previously. For the first time the dialogues become important not only for what they reveal about character, but also for their content. A system of moral and social values is always at least implicit in Jane Austen's novels, but in none of the other novels is it given such prominence, not even in *Sense and Sensibility*, which in its moral seriousness resembles *Mansfield Park* most closely. The number of principals in the cast of characters is enlarged. Attention is directed not just to the heroine, but to a whole group of young people who are products of three different attitudes towards education.[30] Their contrasting systems of values form the basis of all the conflicts that arise. Halfway through the novel the focus shifts from the young people as a group to the heroine, Fanny Price.

Fanny is the outsider, the poor relation brought to Mansfield Park and taken into the Bertram Family. In this novel there is little room for the high comedy associated with *Pride and Prejudice*; however, the structure of *Mansfield Park* as a whole is ironic. Mansfield Park symbolizes traditional moral and social values, and the importance of upholding and preserving these values. The estate as a symbol of these values is as much the focus of interest as the novel's heroine. From the beginning, especially through the offices of Mrs Norris, it is made clear to Fanny that she is not the equal of the Bertram children, the legitimate heirs to the estate and all that it represents. The central irony of the plot is that Fanny is indeed not their equal, though not in the sense suggested by Mrs Norris, who never misses an opportunity of reminding Fanny of her inferiority. Fanny shows herself superior to all the other characters by consistently respecting and actively trying to uphold the traditional values symbolized by Mansfield Park. The plot requires a very different treatment from that of *Pride and Prejudice*. More than half of the story is given over to events in which Fanny functions primarily as an observer. This part is devoted to the delineation of the characters of several young people with whom Fanny is implicitly compared, and whose values often differ from hers. The principals include Mary and Henry Crawford and the Bertram children, Tom, Edmund, Julia and Maria. The Crawfords are the products of a sceptical modern philosophy associated in general with their circle of acquaintance in London and in particular with the marriage of their uncle and aunt. Their arrival in the neighbourhood of Mansfield Park brings with it a set of worldly, cynical and egotistical values that threaten those that have prevailed up to this time. The Bertram sisters are the most susceptible to this threat, for their fashionable education has had no firm moral basis. On the contrary, emphasis was laid on the development of accomplishments appropriate at the time to young ladies of their social position. As a result their values are superficial. They ignore or, more often, fail to see the moral implications of their behaviour. Their eldest brother Tom has long since proved himself morally bankrupt, and, therefore, is absent during that phase of the action when the others are still being put to the test. Even Edmund falls victim to temptation, though he is closer in his own thinking to Fanny's right-mindedness than any of the others.

Jane Austen successfully overcomes the difficulties inherent in portraying the characters of the six young people, their relations and systems of values, while at the same time maintaining the focus on the moral seriousness of the whole. Since Fanny is often on the periphery of events, much of the story is related from the narrator's point of view. Even in the second half of the novel, where Fanny is the center of interest, the narrator has a prominent role, for the heroine has no one with whom she can talk except Edmund, and she cannot talk with him about what concerns her most; therefore, the narrator is necessary in order to provide inside views and analyses of Fanny's thoughts and feelings as well as those of the other characters. In addition, Jane Austen makes use of two long episodes to reveal character and conflicting values. The first of these is an excursion to Sotherton, the estate of Mr Rushworth, to whom Maria becomes engaged before discovering a more attractive alternative in Henry Crawford. The second involves the production of a translation of Kotzebue's *Lovers' Vows*. In these two episodes Jane Austen expands the possibilities of the narrative techniques she has used previously by increasing the number of principals, extending the action over several chapters, and exploiting the possibilities of symbolic situation. Her handling of these episodes reflects how much she has developed since composing

Sense and Sensibility. The episodes are far too long to be considered in detail, but the passages discussed below illustrate her method.

A conflict between traditional and modern values is central to the novel's plot. Fanny and Miss Crawford are diametrically opposed in their views, but all the young people are affected by the conflict. The key issues are brought out already or at least foreshadowed in the episode at Sotherton. Mrs Rushworth has been showing the young people around the house of her son's estate when they finally come to a chapel. Fanny is disappointed and remarks to Edmund, 'This is not my idea of a chapel. There is nothing awful here, nothing melancholy, nothing grand' (*MP* 114).[31] Mrs Rushworth points out that the chapel ceased being used in the last generation, which moves Miss Crawford to observe, 'Every generation has its improvements' (*MP* 115). This observation touches on the crux of the problem: the idea of 'improvements' implies a challenge to the established order. Later Henry Crawford makes numerous suggestions for 'improving' the parsonage that Edmund will be taking over (Chapter 25). That 'improvements' are not something inherently positive is a point implicit in the scene which follows Miss Crawford's remark as well as in the plot of the novel as a whole:[32]

'It is a pity,' cried Fanny, 'that the custom should have been discontinued. It was a valuable part of former times. There is something in a chapel and chaplain so much in character with a great house, with one's ideas of what such a household should be! A whole family assembling regularly for the purpose of prayer, is fine!'

'Very fine indeed!' said Miss Crawford, laughing, 'It must do the heads of the family a great deal of good to force all the poor housemaids and footmen to leave business and pleasure, and say their prayers here twice a day, while they are inventing excuses themselves for staying away.'

'*That* is hardly Fanny's idea of a family assembling,' said Edmund. 'If the master and mistress do *not* attend themselves, there must be more harm than good in the custom.'

'At any rate, it is safer to leave people to their own devices on such subjects. Every body likes to go their own way—to choose their own time and manner of devotion. The obligation of attendance, the formality, the restraint, the length of time—altogether it is a formidable thing, and what nobody likes: and if the good people who used to kneel and gape in that gallery could have foreseen that the time would ever come when men and women might lie another ten minutes in bed, when they woke with a headache, without danger of reprobation, because chapel was missed, they would have jumped with joy and envy. Cannot you imagine with what unwilling feelings the former belles of the house of Rushworth did many a time repair to this chapel? The young Miss Eleanors and Mrs Bridgets—starched up into seeming piety, but with heads full of something very different—especially if the poor chaplain were not worth looking at—and, in those days, I fancy parsons were very inferior even to what they are now.'

For a few moments she was unanswered. Fanny coloured and looked at Edmund, but felt too angry for speech; and *he* needed a little recollection before he could say, 'your lively mind can hardly be serious even on serious subjects. You have given us an amusing sketch, and human nature cannot say it was not so. We must all feel *at times* the difficulty of fixing our thoughts as we could wish; but if you are supposing it a frequent thing, that is to say, a weakness grown into a habit from neglect, what could be expected from the private devotions of such persons? Do you think the minds which are suffered, which are indulged in wanderings in a chapel, would be more collected in a closet?'

'Yes, very likely. They would have two chances at least in their favour. There would be less to distract the attention from without, and it would not be tried so long.'

'The mind which does not struggle against itself under one circumstance, would find objects to distract it in the *other*, I believe; and the influence of the place and of example may often rouse better feelings than are begun with. The greater length of the service, however, I admit to be sometimes too hard a stretch upon the mind. One wishes it were not so—but I have not yet left Oxford long enough to forget what chapel prayers are.'

While this was passing, the rest of the party being scattered about the chapel, Julia called Mr Crawford's attention to her sister, by saying, 'Do look at Mr Rushworth and Maria, standing side by side, exactly as if the ceremony were going to be performed. Have they not completely the air of it?'

Mr Crawford smiled his acquiescence, and stepping forward to Maria, said, in a voice which she only could hear, 'I do not like to see Miss Bertram so near the altar.'

Starting, the lady instinctively moved a step or two, but recovering herself in a moment, affected to laugh, and asked him, in a tone not much louder, 'if he would give her away?'

'I am afraid I should do it very awkwardly,' was his reply, with a look of meaning.

Julia joining them at the moment, carried on the joke.

'Upon my word, it is really a pity that it should not take place directly, if we had but a proper license, for here we are altogether, and nothing in the world could be more snug and pleasant.' And she talked and laughed about it with so little caution, as to catch the comprehension of Mr Rushworth and his mother, and expose her sister to the whispered gallantries of her lover, while Mrs Rushworth spoke with proper smiles and dignity of its being a most happy event to her whenever it took place.

'If Edmund were but in orders!' cried Julia, and running to where he stood with Miss Crawford and Fanny; 'My dear Edmund, if you were but in orders now you might perform the ceremony directly. How unlucky that you are not yet ordained, Mr Rushworth and Maria are quite ready.'

Miss Crawford's countenance, as Julia spoke, might have amused a disinterested observer. She looked aghast under the new idea she was receiving. Fanny pitied her. 'How distressed she will be at what she has said just now,' passed across her mind. (*MP* 115–117)

The narrator need hardly intervene at all in the first part of this scene. Fanny's and Edmund's responses place Miss Crawford for the reader. The narrator first interrupts the dialogue after Miss Crawford's assertion that 'in those days I fancy parsons were very inferior even to what they are now.' She has misjudged her audience and damned herself in the process. Her own cynical views prevent her from successfully anticipating the responses of her listeners. That her observation borders on insult and even blasphemy in the view of her auditors becomes evident to Miss Crawford in the course of the ensuing scene. Edmund's and Fanny's immediate reaction is silence. They are no more prepared for Miss Crawford's remark than she is for their reaction. Edmund's

c

efforts to smooth things over cause Miss Crawford to realize that the conversation has taken an unfortunate turn, but she remains for the moment unsure as to why this is so. With the aid of his knowledge of what has been happening in the text up to this point and the additional perspective afforded by the narrator, the reader cannot miss the implications of what is being said nor the fact that the participants in this conversation are failing to communicate effectively with one another because of their fundamentally different views on religion. Before the issues raised by this conversation are clarified for all the parties concerned and the tensions generated by it alleviated, the author shifts attention to the others present in the chapel.

In this part of the scene the narrator is introduced more often, for there is no one else to share with the reader the ironies of the situation. Henry Crawford's predeliction for flirting leads him to encourage the engaged Maria's interest, though he has earlier devoted most of his attentions to Julia. Maria is flattered and responsive, and her sister understandably jealous. The narrator is being doubly ironic when he observes, 'Julia joining them at the moment, carried on the joke.' She carries on the one joke, but misses the second, which is a private one between her sister and Henry Crawford. Moreover, although she carries on the joke, her motives may be attributed to more than an innocent desire to be witty. In this exchange, as in the previous one, there are various degrees of understanding. Mrs Rushworth and her son catch only a little of what is going on, and as a consequence they are unable to ascribe any particular significance to it beyond the questionable propriety of the remarks which they hear; Julia can better appreciate the implications of the situation, but she is still an outsider. However, even Maria and Mr Crawford are too preoccupied with their mutual flirtation to recognize the full significance of what is happening. The reader has more perspective on the situation.

The young people are brought together in the chapel and given the opportunity to consider the results of one of the 'improvements' on the estate, that is, the fact that the chapel is no longer used. The interaction of the characters in this scene prefigures their subsequent behaviour. Moreover, it symbolically suggests the immoral tendencies that threaten the destruction of traditional values. The chapel has already fallen into disuse. Miss Crawford summarily dismisses the importance of the traditional function the chapel earlier had served in the lives of those connected with the estate. Julia, Maria and Mr Crawford show little regard for the sanctity of the chapel, and the reader gains the impression from their behaviour that the young people feel freed from the restraints normally imposed by tradition. Edmund sympathizes with Fanny's response to the situation, but in her opinions she is actually completely isolated from the others. This point is emphasized when the author once again shifts the focus near the end of this scene to include all of those present and to stress once more how far apart Fanny and Miss Crawford are in their thinking. Miss Crawford is taken by surprise at the news that Edmund is going into orders. Whereas Fanny pities her with a true Christian charity, Miss Crawford's own motives are more egotistical and materialistic. The scene as a whole suggests the threat that the Crawfords represent to a stable set of values rooted in tradition: Miss Crawford directly opposes a tradition which Fanny and Edmund have learned to value, and Mr Crawford symbolically and literally distracts Maria, who soon will stand before the altar. With the exception of Fanny, all of those present are culpable—even Edmund, whose motives in relieving the tension generated by Miss Crawford's remarks arise in part from a growing interest in her. No one, however, is more culpable and therefore more dangerous than the Crawfords themselves.

Mansfield Park is not a symbolic novel in the sense that Henry James's *Wings of the Dove* and *The Golden Bowl* are symbolic; however, as the preceding scene and the one to be considered below illustrate, Jane Austen creates symbolic situations in order to throw more light on the behaviour of her characters and to foreshadow how they are likely to behave in the future. This use of symbolism is new in her fiction. In *Pride and Prejudice* the author employs the thesis that manners mirror moral character, and the reader learns that one is usually an index of the other. In *Mansfield Park* Jane Austen's view of human nature is more complex, and symbolism is one of the means employed to reveal this complexity. Some minutes after the scene in the chapel, the setting of the action at Sotherton has changed, and Fanny is sitting outside alone when Maria in the company of Henry Crawford and her fiancé approach. Maria and Mr Crawford soon contrive to be rid of Mr Rushworth by sending him back to fetch a key, so that they can all pass through the gate. This scene is symbolic in much the same manner as the last. Maria wants to be completely unrestricted in her actions; she does not want any gates standing in her way. When Mr Rushworth departs to get the key, the symbolic gate is opened, and Fanny is an unwilling witness to what follows.

'Naturally, I believe, I am as lively as Julia, but I have more to think of now.'

'You have undoubtedly—and there are situations in which very high spirits would denote insensibility. Your prospects, however, are too fair to justify want of spirits. You have a very smiling scene before you.'

'Do you mean literally or figuratively? Literally I conclude. Yes, certainly, the sun shines and the park looks cheerful. But unluckily that iron gate, that ha-ha, give me a feeling of restraint and hardship. I cannot get out, as the starling said.' As she spoke, and it was with expression, she walked to the gate; he followed her. 'Mr Rushworth is so long fetching this key!'

'And for the world you would not get out without the key and without Mr Rushworth's authority and protection, or I think you might with little difficulty pass round the edge of the gate, here with my assistance; I think it might be done, if you really wished to be more at large, and could allow yourself to think it not prohibited.'

'Prohibited! nonsense! I certainly can get out that way, and I will. Mr Rushworth will be here in a moment you know—we shall not be out of sight.'

'Or if we are, Miss Price will be so good as to tell him, that he will find us near that knoll, the grove of oak on the knoll.'

Fanny feeling all this to be wrong, could not help making an effort to prevent it. 'You must hurt yourself, Miss Bertram,' she cried, 'you will certainly hurt yourself against those spikes—

you will tear your gown—you will be in danger of slipping into the ha-ha. You had better not go.'

Her cousin was safe on the other side, while these words were being spoken, and smiling with all the good-humour of success, she said, 'Thank you, my dear Fanny, but I and my gown are alive and well, and so good bye.'

Fanny was again left to her solitude, and with no increase of pleasant feelings, for she was sorry for almost all that she had seen and heard, astonished at Miss Bertram, and angry with Mr Crawford. (*MP* 126–127)

Fanny had already been abandoned by Edmund and Miss Crawford, who intended to be 'back in a few minutes' (*MP* 124); and now she is once again left alone. Like the scene at the chapel, this scene foreshadows what is to come. Here Fanny is isolated from the others, as she will continue to be throughout most of the novel. Her physical separation in this scene prefigures her emotional and moral isolation, which will become increasingly obvious in the course of the action. One by one the other members of the group will give in to the influence of the Crawfords. Maria's conduct here is an early indication of how little resistance the Crawfords are likely to meet, and more significantly, how dangerous their influence on the young people of Mansfield Park may prove to be. Maria behaves foolishly without perceiving her moral error. She playfully goes along with Henry Crawford's flirtation, ignoring any questions of its propriety. By contrast, Fanny is only too much aware of the possible moral consequences of Maria's behaviour. The recording of Fanny's reaction suffices to place this dialogue between Maria and Mr Crawford in its proper moral context; otherwise, there is no occasion in this scene for the narrator to intrude. Much more is implied than actually said. It is one of the rare examples in Jane Austen of a conversation in which the two participants understand one another perfectly. Maria and Mr Crawford have no difficulty in anticipating how the other is likely to react, nor do they have any problems in assigning the appropriate meaning to what they hear. However, they are unaware of a second level of meaning—the moral implications of their conversation and conduct. But the reader can hardly overlook this level of meaning, since it is evident in Fanny's reaction to what she hears and sees and in the symbolic character of the whole situation.

Jane Austen's most elaborate use of symbolism occurs in the long episode involving the production of a play at Mansfield Park. The preparations for this event bring the action to its first climax. Questionable interpretations of *Mansfield Park* are usually based on a misreading of this part of the novel. In this episode Jane Austen portrays the extent to which the traditional values of Mansfield Park have been eroded.[33] The play itself becomes a symbol of all the outside forces that have invaded the estate and, that, as a consequence, pose a threat to its values. The idea of the play is initiated by Tom Bertram, who has long since demonstrated that he has no sense of moral values, and his aristocratic friend John Yates, who is typical of the 'wrong' kind of company Tom is accustomed to keeping. The idea is actively supported by the Crawfords, and with little effort the others are quickly drawn into the plan, with the predictable exceptions of Fanny and Edmund. From the moral standpoint there are several objections to the plan. First of all, the head of the household—the guardian of Mansfield Park's traditions—is absent; and if he were present, as Tom well knows, he would never give his permission. He would object to the expensive liberties to be taken with his house; he would further object to his daughters—especially the engaged Maria—displaying themselves; and, finally, he would object to the unfortunate choice of Kotzebue's *Lovers' Vows*, a sentimental and sensational drama. But there is an even more serious problem that Sir Thomas would discover only after preparations were under way. The preparations, rehearsals, and everything involved in leading up to the play—release the young people from the normal moral and social constraints. The roles they play in the drama come to stand for the roles they are playing in real life, with the important and dangerous difference that they are just acting and, therefore, not inhibited by the usual conventions of propriety. The point, of course, is that they are not really acting, merely behaving without the customary restraints of social convention: Fanny says that she cannot act at all. By contrast, Henry Crawford is acknowledged by everyone except for the jealous Mr Rushworth to be by far the most accomplished actor. Maria incessantly and needlessly rehearses her scenes with him. In the end, even Edmund gives in to temptation and accepts a role in which he is supposed to make love to Miss Crawford. At the very last moment before the first full-scale rehearsal, even Fanny is pressed at Edmund's bidding into taking on a role. At this climactic point, the legitimate head of the household returns unexpectedly. The Crawfords quickly depart from the scene and Mr Yates is soon to follow. Sir Thomas spends his first few days at home trying to restore order. Disaster has apparently been avoided. Jane Austen resorts to the dramatic coincidence of Sir Thomas' return in order to highlight the extent to which the situation has deteriorated and to underline the fact that there is no one else left to set things right. But the damage has been more serious than Sir Thomas realizes. He can restore the appearance of order, but, as he subsequently comes to recognize, his return came too late for him to do anything more.

The treatment of the novel's main characters and themes is for Jane Austen largely experimental. The number of major characters is in itself a departure from earlier practice. The passive, insecure heroine contrasts sharply with the naïve Catherine, the rational Elinor, and the lively and witty Elizabeth. And most importantly, the decision to employ symbolism as a means of revealing character and the moral issues that are central to the story represents a new phase in Austen's artistic development. These authorial commitments lead to a method of dramatic presentation quite different from that of *Pride and Prejudice*. Dramatic scenes are used in both novels to reveal character; but, while such scenes in *Pride and Prejudice* are employed to reinforce the ambiguities of Elizabeth and Darcy's attitudes towards one another, dramatic scenes are introduced in *Mansfield Park* to highlight the moral conflicts. There are two key reasons for choosing this method of presentation. First of all, in contrast to *Sense and Sensibility* and, to a lesser extent,

Pride and Prejudice, characters are not simply divided between the 'bad' and the 'good'. For the most part, irony is directed at human weakness rather than at individuals—Mrs Norris being the obvious exception. Secondly, in Fanny the reader has a less reliable guide than he has in the heroine of *Sense and Sensibility*. Elinor is the spokesman for a standard according to which character and conduct are judged. Fanny is far less sure of her judgements. She is aware that she allows her emotions to interfere with her ability to see clearly. She has to struggle repeatedly with a conflict of conscience—either in observing the behaviour of others or in trying to respond correctly to demands being made upon her. It is not of course that Fanny is in error. She embodies a set of values just as clearly defined as Elinor's; however, Fanny lacks Elinor's self-assurance. Consequently, Fanny is very reluctant to judge others; her judgements are more often implied than stated. The reader is never in as much doubt as the heroine is about the seriousness of the threat to Mansfield Park or the rightness of Fanny's judgements concerning her own conduct or that of others; for he has a perspective not available to any of the characters in the novel, and the correctness of Fanny's perceptions of behaviour and events is confirmed consistently by the narrator and by the symbolic implications of the dramatic scenes. *Mansfield Park* is a didactic novel, but the didactic element is seldom made explicit. Irony is fundamental to this didactic intent. The basis of much of this irony is the grouping together of characters with differing views. Out of these confrontations arise the conflicts which are first clarified and then resolved positively or negatively in the course of the action. As the action unfolds, the reader becomes involved in the process of reassessing the relative merits of each of the main characters. The young, plain heroine with no fortune and little more claim to social status turns out to be more admirable than those born into much more favourable circumstances.

Emma represents a successful synthesis and development of methods Jane Austen has employed previously. Emma Woodhouse is a far more complex heroine than any of her predecessors, and the focus of attention is on her mental life throughout the novel. The author has made her task all the more difficult by choosing a heroine who in some respects is not at all sympathetic. Emma's indulgence in flights of fancy and her sense of superiority cause her to misguide Harriet Smith and to treat others unjustly. Emma's attitude is not simply derived from a reading of Sentimental fiction, as Catherine Morland's is in *Northanger Abbey*, or from a romantic sensibility like Marianne Dashwood's in *Sense and Sensibility*. Its origins may be traced to too much beauty, too much cleverness and too much independence. Her development most closely resembles Elizabeth Bennet's; however, the parallel should not be over-stressed, for by the middle of *Pride and Prejudice* Elizabeth perceives her error; while Emma holds onto, and nurtures, her illusions until the novel's dénouement. Elizabeth comes to realize that she has allowed pride to interfere with her judgement. Emma's errors of judgement are much graver, and, as a result, much more difficult for the heroine to accept. The action of the novel reaches its climax when Emma realizes the extent to which she has been mistaken in her judgements.

Most of the irony in this novel centres in Emma's personality. In part this is due to the reader's more objective angle of vision, which is discussed below. In part it is due to the fact that most of the complications which develop in the course of the action stem from the heroine's errors in judgement. The reader soon learns that Emma's views and judgements are inconsistent with an objective reality; however, he only learns the degree of her error from the subsequent action. The typical ironic pattern: the reader suspects Emma is in error; his suspicions are confirmed; Emma perceives the error herself. The pattern is repeated frequently. The reader's knowledge does not approach that of the narrator's before the climactic turning point in the action. The plot develops in three stages, and each of these stages is associated with a new suitor for Emma's protégée Harriet Smith. Emma sees in Harriet a young woman, who lacks only a little education and refinement to make her the perfect wife for Mr Elton; therefore, Emma takes on the role of mentor and guide to her friend without discovering in the process that Harriet is actually an unexceptional, easily influenced, and somewhat stupid young girl. Harriet's beauty and talents, like the possibility of a marriage with Mr Elton, are products of Emma's imagination. She creates fictions out of the rather mundane world of her country village. Her motives stem partly from snobbery and partly from pride in her own cleverness in perceiving the possibility of such a match. She dissuades Harriet from marrying Robert Martin, for in Emma's opinion Martin is too far below her friend socially. During the first phase of the action, Emma is shocked to discover that Mr Elton has dared to presume that she might think of him as her equal. For Emma's second candidate for a marriage with Harriet the situation is different. For a time, Emma herself is taken in by the new candidate's flattery; however, nothing comes of this or of Emma's second plan for Harriet, because Frank Churchill has long since been secretly engaged. At this stage of the story, Harriet no longer needs Emma's encouragement, for she has come to accept much of the argument which underlies Emma's conviction that Harriet is destined to marry well. As a consequence, in the final phase of the action and without Emma's intervention, Harriet discovers in Mr Knightley her future husband. This development comes as more of a shock to Emma than anything she has previously experienced, and it forces her to re-examine her own feelings and to reconsider much of what she has thought and done in the past. Like Jane Austen's other heroines, Emma progresses from illusion to reality. But Emma differs from the other heroines in the energy she expends to create and maintain her illusions. Even at those points in the action where she regrets having given in to fancy and having encouraged Harriet to pursue an unobtainable goal, Emma continues at the same time to indulge in further speculations. The reader is never taken in completely by Emma's flights of fancy, for he has a critical perspective from which he can evaluate Emma's powers of discernment.

Jane Austen's solution to the problem of portraying such a potentially unsympathetic heroine is to present most of the story from Emma's angle of vision, filtered through the ironic lens of the narrator. In addition, the character Mr

Knightley provides the reader with a more reliable guide than he has in Emma to an accurate assessment of the situation. Knightley's view of Emma is not uncritical. On the contrary, he feels compelled to chastise her on several occasions. Nevertheless, it is evident that he has a high regard for Emma despite her weaknesses, and the reader comes to share this regard. From his close observations of the workings of Emma's mind, the reader learns that Emma's errors may be attributed to human failings but not to evil intent. Emma does not hurt anyone intentionally, though her snobbishness and pride blind her to the obvious, and lead her to do harm and to treat others unjustly. The inevitable conflicts generated by Emma's attitude are reflected in the inside views of her mental life.

She was not struck by any thing remarkably clever in Miss Smith's conversation, but she found her altogether very engaging—not inconveniently shy, not unwilling to talk—and yet so far from pushing, shewing so proper and becoming a deference, seeming so pleasantly grateful for being admitted to Hartfield, and so artlessly impressed by the appearance of every thing in so superior a style to what she had been used to, that she must have good sense and deserve encouragement. Encouragement should be given. Those soft blue eyes and all those natural graces should not be wasted on the inferior society of Highbury and its connections. The acquaintance she had already formed were unworthy of her. The friends from whom she had just parted, though a very good sort of people, must be doing her harm. (*E* 53–54)[34]

In this passage Emma gives herself away at every turn, revealing a snobbishness and an egotism which are far removed from the altruistic and generous motives she would ascribe to her own behaviour. She condemns Harriet's past acquaintances without ever having met them herself, and she contemplates the important role she will play in Harriet's future. Whether or not Harriet desires such a future or can live up to the great expectations of her self-appointed mentor are questions Emma does not bother to consider. This example of an inside view differs from those in the other novels. Like Jane Austen's other heroines, Emma examines the implications of what she has observed and experienced. But here, in contrast to its function in the other novels, the inside view serves not so much to enlighten the reader about the significance of past events or behaviour as to give insight into the nature of Emma's own attitudes. The ironic perspective from which her thoughts are presented as well as the context of the novel as a whole highlights the discrepancies between Emma's values and the system of norms and values adhered to by Knightley and supported by the narrator.

Now, it so happened that in spite of Emma's resolution of never marrying, there was something in the name, in the idea of Mr Frank Churchill, which always interested her. She had frequently thought—especially since his father's marriage with Miss Taylor—that if she *were* to marry, he was the very person to suit her in age, character and condition. He seemed by this connection between the families, quite to belong to her. She could not but suppose it to be a match that every body who knew them must think of. That Mr and Mrs Weston did think of it, she was strongly persuaded; and though not meaning to be induced by him, or by any body else, to give up a situation which she believed more replete with good than any she could change it for, she had a great curiosity to see him, a decided intention of finding him pleasant, of being liked by him to a certain degree, and a sort of pleasure in the idea of their being coupled in their friends' imaginations. (*E* 139–140)

The contrast between the content of Emma's thoughts and the form in which they are expressed is indicative of the heroine's habit of deluding herself. The substance of her reflections is quite simple: if Frank Churchill discovers an interest in her, Emma will be more than ready to abandon her decision not to marry. Her unwillingness to be completely honest even with herself on this point is signalled by the narrator's opening remark: 'Now, it so happened that in spite of Emma's resolution of never marrying, there was something in the name, in the idea of Frank Churchill, which always interested her.' The narrator understates the import of Emma's thoughts. From what follows it is evident that Emma is intrigued by the personality of someone she has yet to meet and the possibility of finding in him a suitor to her liking. She speculates about her own future in much the same manner as she speculates about the future of others. On the basis of very little information she arrives at an opinion. The form given her thoughts underlines the absence of any logic in her reasoning. Implicitly or explicitly her thoughts are put into the subjunctive mood. Emma's line of thought departs further and further from an objective reality. She speculates about what might happen until she reaches the conclusion that it most likely will happen. Although she is careful to modify and qualify her speculations, the impulse behind these thoughts is stronger than any restraint her reason might impose. The reader is not taken in by Emma's fancies. As in the preceding passage, discussed above, Emma gives herself away. The powers of her imagination prevail over those of her reason.

Emma's speculations about the role Frank Churchill might one day play in her life seem harmless enough; however, her speculations in this instance reflect a habit of mind which does in fact lead Emma to cause others pain and unhappiness. This less attractive side of Emma's personality is not hidden from the reader; but, since the unpleasant consequences of Emma's conduct are hardly in the forefront of her thoughts and the reader more or less shares her angle of vision, he only becomes acquainted with this aspect of Emma's personality gradually. It is most visible in her relationship to Harriet, but, as the story develops, the reader comes to realize that Harriet is not the only one to suffer because of Emma's willfulness. As in *Pride and Prejudice*, the way is carefully prepared for the reader's revaluation of what he has experienced from the heroine's point of view. From the opening pages of the novel, the evidence against Emma's view of her own conduct begins accumulating, but the significance of what is implied and the degree to which Emma errs does not become clear before the story reaches its climax. The passages discussed below illustrate how the author prepares the ground for the reader's realization that the heroine has caused much more harm than Emma herself would be willing to admit.

Knightley is more than a little displeased with Emma when he learns that she has discouraged Harriet from marrying Robert Martin. For her part, Emma is reluctant to admit to any responsibility in the matter, but she goes on to add that Mr Elton would be a more suitable match for Harriet in any case. Knightley tries to make it clear to Emma that Mr Elton would never seriously entertain such an idea. The conversation ends in frustration for both parties. Emma's reaction is recorded in an inside view.

He had frightened her a little about Mr Elton; but when she considered that Mr Knightley could not have observed him as she had done, neither with the interest, nor (she must be allowed to tell herself, in spite of Mr Knightley's pretensions) with the skill of such an observer on such a question as herself, that he had spoken hastily and in anger, she was able to believe, that he had rather said what he wished resentfully to be true, than what he knew anything about. He certainly might have heard Mr Elton speak with more unreserve than she had ever done, and Mr Elton might not be of an imprudent, inconsiderate disposition as to money-matters; he might naturally be rather attentive than otherwise to them; but then, Mr Knightley did not make due allowance for the influence of a strong passion at war with all interested motives. Mr Knightley saw no such passion, and of course thought nothing of its effects; but she saw too much of it, to feel a doubt of its overcoming any hesitations that a reasonable prudence might originally suggest; and more than a reasonable, becoming degree of prudence, she was very sure did not belong to Mr Elton. (*E* 93)

This view into the workings of Emma's mind highlights the pride she takes in her own perceptive powers. Despite her undoubted respect for Knightley and the likelihood that he is in a better position than she is to predict how Mr Elton might act, she succeeds in convincing herself that her own intuitions are a more reliable guide than Knightley's knowledge. Her self-confidence grows as she allows her thoughts to take their course. Upon Knightley's departure, 'Emma remained in a state of vexation too; but there was more indistinctness in the causes of hers, than in his. She did not always feel so absolutely satisfied with herself, so entirely convinced that her opinions were right and her adversary's wrong, as Mr Knightley' (*E* 92). But it does not take long for Emma to overcome this feeling of uncertainty. The carefully balanced organization of this inside view is deceptive, for it suggests that Emma is trying to re-examine rationally and objectively her own views and those of Knightley. This of course is far from being the case. Emma may succeed in deceiving herself on this point, but the reader is not likely to be misled. It is too apparent that Emma is weighting the scales in her favour. Moreover, the arguments in support of her position are all based on Emma's conviction that she is a more astute observer than Knightley. The weakness of Emma's position is underscored by what she considers her decisive argument: 'Mr Knightley did not make due allowance for a strong passion. . . .' Like the passage as a whole, this remark reveals more about Emma than about anything else. For the time being, the reader remains in the dark as to what the consequences might be of Emma's obstinacy and her unwillingness to accept—or often even to recognize—the obvious.

In general, Emma is far more certain than the reader has any cause to be about what the future might bring. Emma's self-assurance as well as the powers of her imagination are seldom so much in evidence as when the topic of conversation turns to the 'future'. When Harriet asks Emma whether she would not prefer marriage to becoming an old maid, like Miss Bates, Emma replies:

'Never mind, Harriet, I shall not be a poor old maid; and it is poverty only which makes celibacy contemptible to a generous public! A single woman, with a very narrow income, must be a ridiculous, disagreeable, old maid! the proper sport of boys and girls; but a single woman, of good fortune, is always respectable, and may be as sensible and pleasant as anybody else. And the distinction is not quite so much against candour and common sense of the world as appears at first; for a very narrow income has a tendency to contract the mind, and sour the temper. Those who can barely live, and who live perforce in a very small, and generally very inferior, society, may well be illiberal and cross. . . .'

'Dear me! but what shall you do? how shall you employ yourself when you grow old?'

'If I know myself, Harriet, mine is an active, busy mind, with a great many independent resources; and I do not perceive why I should be more in want of employment at forty or fifty than one-and-twenty. Woman's usual occupations of eye and hand and mind will be as open to me then, as they are now; or with no important variation. If I draw less, I shall read more; if I give up music, I shall take to carpetwork. . . .'

'Do you know Miss Bates' niece? That is, I know you must have seen her a hundred times—but are you acquainted?'

'Oh! yes; we are always forced to be acquainted whenever she comes to Highbury. . . .' (*E* 109–110)

This scene illustrates well the care taken by the author to prepare the way for later developments in the action. As in the other passages discussed above, though in a less obvious manner, Emma says more about herself than she is conscious of doing. Although Harriet fails to notice it, Emma allows the less attractive side of her personality to surface in this scene. Here as elsewhere in the novel, pride and prejudice hinder the heroine in her efforts to make accurate assessments of herself and others. The general tendency of Emma's remarks is to underscore the superiority of her situation and prospects. In her view, the decision of whether or not to marry is less crucial for her than it is for those who do not enjoy the privileges of wealth and rank. This observation cuts two ways. On the one hand, the validity of Emma's observation is beyond question; on the other hand, it suggests Emma's prejudices against those who do not enjoy such privileges. Objective observation shades over into subjective opinion, for example, when Emma remarks, 'a very narrow income has a tendency to contract the mind'. For the time being, the reader may pass over the implications of Emma's comments, for the narrator does not intervene to direct attention to the underlying significance of what Emma is saying. However, when the topic of conversation shifts to Miss Bates's niece, Jane Fairfax, the reader is put on his guard to question the significance of the implied comparison between Jane and Emma. The heroine has just explained why the decision not to marry would constitute no real problem for her. A woman with her resources, interests, and accomplishments need have no concern as to what the future might have in store for her. Already, the reader has reason to doubt that Emma will one day take to carpet-work. What the reader has yet to learn is that it is Jane and not Emma who in fact has the capacity to realize the future which Emma has envisaged for herself. Jane is the truly accomplished young woman Emma imagines herself to be. At first glance, Emma's conversation with Harriet seems innocent enough; however, in the light of the subsequent action, it is evident that the author provides in this scene insight into the motives behind Emma's cruel treatment of Miss Bates and her disinclination to have any contact with Jane Fairfax. Emma's antipathy towards Miss Bates's niece is made sufficiently explicit in the remark, 'we are always forced to be acquainted whenever she comes to Highbury'; however, the reader has to wait for further developments in the action before he can comprehend the motivation behind Emma's attitude.

In *Emma* the author departs once again from her earlier practice. Most of the methods of presentation found in Jane Austen's previous novels occur again in *Emma*, but the presentation of events from the heroine's unreliable point of view is a distinctive new feature. Most of the ironies derive from the contradictions between Emma's observations and an objective reality. Foolish characters such as Mrs Elton are given less prominence than in previous novels, partly because they are of little consequence to Emma, and partly because the heroine's own foolish behaviour is the centre of attention. The reader's superior knowledge allows him a critical view of Emma's behaviour and her powers of discernment. Emma is not undiscerning; she is capable of seeing faults in herself as well as in others, but only if she is not already blinded by ideas formed before she has been confronted with reality. She becomes preoccupied with restructuring the little world in which she lives, so that it will conform to her preconceptions.

Persuasion differs from *Emma* in its subject matter, style,

D

and length. It has often been suggested that *Persuasion* is finished but not completed; and that if Jane Austen's health had not already been failing when she laid the manuscript aside eleven months before her death, she would have probably revised it. Such speculation is of little use except as a reminder that the structure of *Persuasion* as a whole is less satisfactory than that of *Emma*. For each of the three novels conceived and completed during her last years, Jane Austen selects a story which constitutes a new challenge, posing a new set of problems in narrative presentation. *Mansfield Park* requires the portrayal of a wide spectrum of attitudes embodied in several main characters. The author's solution is the employment of two long dramatic episodes in which the characters are allowed to reveal themselves. The central problem in *Emma* is the reader's acceptance of a potentially unsympathetic and egotistical heroine. Jane Austen resolves this problem by presenting much of the story from Emma's angle of vision, and reinforcing the more positive qualities in the heroine's personality through Knightley's admiration of them. Knightley serves as a guide to the reader as well as to Emma. In *Persuasion* there is also a wide variety of attitudes among the characters, but these are not the source of the conflicts which arise in the novel. They serve as the context within which the rationality and sensitivity of the heroine's own manner of thinking is highlighted. As in *Emma*, the story is related for the most part from the heroine's angle of vision; however, it need not be filtered through the ironic lens of the narrator, for Anne Elliot has long since undergone the process of education experienced by Jane Austen's other heroines, moving from a state of illusion to a sense of reality and self-awareness.

As the novel opens, Anne is twenty-seven, a dangerous age for Austen women. At about this age, Charlotte Lucas marries the foolish Mr Collins. Marianne Dashwood laments that a 'woman of seven and twenty . . . can never hope to feel or inspire affection again' (*SS* 70). The one serious romance which Jane Austen seems to have experienced occurred when she was about this age.[35] At nineteen Anne fell in love with Wentworth, a young naval officer with little claim to social status and less to fortune. His ambition was to make a fortune for himself in the navy, but this was not enough for Anne's family, nor, in particular, for her godmother and closest confident, Lady Russell. As a consequence, Anne allows herself to be persuaded that the match would be imprudent. From the novel's opening chapters the reader learns that circumstances will bring Anne—now twenty-seven—and Wentworth together again for the first time in eight years, and that Anne is still very much in love with Wentworth. This situation points to the central problem with which Jane Austen was confronted in choosing this story. Most of the action familiar from the other novels has already taken place. Anne has already gained the necessary insights into herself and others to achieve the balance of elegance and understanding valued by the author. The character of the heroine does not really undergo any further changes in the course of the novel, apart from an increase in her awareness of how much she still loves Wentworth. By contrast, Wentworth does change in some respects, but his development takes place at such a distance from the reader that it is far from the centre of the action. As a result, the novel has a certain static quality. The focus is less on the development of the action than on the quality of Anne's mind. The outcome of the novel is never really in doubt, though the reader is more certain about this than the heroine is. This is partly explained by the reader's familiarity with literary convention and the likely pattern the action will follow, and partly by the additional knowledge he gains of Wentworth's thoughts. In introducing complications into her plot, Jane Austen relies too much on contrivance and coincidence; examples are Mr Elliot's appearance at Lyme and Anne's conversations with Mrs Smith. But it would be an error to stress these weaknesses, since the centre of interest lies elsewhere, namely, in Anne's consciousness. The reader participates directly in the process whereby Anne gradually finds more reason to hope for a reunion. Actually, the fundamental irony in the novel is the fact that it takes Anne and Wentworth so long to discover the obvious.

Persuasion is much shorter than *Emma* or *Mansfield Park*, and, as a consequence, the author relies more on the narrative summary of events and emotions. The story is related for the most part from Anne's point of view, but the narrator adds an ironic perspective through a word, a phrase, or the selection of details included in the summary. The resulting ironies do not derive primarily from Anne's personality, for her minor failings are not symptomatic of more serious weaknesses.[36] On the other hand, it is an oversimplification to argue as Mudrick does that Anne is 'unsubjected to the temper of Jane Austen's irony.'[37] As Babb has pointed out, 'irony crops up whenever Anne is under real stress.'[38] Upon overhearing Wentworth's praise of Louisa Musgrove's enthusiasm, 'Anne could not immediately *fall into a quotation again*. The sweet scenes of autumn were for a while put by— unless some *tender* sonnet, *fraught* with the *apt analogy* of the declining year, with declining happiness, and the images of youth and hope, and spring, all gone together, *blessed* her memory' (*P* 107).[39] It is unlikely that Anne can find any consolation in the fact that Wentworth is apparently lost to her forever. The italicized words signal an ironic distancing of the reader from Anne's feelings. A little later in this same scene, Anne overhears an exchange between Louisa and Wentworth, and the narrator's comments blend once again with Anne's.

The sounds were retreating, and Anne distinguished no more. Her own emotions still kept her fixed. She had much to recover from, before she could move. The listener's proverbial fate was not absolutely hers; she had heard no evil of herself,—but she had heard a great deal of very painful import. She saw how her own character was considered by Captain Wentworth; and there had been just that degree of feeling and curiosity about her in his manner, which must give her extreme agitation. (*P* 111)

The 'proverbial fate' is clearly the narrator's comment and not Anne's. The author employs the awkward device of over-heard conversation here and elsewhere in the novel in order to provide Anne with some insights into Wentworth's thoughts, and, in the key scene leading up to the climax, in order to give Wentworth the encouragement to make a second proposal of marriage.[40] Much later in the course of the action, Anne learns that, contrary to her expectations, Louisa has decided to marry Captain Benwick.

> She saw no reason against their being happy. Louisa had a fine naval fervour to begin with, and they would soon grow more alike. He would gain cheerfulness, and she would learn to be an enthusiast for Scott and Lord Byron; nay, that was probably learnt already; of course they had fallen in love over poetry. The idea of Louisa Musgrove turned into a person of literary taste, and sentimental reflection was amusing, but she had no doubt of its being so. The day at Lyme, the fall from the Cobb, might influence her health, her nerves, her courage, her character to the end of her life, as thoroughly as it appeared to have influenced her fate.
>
> The conclusion of the whole was, that if the woman who had been sensible of Captain Wentworth's merits could be allowed to prefer another man, there was nothing in the engagement to excite everlasting wonder; and if Captain Wentworth lost no friend by it, certainly nothing was to be regretted. No, it was not regret which made Anne's heart beat in spite of herself, and brought colour into her cheeks when she thought of Captain Wentworth unshackled and free. She had some feelings which she was ashamed to investigate. They were too much like joy, senseless joy! (*P* 178)

In this passage it is the whole pattern of Anne's thought rather than any comment by the narrator which is revealing. Like Emma, but in a much more readily excusable manner, Anne gives herself away at every turn in her thoughts. She is completely preoccupied with Wentworth and the possibility that she may still have reason to hope. It may be a 'wonder' to her that Louisa could prefer another, but it is not to the reader. None of the other characters, including Louisa, is in as good a position as Anne's to appreciate Wentworth's true merits. In contrast to the irony of the presentation of the heroine of *Emma*, the irony here is very mild, for Anne's inability to be objective at this particular moment and on many similar occasions does not threaten harm to anyone, not even to herself. As in *Emma*, the action is organized about what Anne does, says, and thinks; but because the heroine sees so much more clearly than her predecessor, and has achieved an ideal of elegance and moral understanding, the irony is much gentler.

Anne's uncertainty about Wentworth's attitude towards her is essential for the development of the action. Wentworth, therefore, must be kept at some distance from the reader in order that the questions and conflicts which arise in Anne's mind may be given substance. The problem is similar to the problems of presenting Darcy, Frank Churchill, and Knightley. The reader knows little more of these characters than the heroine does. This statement is less true of Knightley than of the others, but even in this case the reader experiences little of what Knightley feels. In the previous novels, the uncertainty of the heroines stems in large part from false assumptions and errors of judgement, so that whenever Darcy or Churchill appears Elizabeth or Emma is likely to misinterpret his behaviour. Anne is far less likely to make such errors of judgement; therefore, it is necessary for Wentworth to be kept at even greater distance from Anne and from the reader. Quite early a brief inside view of Wentworth's thoughts indicates to the reader that Anne has not become indifferent to Wentworth, but the degree of his interest is left unexpressed (*P* 86). In *Pride and Prejudice*, the reader has the possibility of forming an opinion of his own based on what Darcy says. In retrospect, it becomes evident that Elizabeth was in error. In *Persuasion*, such independent assessments of Wentworth are more difficult, since he utters only a little over two thousand words, two-thirds of these not addressed to the heroine.[41] It is not possible for the author to follow her own precedent from *Pride and Prejudice*, for a series of conversations between the two principals, who are not given to misconstruing the remarks of others, could not lead to the uncertainties and misunderstandings the action requires. Jane Austen's alternative is to create uncertainties through situations. As a consequence, the action in this novel depends more on coincidence, overheard conversation, and melodramatic incident. Mr Elliot appears on the scene at Lyme just in time to cause Wentworth to discover that Anne has regained her lost bloom. Also at Lyme,

Louisa has an accident which gives her the opportunity to be more with Benwick and less with Wentworth. In Bath, Anne renews her acquaintance with her old school friend, Mrs Smith, who just happens to be now living there. During their first meetings, Mrs Smith withholds information concerning Mr Elliot's true character. Her subsequent explanation for remaining silent for so long is that according to rumour Anne is soon to make known her engagement to Mr Elliot. Mrs Smith has been hoping that Anne's anticipated marriage might bring some relief to her difficult financial situation. Apparently, Mrs Smith is introduced into the narrative to strengthen Anne in her resolve not to marry Mr Elliot. It is questionable whether Anne needs such additional support. Mrs Smith's revelations recall Colonel Brandon's in *Sense and Sensibility*. In both instances, the heroine's suspicions about a particular character are confirmed, but the revelations in the two novels seem melodramatic, and serve primarily to clear the stage for the final act.

Having chosen to write a novel about the silences which may exist between two mature individuals who in fact are destined for one another, the author finds it necessary to employ coincidences and melodramatic incidents in order to give her story some dimension and depth. These devices serve as a substitute for the conversations or philosophical confrontations which might also have generated the conflicts necessary for the development of the action. They have two functions. First, they extend Anne's range of vision. Since the reader's point of view is very close to Anne's, his perspective is also broadened. Considered in this light, an overheard bit of conversation becomes important, for it causes the reader as well as Anne to revaluate what has already been learned. Second, these devices are used to create, and then to eliminate the possibility of an alternative to a marriage between Anne and Wentworth. The impulses for such an alternative must come from outside, since, as Anne suggests in her comments on woman's constancy, it is not in her nature to fall in love a second time (*P* 236–238). Moreover, the melodramatic elements form the basis of the central ironies of the plot. In Jane Austen's other novels much of the irony

derives from the heroine's errors of judgement or her tendency to reinterpret the facts in terms of her own preconceptions. By contrast, Anne's errors are due simply to a lack of
information.

The distinctive features of Jane Austen's method in
Persuasion are the result of the author's concentration on
Anne's mental life. Throughout the novel the reader's
knowledge is only incidentally and not consistently superior to
Anne's. The occasional mild irony directed at the heroine
does not distance the reader sufficiently to cause him to
question Anne's judgement. The frequent use of inside
views allows the reader to reconsider the facts as well as to
observe the qualities of Anne's mind. The ironies used in the
portrayal of the secondary characters corroborate and
reinforce the opinions Anne forms of them. The ironies
central to the plot do not stem directly from Anne or Wentworth. These ironies are largely external. Circumstances
bring Anne and Wentworth together, cause them to separate,
introduce what appear to be insuperable barriers to their
marriage, and finally give each of them the courage to say
what he feels. The situations which arise as the plot unfolds
serve to clarify how much they are in fact in love with each
other. The uncertainties, misgivings, and despair Anne
experiences are, as the reader learns from the concluding
pages, shared by Wentworth. In her handling of individual
scenes and in her method of portraying the secondary
characters, Jane Austen deviates little from what she has
done previously, but her choice of subject matter and her
externalization of the novel's major conflicts represent a
new direction in the author's work.

Irony, then, is the structuring principle of all Jane Austen's
novels. The central ironies derive either from the heroine's
inability to distinguish between illusion and reality or
from the limitations placed on her knowledge. The reader in
general knows more than the heroine, but the extent of his
superior knowledge varies from novel to novel. He gains
his superior knowledge through the introduction of dramatic
scenes, shifts in the point of view, and interventions on the
part of the narrator. All these means are employed by the

author at times to place character and conduct in an ironic perspective. Inside views are used to reveal the workings of the heroine's mind. Her thoughts may or may not be tempered by the narrator's irony. The pattern of the ironies is not arbitrary; it is based on a particular *Weltanschauung* with a fixed set of values.[42]

II

Putting the Reader in his Place

Inside Views and Dramatic Scenes

In this chapter I want to look more closely at the relationship between the text and the reader in some narrative
passages and dramatic scenes. Jane Austen has been accused
of a fundamental incoherence of point of view; however, if
her commitment to maintaining a consistently ironic perspective is kept in mind, apparent inconsistencies in the
point of view are for the most part eliminated.[1] In the first
chapter it was pointed out that irony is central to the plot
structure of each of the novels with the qualified exception
of *Sense and Sensibility*. It is also the organizing principle
of the dramatic scenes and many of the inside views into the
mental life of the heroines. Jane Austen has the advantage
over the reader in that she knows at any given point in the
narrative the extent of the reader's familiarity with the
characters and events being portrayed, and, as a consequence,
she can anticipate what the reader's expectations and possible
responses are likely to be. This is of course true of any
narrative. What makes Jane Austen's work distinctive is the
subtlety with which she takes advantage of this relationship
between the author and the reader. With the exception of
Northanger Abbey, this relationship is basically the same in all
of the novels. The narrator's position is clearly defined and
unchanging. He has limited omniscience, that is, he does
not tell all he presumably knows. The necessity of controlling
the distance between the reader and the events being portrayed determines what is revealed and what is withheld.
This of course includes what is implied but left unsaid.

Each of the heroines undergoes an educational process which leads her to perceive her own error in the light of an objective reality. The extent to which the reader participates in this process varies from novel to novel. He becomes, for example, more involved in Emma's mental life than in Catherine Morland's. Enough distance is established to prevent the reader from viewing the heroine uncritically, but not so much as to lose the reader's sympathy for her. In other words, the primary source of Jane Austen's irony derives from knowledge or a lack of it. This is true not only in regard to the heroines but in regard to the other characters as well. The author builds up the ironies in her novels on the discrepancies between the reader's knowledge and that of the characters on the one hand and the reader's knowledge and that of the narrator on the other. This principle underlies Jane Austen's handling of narrative as well as dramatic passages. She succeeds in combining the two literary traditions represented by Fielding and Richardson, employing narrative commentary while at the same time achieving much of what Ian Watt termed 'Richardson's psychological closeness to the subjective world of the characters.'[2] Her commentary, which is less obtrusive than Fielding's, provides an ironic perspective on the heroines' evaluation of their own behaviour and that of others. Some of the commentary is stated directly by the narrator, but it is often merely implied through juxtaposition, selection, or the indirect presentation of conversation. In the following analysis of some dramatic and narrative passages, I want to show how this narrative perspective is achieved. In *Aspects of the Novel*, E. M. Forster notes that all of Jane Austen's 'characters are round, or capable of rotundity.'[3] A close examination of how irony functions in her texts should clarify some of the ways in which this illusion of 'rotundity' is created.

In any given dramatic exchange, one of Jane Austen's characters is likely to have 'superior' knowledge, which is not the same as to suggest that he is morally or socially superior. Quite the contrary may in fact be the case. Rarely in Jane Austen are both parties equally informed and equally in control of the situation. In *Persuasion*, where this might be most likely to occur, the principals, Anne Elliot and Captain Wentworth, are simply not given the opportunity to converse at length with one another. Elizabeth Bennet's confrontation with Lady Catherine comes close to being an exception, for both parties think of themselves as being in control of the situation (*PP* 361–368).[4] The author prefers situations in which one of the parties dominates. This dominance may have positive or negative consequences, but in either case it is most probable that effective communication takes place only in one direction. The dominant speaker may be aware of some weakness in his listener's character, such as pride or foolishness, or may know that he himself is lying or at least withholding information—to cite only a few of the possibilities. One speaker's knowledge is superior to the other's, but the reader's knowledge is superior to them both. This superiority is partly due to the reader's experience of the text up to this point, and to the explicit or at least implicit commentary in the scene itself. The pattern provides the basis for the local ironies.[5] Jane Austen's effectiveness as a novelist depends on her ability to co-ordinate these local ironies with the structural ironies discussed in the last chapter, so that they contribute to a unified, clearly defined fictional world.

In *Northanger Abbey* the local ironies are achieved at the expense of unity. Catherine Morland has little experience and few opinions of her own, so that she is easily influenced and susceptible to the opinions of others. Initially she has little basis for evaluating behaviour except for her own natural and unconscious tendency to do whatever is right and proper. These features of Catherine's personality are brought out in dramatic scenes.

'Blaize Castle!' cried Catherine; 'what is that?'

'The finest place in England—worth going fifty miles at any time to see.'

'What, is it really a castle, an old castle?'

'The oldest in the kingdom.'

'But is it like what one reads of?'

'Exactly—the very same.'

'But now really—are there any towers and long galleries?'

'By dozens.'

'Then I should like to see it; but I cannot—I cannot go.'

'Not go!—my beloved creature, what do you mean?'

'I cannot go, because'—(looking down as she spoke, fearful of Isabella's smile) 'I expect Miss Tilney and her brother to call on me to take a country walk. They promised to come at twelve, only it rained; but now, as it is so fine, I dare say they will be here soon.'

'Not they indeed,' cried Thorpe; 'for, as we turned into Broadstreet, I saw them—does he not drive a phaeton with bright chestnuts?'

'I do not know indeed.'

'Yes, I know he does; I saw him. You are talking of the man you danced with last night, are not you?'

'Yes.'

'Well, I saw him at that moment turn up the Lansdown Road, —driving a smart-looking girl.'

'Did you indeed?'

'Did upon my soul; knew him again directly, and he seemed to have got some very pretty cattle too.'

'It is very odd! but I suppose they thought it would be too dirty for a walk.' (*NA* 101–102)

This scene is characteristic of Jane Austen's use of dramatic scenes in *Northanger Abbey*. It lacks the complexity of similar scenes in the later novels, but in other respects the technique of dramatic presentation is the same. The scene may be analysed in terms of Catherine's response, John Thorpe's response, and the reader's response. It is a good illustration of Jane Austen's use of implicit commentary. The reader cannot miss the single-minded purpose of John Thorpe's remarks even if the reader does not happen to know that Blaize Castle was first built in the eighteenth century. The lies, the exaggerations, and the silent support of his sister are all selfishly intended to produce one effect. Catherine, however, remains innocent of Thorpe's duplicity. Communication fails to function effectively in this scene for two reasons. First of all, Thorpe's comments are inappropriate to the social situation. Apart from the fact that he is lying, such phrases as 'upon my soul' and 'got some very pretty cattle' indicate that Thorpe is using a vulgar register, which is completely out of place in polite conversation. More importantly, Thorpe takes advantage of Catherine's naïveté. He realizes that 'lying' is not among the possible interpretations which Catherine is likely to assign to his remarks, because she is not capable of seriously doubting the veracity of his comments even though they take her by surprise. Unbeknownst to Catherine, Thorpe alters the ground rules of their conversation. He has no intention of being open and informative, which is presumably what Catherine would expect. The reader of course is not taken in, but Catherine is persuaded. Catherine's remarks on the other hand do not carry the force she intends them to have. Since she is unaware of the 'new' rules governing their conversation, she cannot possibly succeed; moreover, even if she were aware of them, it would be inconsistent with her character to place self-interest above honesty. Therefore, her objections are not taken seriously, but for the time being she is oblivious to this fact. From his position of superior knowledge, the reader perceives what is happening more clearly than any of the participants.

Manipulation of the heroine's responses by another character is a feature of several of the dramatic scenes in *Northanger Abbey*, but the motives for such manipulation are not always so questionable. The most important event in Catherine's education is getting to know Henry Tilney. He enjoys playing the mentor and guiding Catherine to greater self-awareness.

'. . . But you must be aware that when a young lady is (by whatever means) introduced to a dwelling of this kind, she is always lodged apart from the rest of the family. While they snugly repair to their own end of the house, she is formally conducted by Dorothy the ancient housekeeper up a different staircase, and along many gloomy passages, into an apartment never used since some cousin or kin died in it about twenty years before. Can you stand such a ceremony as this? Will not your mind misgive you, when you find yourself in this gloomy chamber—too lofty and extensive for you, with only the feeble rays of a single lamp to take in its size—its walls hung with tapestry exhibiting figures as large as life, and the bed, of dark green stuff or purple velvet, presenting even a funereal appearance. Will not your heart sink within you?'

'Oh! but this will not happen to me, I am sure.'

'How fearfully will you examine the furniture of your apartment!—And what will you discern?—Not tables, toilettes, wardrobes, or drawers, but on one side perhaps the remains of a broken lute, on the other a ponderous chest which no efforts can open, and over the fireplace the portrait of some handsome warrior, whose features will so incomprehensibly strike you, that you will not be able to withdraw your eyes from it. Dorothy, meanwhile, no less struck by your appearance, gazes on you with great agitation, and drops a few unintelligible hints. To raise your spirits, moreover, she gives you reason to suppose that the part of the abbey you inhabit is undoubtedly haunted, and informs you that you will not have a single domestic within call. With this parting cordial she curtseys off—you listen to the sound of her receding footsteps as long as the last echo can reach you—and when, with fainting spirits, you attempt to fasten your door, you discover, with increased alarm, that it has no lock.'

'Oh! Mr Tilney, how frightful!—This is just like a book!' (*NA* 164–165)

Two different worlds come into innocent conflict in this scene: the world of the romantic, naïve Catherine and that of the more experienced and sensible Henry Tilney. The latter is of course very much aware of how Catherine will interpret his remarks, and he does nothing to discourage these misinterpretations. Much of the irony in this scene derives from Catherine's readiness—perhaps even very strong desire—to believe what she hears even though common sense argues against it. At the moment she is not herself conscious of the degree of truth she ascribes to Henry's remarks. That she in fact does this is suggested by her obvious enthusiasm in this scene and confirmed by her behaviour later at the abbey. To her embarrassment she discovers at the abbey that she was completely wrong in her interpretation of Henry's remarks. Subsequent experience invalidates Catherine's interpretation of Henry's comments as factual. Viewing the dialogue the other way around, Catherine's remarks are not understood in the manner she anticipates. She assumes her comments will be taken at their face value, but such an interpretation on Henry's part would be inconsistent with his experience of the world. He realizes that underlying her expressions of doubt and disbelief is the hope that all he has related is true. The reader shares with Catherine the knowledge that Henry's description is indeed 'just like a book', or, more precisely, just like one of the 'horrid' novels mentioned previously in *Northanger Abbey*;[6] however, unlike the heroine, the reader also knows that it is in fact a 'fiction'.

This scene between Henry Tilney and Catherine completes the preparations for Catherine's quixotic adventures at the abbey, which, in turn, serve as a climax to the novel's second main theme: the difference between the fictional and real worlds. Catherine's novel reading as well as her introduction to a new circle of acquaintances becomes a part of her education, in which she learns to differentiate literature from life. But she first gains this insight after comprehending the foolishness of her behaviour at the abbey. In the Bath chapters the topic of fiction is used to differentiate character.[7] The reader is placed in a position from which he can evaluate and judge character by the individual's ability to read and discuss fiction with discernment and a sense of literary merit.[8] Catherine is also placed in such a position; however, she lacks the experience to make such judgements. Henry Tilney gives her some guidance, but initially her response is completely uncritical.

'Have you gone on with Udolpho?'

'Yes, I have been reading it ever since I woke; and I am got to the black veil.'

'Are you, indeed? How delightful! Oh! I would not tell you what is behind the black veil for the world! Are not you wild to know?'

'Oh! yes, quite; what can it be?—But do not tell me—I would not be told on any account. I know it must be a skeleton, I am sure it is Laurentina's skeleton. Oh! I am delighted with the book! I should like to spend my whole life in reading it. I assure you if it had not been to meet you, I would not have come away from it for all the world.'

'Dear creature! how much I am obliged to you; and when you have finished Udolpho, we will read the Italian together; and

I have made out a list of ten or twelve more of the same kind for you.'

'Have you, indeed! How glad I am!—What are they all?'

'I will read you their names directly; here they are, in my pocket-book. Castle of Wolfenbach, Clermont, Mysterious Warnings, Necromancer of the Black Forest, Midnight Bell, Orphan of the Rhine, and Horrid Mysteries. Those will last us some time.'

'Yes, pretty well; but are they all horrid, are you sure they are all horrid?'

'Yes, quite sure; for a particular friend of mine, a Miss Andrews, a sweet young girl, one of the sweetest creatures in the world, has read every one of them.' (*NA* 60–61)

The chapter from which this dialogue is taken begins: 'The following conversation, which took place between the two friends in the Pump-room one morning, after an acquaintance of eight or nine days, is given as a specimen of their very warm attachment, and of the delicacy, discretion, originality of thought, and literary taste which marked the reasonableness of that attachment' (*NA* 60). This comment from the narrator establishes the ironic angle of vision. In its obviousness and directness this use of explicit commentary is unlike anything employed in the later novels; however, it is consistent with the simple manner in which the scene that follows is developed, and in keeping with the burlesque character of the opening chapters. Isabella's and Catherine's conversation is punctuated with sentence fragments and exclamations, which indicate their inability to pursue a serious critical discussion on fiction. Nevertheless, despite its simplicity (like the scenes between John Thorpe and Catherine and between Henry Tilney and the heroine already considered) this scene exemplifies a method of presentation used repeatedly in all of the later novels. As usual, the reader's knowledge is superior to that of either of the participants in the dialogue. He perceives that Isabella has nothing more intelligent to say about fiction than Catherine. What opinions Isabella has, she has from Miss Andrews, and, as becomes evident in the course of this scene, what Miss Andrews knows is what is current.[9] Miss Andrews is not, for

E

example, familiar with Richardson's *Sir Charles Grandison* (1753–1754).[10] Unlike the reader, Catherine attributes to Isabella's comments on fiction the same value which Isabella herself would give them. Isabella intends to interest Catherine in what she herself is interested in, and she meets no resistance. As in the scenes discussed above, Catherine is manipulated without being conscious of it. Isabella's motives are less unkind, but just as egotistical as her brother's; and like her brother, she is able to anticipate Catherine's possible responses and to eliminate any doubts her listener might have before Catherine has had a chance to reflect at all upon what Isabella is saying. As is true with her brother, the degree of truth contained in Isabella's comments is for her irrelevant and for Catherine unknown. Isabella does not have ten titles on her list, not to mention twelve.

As was pointed out in Chapter 1, Jane Austen alters her method of presentation at about the middle of *Northanger Abbey*. As in Fielding's *Joseph Andrews* (1742), parody gives way to another kind of narrative. There are of course many connections between the early and late chapters, but the overall effect is weakened by the changes in method and emphasis. From the point of view of style, the novel is of particular interest, because the author's techniques are more transparent than in the other novels. This is partly because Jane Austen is experimenting and trying out a number of different strategies of presentation, and partly because of the subject matter, which requires a less serious and consistent treatment. The narrative perspective used in the first half of the novel anticipates her heavy reliance on dramatic scene in *Pride and Prejudice*; whereas, the reader's angle of vision in the second half anticipates the method used throughout in *Emma*. Similarly, the structure of the dramatic scenes, where one of the parties has little insight into the implications of what is being said, is typical of the dramatic scenes in the later novels as well. In many of these scenes what is being said has very little to do with what is being thought or felt. All the rules governing conversation are broken at one time or another by one or more of Jane Austen's characters. This explains why the process of communication generates more misunderstanding than enlightenment among her characters. The point in which *Northanger Abbey* differs most obviously from the other novels is in the development of the novel's structural ironies. Even in retrospect it is difficult for the reader to resolve the problems related to the novel's conflicting themes.[11] On the first page he is confronted with what appears to be an *antinovel*. But this theme is not developed systematically. Later the focus on Catherine as an individual, and General Tilney's treatment of her, present difficulties, because the reader has not been prepared for either of these developments. Interpreting *Northanger Abbey* as the education of the reader as well as the education of Catherine fails to resolve all of these difficulties. The strengths as well as the weaknesses of this novel indicate that the author is still in the process of completing her own education.

Both *Sense and Sensibility* and *Pride and Prejudice* were written and rewritten over a number of years, but the former seems to have been less thoroughly revised than the latter.[12] It is a mixture of a mature and an immature Jane Austen. Her mature style is most evident in her treatment of individual scenes and her portrayal of some of the secondary characters. Her less mature style is suggested by the melodramatic developments in the plot, the unresolved technical difficulties of presenting two parallel stories from the point of view of only one of the main characters, the simplistic categorization of characters into the good and the bad (the bad are objects of her irony, the good are not), and the unnaturally long speeches of Marianne and, especially, Elinor. In making this list of 'immature' features, I am simplifying and overstating my case; however, even the most cursory reading of the text reveals qualitative differences between, for example, the first and the second chapters. These differences can be seen in the alternative means Jane Austen employs to portray the secondary characters.

If irony is not the structuring principle of the plot, it is an essential element in the characterization of the secondary figures. The following comparison of the author's introduction of the Palmers and her portrayal of a serious discussion

relating to family matters, which takes place at the Dashwoods', illustrates qualitative differences in the means
employed to achieve ironic effects.

Mrs Palmer was several years younger than Lady Middleton,
and totally unlike her in every respect. She was short and plump,
had a pretty face, and the finest expression of good humour in
it that could possibly be. Her manners were by no means so elegant
as her sister's, but they were much more prepossessing. She
came in with a smile, smiled all the time of her visit, except when
she laughed, and smiled when she went away. Her husband was
a grave looking young man of five or six and twenty, with an air
of more fashion and sense than his wife, but of less willingness
to please or be pleased. He entered the room with a look of self-
consequence, slightly bowed to the ladies, without speaking a
word, and, after briefly surveying them and their apartments,
took up a newspaper from the table and continued to read it as
long as he staid.

Mrs Palmer, on the contrary, who was strongly endowed by
nature with a turn for being uniformly civil and happy, was
hardly seated before her admiration of the parlour and every
thing in it burst forth.

'Well! what a delightful room this is! I never saw anything
so charming! Only think, mama, how it is improved since I
was here last! I always thought it such a sweet place, ma'am
(turning to Mrs Dashwood,) but you have made it so charming!
Only look, sister, how delightful every thing is! How I should
like such a house for myself! Should not you, Mr Palmer?'

Mr Palmer made her no answer, and did not even raise his
eyes from the newspaper.

'Mr Palmer does not hear me,' said she, laughing, 'he never
does sometimes. It is so ridiculous!'

This was quite a new idea to Mrs Dashwood, she had never
been used to find wit in the inattention of any one, and could not
help looking with surprise at them both. (*SS* 130–131)

This introduction of the Palmers establishes their characters.
The pattern of their future behaviour is predictable. Mr
Palmer will hold himself aloof whenever it is not possible to
avoid such social confrontations entirely. Mrs Palmer will
show herself a master at indiscretion. She is talkative without
saying much, and neither Elinor nor Marianne can be ex-

pected to have much patience with her. Her primary function in the narrative is to create awkward moments by asking indelicate questions. The ironic commentary is both implicit and explicit. The first reference to Mr and Mrs Palmer forewarns the reader not to expect too much from the new arrivals: 'It is only the Palmers' (*SS* 130). Mrs Palmer confirms what is implied here as soon as she opens her mouth. The impression that Mrs Palmer is a silly woman who talks nonsense is reinforced by the brief inside view of what Mrs Dashwood—a woman not known in general for her quick insight into character—is thinking. Elinor's mother cannot help suspecting that there is a certain amount of foolishness in what is being said. The content of Mrs Palmer's conversation is not of particular importance. Its primary function is phatic, that is, its purpose is simply to establish and maintain social contact; and, in this respect, it functions effectively. But her comments have a second function which Mrs Palmer is not aware of, namely, to project an image of silliness. This scene exemplifies a situation in which the auditors have an advantage over the speaker, for Mrs Palmer is not capable of anticipating what interpretation her listeners will assign to her remarks. Such situations occur often in Jane Austen, for example, in the characterizations of Mr Collins and Mrs Norris. As a rule, however, the image projected is more complex and not so easily identified and specified as in this instance.

In her portrayal of the Dashwoods, Jane Austen uses a much more complex means of revealing character, though the characters themselves are not necessarily more complex than the Palmers. In Chapter 2 of *Sense and Sensibility*, the narrator's comments make explicit what Mr and Mrs Dashwood are thinking but incapable of stating directly. A tone of hypocrisy and self-interest dominates this scene. Neither Mrs Dashwood nor her husband wants to do anything financially for his half-sisters and their mother; on the other hand, they would like to have the comforting feeling that in doing nothing, they have, nevertheless, done the right thing. This is brought out clearly in the dialogue between them. Mr Dashwood makes a series of assertions which fail to function as such, because they are weakened by the qualifying, sometimes subjunctive mood in which they are expressed. In the process of reflecting on his wife's possible response and deciding how to formulate his message, he selects a form which is least likely to offend her while at the same time retaining the conviction that he has said what was necessary under the given circumstances.

Perhaps it would have been as well if he had left it wholly to myself. (*SS* 44)

Perhaps then, it would be better for all parties if the sum were diminished one half. (*SS* 44)

I do not know whether, upon the whole, it would not be more advisable to do something for their mother while she lives rather than for them.... (*SS* 45)

As his wife slowly brings Mr Dashwood to realize that he need not do anything at all for his relatives, his assertions become more forceful and the subjunctive disappears from his speech. Gradually he perceives that he and his wife are actually very close to one another in their thinking about the matter, and that he need not be afraid of how she is going to react to his remarks. The irony of course being that what he eventually ends up considering his opinion is the complete opposite of what he initially thought and felt to be his duty.

It will certainly be much the best way. A present of fifty pounds, now and then, will prevent their ever being distressed for money, and will, I think be amply discharging my promise to my father. (*SS* 46)

I believe you are perfectly right. My father certainly could mean nothing more by his request to me than what you say. I clearly understand it now, and I will strictly fulfil my engagement by such acts of assistance and kindness to them as you have described. (*SS* 47)

Mrs Dashwood, for her part, is never in any doubt as to what conclusion this conversation with her husband should have.

Aware that her husband has certain scruples which must be overcome, she directs the conversation in such a manner that in the end Mr Dashwood is convinced he has no other choice—a conviction which is all the easier, since he was inclined to it from the beginning. In this respect it parallels the opening scene of *Pride and Prejudice*, in which Mrs Bennet attempts to persuade her husband to do something he has long since decided to do. The scene ends with her apparent failure. In contrast, Mrs Dashwood sets out to persuade her husband to act in a way he himself would like to act if he can only find sufficient reason for doing so. His wife's reasons are more than sufficient. All her remarks amount to the same implied question: is it really necessary? In effect each of her statements is an additional argument why it is impossible to provide any financial assistance at all. The strength of these arguments is underlined by the manner in which they are formulated.

He did not know what he was talking of, I dare say; ten to one but he was light-headed at the time. (*SS* 43–44)

Well, then, *let* something be done for them; but *that* something need not be three thousand pounds. (*SS* 44)

There is no knowing what *they* may expect, . . . but we are not to think of their expectations: the question is, what you can afford to do. (*SS* 44)

Mrs Dashwood leaves no room for misunderstanding or contradiction. Her husband cannot possibly miss the import of her remarks. He does fail to perceive (what Mrs Bennet also fails to recognize) that he is being manipulated. As Mrs Dashwood perceives that she is gaining ground, she alters her tactics. Whereas initially she formulates her remarks in such a manner that her husband does not dare to contradict her, at about midpoint in the discussion her tone shifts.

To be sure it would. . . . (*SS* 44)

To be sure it is. . . . (*SS* 45)

To be sure . . . it is better than parting with fifteen hundred pounds at once. (*SS* 45)

To be sure it will. Indeed, to say the truth, I am convinced within myself that your father had no idea of your giving them any money at all. (*SS* 46)

In the latter part of their conversation, as the above quotations suggest, Mrs Dashwood appears willing to accept her husband's opinion; however, what follows in each instance makes clear that this is not the case at all. The initial verbal signals seem to point in the direction of being in agreement with her husband, but, in fact, they are simply Mrs Dashwood's indirect method of making assertions without alienating her husband in the process. In the end the decision is made for him, but Mr Dashwood remains ignorant of this fact. The narrator's remarks clarify the degree of Mrs Dashwood's success. In introducing this scene, the narrator records Mrs Dashwood's opinion of the whole affair. She has no intention of arriving at a compromise solution to the problem. She is not willing to give an inch or, more accurately, a pound. As the scene opens, therefore, Mrs Dashwood's intransigence is known to the reader but not to Mr Dashwood. In the course of the ensuing discussion, the narrator intrudes only once, at that point where Mrs Dashwood appears willing to make a reasonable compromise.

His wife hesitated a little, however, in giving her consent to this plan. (*SS* 45)

At this point nothing more need be said. The narrator's introductory comments have already established the ironic context in which the entire scene is to be viewed. The narrator intervenes once again at the conclusion of this scene.

This argument was irresistible. It gave to his intentions whatever of decision was wanting before; and he finally resolved, that it would be absolutely unnecessary, if not highly indecorous, to do more for the widow and children of his father, than such kind of neighbourly acts as his wife pointed out. (*SS* 47)

In light of the general tendency of the preceding discussion, it is not difficult for the reader to imagine what kinds of 'neighbourly acts' Mrs Dashwood is likely to point out to her husband. As at the end of the first chapter of *Pride and Prejudice*, the narrator confirms what the reader comes to suspect in the course of this scene. Nothing in the Dashwoods' relationship to one another is going to change, nor is it probable that they will discover at some time in the future a sense of obligation and duty to anyone except themselves. A pattern of behaviour is fixed in much the same manner as it is fixed in the relationship of Mr and Mrs Palmer or Mr and Mrs Bennet.

As early as *Northanger Abbey* Jane Austen makes occasional use of inside views. As a rule they are introduced when the heroine is considering the implications of something she has learned or observed. The process of communication takes place between the heroine and the reader, the heroine usually having no one with whom she can talk openly about the subject. Her thoughts may be more or less formally structured, and more or less logically ordered. In *Sense and Sensibility* these inside views tend to be unnaturally rigid in their structure.

However small Elinor's general dependence on Lucy's veracity might be, it was impossible for her on serious reflection to suspect it in the present case, where no temptation could be answerable to the folly of inventing a falsehood of such a description. What Lucy asserted to be true, therefore, Elinor could not, dared not longer doubt; supported as it was too on every side by such probabilities and proofs, and contradicted by nothing but her own wishes. Their opportunity of acquaintance in the house of Mr Pratt was a foundation for the rest, at once indisputable and alarming; and Edward's visit near Plymouth, his melancholy state of mind, his dissatisfaction at his own prospects, his uncertain behaviour towards herself, the intimate knowledge of the Miss Steeles as to Norland and their family connections, which had often surprised her, the picture, the letter, the ring, every fear of condemning him unfairly, and established as a fact, which no partiality could set aside, his ill-treatment of herself. (*SS* 157)

This is only the first part of a long inside view of Elinor's thoughts in which her reaction to the unpleasant news of Edward Ferrars' engagement is recorded. This excerpt, however, is representative not only of the whole passage, but of the inside views in general used in the portrayal of Elinor. The similarity of many syntactic constructions, that is, the clauses which are more or less equally weighted, creates much implicit parallel.[13] These implicit parallels are reinforced by the explicit parallels: conjunctions, alliterations, and, in particular, the dependence of more than one verb on the subject. The overall impression is one of ideas weighed carefully and thought over. The style, like the style of countless other passages in *Sense and Sensibility*, seems closer to an eighteenth-century sermon or moral disquisition than to Jane Austen's later novels. The style is formal, but not really inconsistent with Elinor's character; however, as Jane Austen develops as an artist, she learns to achieve similar effects with more economy and less rigidity.

> Anne went home to think over all that she had heard. In one point her feelings were relieved by this knowledge of Mr Elliot. There was no longer any thing of tenderness due to him. He stood, as opposed to Captain Wentworth, in all his own unwelcome obtrusiveness; and the evil of his attentions last night, the irremediable mischief he might have done, was considered with sensations unqualified, unperplexed.—Pity for him was over. But this was the only point of relief. In every other respect, in looking around her, of penetrating forward, she saw more to distrust and apprehend. She was concerned for the distrust and pain Lady Russell would be feeling, for the mortifications which must be hanging over her father and sister, and had all the distress of foreseeing many evils without knowing how to avert any one of them. (*P* 183)

Like Elinor, Anne is enlightened, but her reaction is recorded without the unnatural, elaborate rhetoric of the preceding passage. In this passage from *Persuasion*, the explicit parallels seem to emerge naturally from the situation. Mr Elliot is on one side and Captain Wentworth is on the other in her thoughts, but they are not balanced off artificially against each other. Her main concern is what might have happened,

and this concern is made explicit: 'with sensations, unquali-
fied, unperplexed'. The explicit parallels which follow suggest the wide-ranging thoughts stimulated by Anne's newly
gained knowledge. All the explicit parallels refer back to
Anne or to her sensations, and this is the main reason why the
parallels remain so unobtrusive. Another passage from
Sense and Sensibility should make the contrast between
Jane Austen's early and late styles even more apparent.

Elinor made no answer. Her thoughts were silently fixed on
the irreparable injury which too early an independence and its
consequent habits of idleness, dissipation, and luxury, had made
in the mind, the character, the happiness, of a man who, to every
advantage of person and talents, united a disposition naturally
open and honest, and a feeling, affectionate temper. The world
had made him cold-hearted and selfish. Vanity, while seeking
its own guilty triumph at the expense of another, had involved
him in a real attachment, which extravagance, or at least its off-
spring, necessity, had required to be sacrificed. Each faulty propensity in leading him to evil, had led him likewise to punishment.
The attachment, from which against honour, against feeling,
against every better interest he had outwardly torn himself,
now, when no longer allowable, governed every thought; and
the connection, for the sake of which he had, with little scruple,
left her sister to misery, was likely to prove a source of unhappiness to himself of a far more incurable nature. (*SS* 324)

Once again there is much implicit parallel. For example, the
two halves of the last sentence counterbalance one another.
In each main clause the subject ('the attachment' and 'the
connection') is followed by a series of prepositional phrases
which separate the subject from its verb. This is an incidental
kind of parallel which might be passed over unnoticed if
there were not similar patterns throughout the passage,
reinforced by obviously explicit parallels. The triplets in
the second sentence ('idleness', 'dissipation', and 'luxury';
'the mind', 'the character', and 'the happiness') give an
explicit value to the doublets which follow. By implication the first group of three is set off against the second
group; and, in turn, 'person and talents' and 'open and
honest' are opposed to 'extravagant and vain' and 'cold-hearted

and selfish'. The key words that contribute to the impression of explicit parallelism are 'vain', 'vanity', and 'vanity'; 'extravagant', 'extravagance' and 'extravagance'. As the paragraph comes to an end, the evidence is summarized: 'against honour, against feeling, against every better interest'. The repetition of 'against' reinforces the point and the parallel. The self-conscious structuring of this passage suggests that it might date from an early draft of the novel written in letters. It is easier to imagine that Elinor's thoughts might have taken this form while she was composing a letter than on the spur of the moment.

The passages cited in the preceding paragraph illustrate Jane Austen's typical use of the inside view. Nowhere are inside views employed more often than in *Sense and Sensibility*. Whenever they are used in this or the other novels the reader shares with the heroine the experience of gaining some new insight into a situation or character, including the possibility of the heroine's gaining more insight into her own character. With the obvious exception of *Emma*, the reader's knowledge at such points in the narrative is not necessarily superior to the heroine's. Because of the reader's closeness to the heroine's angle of vision in these passages, there is little room for local irony; however, structural irony is likely to occur, since past behaviour and past events are viewed in a new light. The formality of such passages—even where it is rather staid and artificial as in *Sense and Sensibility*—signifies the heroine's efforts to reassess rationally what she has thought up to this time. The reader may assume that the heroine is in error, but such an assumption is usually not based on anything in the passage itself, though the ironic perspective from which some of the inside views are presented encourages circumspection rather than uncritical acceptance on the part of the reader.[14] He may suspect, for example, that more information is necessary before the situation can be judged adequately. Or, the reader's doubts may stem from his preconception of what happens in novels—the expectations made fun of in *Northanger Abbey*. In either case what the reader assumes is not so much the product of reflection but anticipation. He speculates about what he is going to learn next. The reader's acquaintance with the heroine enables him to predict with some certainty how she is likely to behave in a given situation, but he has less basis for predicting what these situations will be. The reader's closeness to the heroine's perspective prevents him from knowing much—if anything at all—apart from what the heroine knows about characters and events which are destined to have a decisive influence on the heroine's life. To summarize, inside views give the reader the opportunity to re-evaluate what he has already learned and to examine the heroine's ability to arrive at a critical assessment of the facts with which she is confronted as well as giving the reader the opportunity to speculate about the future course of events.

In contrast to *Northanger Abbey*, in *Sense and Sensibility* there is a consistent angle of vision. The reader shares with the narrator and Elinor a clearly defined system of values according to which behaviour is judged. This perspective gives a sense of unity to a plot which depends on arbitrary and unexpected developments. The pattern of the developments in the plot is consistent with the moral themes of the novel, but it departs from the reader's expectation of verisimilitude.[15] As a consequence, the structural ironies have a melodramatic or conventional effect which seems out of place in a novel that is 'nearer tragedy than comedy'.[16] The strengths of *Sense and Sensibility* are to be found elsewhere, for example, in the author's treatment of the local ironies, and in particular, in her handling of the dramatic scenes. The best of these scenes reveal Jane Austen's increasing skill in rendering character through dialogue. Explicit commentary is kept to a minimum, and foolishness, egotism, and cupidity are allowed to speak for themselves. By contrast, the inside views of Elinor's mental life still show traces of the early date of the novel's origin. Nevertheless, the inside views as well as the dramatic scenes in *Sense and Sensibility* have the function if not always the form that they are given in the later novels, too.

The first chapter of *Pride and Prejudice* might be summarized as follows:

Mrs Bennet announces that an eligible young bachelor has moved into the neighbourhood, and she suggests to her husband that he should pay a call on their new neighbour, since it almost certainly will be decisive for the future of one of their five daughters. Mr Bennet rejects the proposal.

What is missing from this summary is the irony which operates at three levels: Mrs Bennet's interpretation of other people's remarks and the new situation created by the presence of an eligible young man; Mr Bennet's responses to his wife; and the ironic perspective established by the narrator, which provides the reader with a knowledge superior to Mr Bennet's, whose knowledge is, in turn, superior to his wife's. The opening sentence is an assertion: 'It is a truth universally acknowledged, that a single man in possession of a good fortune must be in want of a wife.' The word order undercuts the validity of the assertion being made, since an illogical conclusion follows upon what appears to be a statement of fact. This statement is not put into Mrs Bennet's mouth, and it is only in the course of the ensuing scene that it becomes clearly identified with her perception of the situation and, more generally, the quality of her mind. As becomes apparent immediately, logic is not one of her strong points. The principals do such a good job of giving themselves away at every turn in this scene that there is little need for the narrator to intervene.

However little known the feelings or views of such a man may be on his first entering a neighbourhood, this truth is so well fixed in the minds of the surrounding families, that he is considered as the rightful property of some one or other of their daughters. (*PP* 51)

Mr Bennet replied that he had not. (*PP* 51)

Mr Bennet made no answer. (*PP* 51)

This was invitation enough. (*PP* 51)

Mr Bennet was so odd a mixture of quick parts, sarcastic humour, reserve, and caprice, that the experience of three and twenty years had been insufficient to make his wife understand his character. *Her* mind was less difficult to develope. She was a woman of mean understanding, little information, and uncertain temper. When she was discontented she fancied herself nervous. The business of her life was to get her daughters married; its solace was visiting and news. (*PP* 53)

The narrator's comments provide a structural frame for the scene between Mr and Mrs Bennet. These subdued remarks are in striking contrast to Mrs Bennet's. Further, they reflect the narrator's partisanship in favour of the husband. The last of the narrator's comments quoted above confirms what is already implicit in Mr Bennet's responses to his wife, that she is to be humoured but not taken seriously. Mrs Bennet's comments are comprised of nonsense, which may be sub-divided into questions, assertions, and hearsay. While her husband has no difficulty in comprehending her point long before she has made it, Mrs Bennet remains ignorant to the end of the true import of her spouse's remarks. Her assertions and relations of hearsay are not taken at face value. She is incapable of anticipating her husband's responses. As communicative acts Mrs Bennet's remarks are not successful, since the receiver, Mr Bennet, refuses to interpret the message as the sender has intended. In the other direction, communication does not function much better. Mr Bennet is obviously aware that his remarks will be misunderstood. The irony of course is that it is Mr Bennet's intention that his remarks be misconstrued. The narrator's comments which underline the ironic implications of this scene provide a perspective of superior knowledge, which the reader shares with the narrator throughout the rest of the novel.

From this perspective the reader has to assess and reassess what he learns. The distance established between him and the heroine places the reader in a more favourable position than Elizabeth Bennet to recognize where there has been misunderstanding, though the ironic implications of such misunderstandings only become evident in retrospect. The action turns on the misunderstandings which exist not only for the reader but also for the participants in the action. The development of the plot depends on the effectiveness of the scenes between Elizabeth and Darcy. These are the reader's best opportunity to assess Darcy's thoughts and feelings. Some critics have argued that Darcy's transformation is unconvincing, that he is manipulated by the author for the sake of the plot and does not come across as a fully-rounded, believable character.[17] This line of argument overlooks two important points. In the first place, the reader views Darcy from Elizabeth's not unprejudiced perspective. Secondly, the changes in his attitude are carefully prepared for. The key scenes involving Darcy and Elizabeth are subject to more than one interpretation.[18] Elizabeth gives them the reading which corresponds to the prejudices she forms at their first meeting. At the first Netherfield ball, Elizabeth overhears Darcy's unflattering comments referring to her. To Bingley's suggestion that Darcy be introduced to Elizabeth, Darcy responds, 'She is tolerable, but not handsome enough to tempt me; and I am in no humour at present to give consequence to young ladies who are slighted by other men. You had better return to your partner and enjoy her smiles, for you are wasting your time with me' (*PP* 59). The original title *First Impressions* carried the connotation in Sentimental fiction of immediate surrender to sensibility, love at first sight—the kind of experience Jane Austen portrayed in *Love and Friendship*.[19] Obviously, Elizabeth and Darcy are not destined to undergo such an experience. Somewhat later in the course of the action, when Sir William Lucas attempts to bring Darcy and Elizabeth together, it becomes clear that Elizabeth's view of Darcy for the time being has been fixed by her 'first impression'; whereas there are hints already at this early stage that his view of Elizabeth has begun to alter under the influence of closer observation.

'My dear Eliza, why are you not dancing? Mr Darcy, you must allow me to present this young lady to you as a very desirable partner.—You cannot refuse to dance, I am sure, when so much beauty is before you.' And taking her hand, he would have given it to Mr Darcy, who, though extremely surprised, was not unwilling to receive it, when she instantly drew back, and said with some discomposure to Sir William,

'Indeed, Sir, I have have not the least intention of dancing.—

I entreat you not to suppose that I moved this way in order to beg for a partner.'

Mr Darcy with grave propriety requested to be allowed the honour of her hand; but in vain. Elizabeth was determined; nor did Sir William at all shake her purpose by his attempt at persuasion.

'You excel so much in the dance, Miss Eliza, that it is cruel to deny me the happiness of seeing you; and though this gentleman dislikes the amusement in general, he can have no objection, I are sure, to oblige us for one half hour.'

'Mr Darcy is all politeness,' said Elizabeth, smiling. 'He is indeed—but considering the inducement, my dear Eliza, we cannot wonder at his complaisance; for who would object to such a partner?'

Elizabeth looked archly, and turned away. Her resistance had not injured her with the gentleman . . . (*PP* 72–73)

The most significant feature of this scene is how little either Elizabeth or Darcy says. Sir William is well-meaning, but his remarks are only a too vivid reminder to Elizabeth of Darcy's previous lack of interest in dancing with her. Her statement 'Mr Darcy is all politeness' is not clearly marked; that is, it signals a number of possible interpretations, ranging from insult to compliment. It is intentionally ironic, but it may be even more ironic than the speaker assumes. The proffered partner may indeed wish to dance with Elizabeth and not only because of the exigencies of the situation created by Sir William and the rules of decorum but for more personal reasons. The reader, however, cannot be certain. Darcy's request for a dance is not given but only referred to. From it the reader might have been able to deduce more concerning Darcy's motives. His thoughts at the end of the scene are recorded by the narrator, but these are a response to Elizabeth's reaction to the situation. What he was thinking prior to her 'resistance' is only hinted at with the phrase, 'not unwilling to receive it', meaning Elizabeth's hand for the dance. The technique of presentation in this scene is more complex than anything in the earlier novels or even in the first chapter of *Pride and Prejudice*, where the speeches of Mr and Mrs Bennet are still clearly marked.

F

None of the participants controls the conversation or fully comprehends its implications, not even the reader. Sir William is completely oblivious to any deeper significance whatever. Darcy may perceive some of Elizabeth's irony, but not all of it, for he is unaware of the fact that she has already formed a very definite opinion of him. Elizabeth fails to recognize that Darcy's invitation might be anything more than a courteous gesture. As the story progresses, Jane Austen continues to utilize the ambiguities of such situations for purposes of characterization and in anticipation of the climactic point where Elizabeth perceives her own error.

> Mr Darcy drawing near Elizabeth said to her—
> 'Do not you feel a great inclination, Miss Bennet, to seize such an opportunity of dancing a reel?'
> She smiled, but made no answer. He repeated the question, with some surprise at her silence.
> 'Oh!' said she, 'I heard you before; but I could not immediately determine what to say in reply. You wanted me, I know to say 'Yes,' that you might have the pleasure of despising my taste; but I always delight in overthrowing those kinds of schemes, and cheating a person of their premeditated contempt. I have therefore made up my mind to tell you, that I do not want to dance a reel at all—and now despise me if you dare.'
> 'Indeed I do not dare.'
> Elizabeth having rather expected to affront him, was amazed at his gallantry; but there was a mixture of sweetness and archness in her manner which made it difficult for her to affront anybody; and Darcy had never been so bewitched by any woman as he was by her. He really believed, that were it not for the inferiority of her connections, he should be in some danger. (*PP* 96)

This scene is a variation on the last one quoted above. This time Darcy himself takes the initiative in asking Elizabeth to dance. Elizabeth attributes a motive to his request which is not impossible but is unlikely in the light of Darcy's further remark, which takes her by surprise. The narrator's comment increases rather than reduces the ambiguities of this scene. On the one hand it brings out clearly Darcy's sense of pride; on the other, it indicates that Elizabeth has become more than a subject of minor interest to him. The key question implied in this scene is why Darcy does not 'dare'. For the time being, it is left unanswered.

> They stood for some time without speaking a word; and she began to imagine that their silence was to last through the two dances, and at first was resolved not to break it; till suddenly fancying that it would be greater punishment to her partner to oblige him to talk, she made some slight observation on the dance. He replied, and was again silent. After a pause of some minutes she addressed him a second time with
>
> 'It is *your* turn to say something now, Mr Darcy—I talked about the dance, and you ought to make some kind of remark on the size of the room, or the number of couples.'
>
> He smiled, and assured her that whatever she wished him to say should be said.
>
> 'Very well.—That reply will do for the present.—Perhaps by and bye I may observe that private balls are much pleasanter than public ones.—But *now* we may remain silent.'
>
> 'Do you talk by the rule then, while you are dancing?'
>
> 'Sometimes. One must speak a little, you know. It would look odd to be entirely silent for half an hour together, and yet for the advantage of *some*, conversation ought to be so arranged as that they may have the trouble of saying as little as possible.'
>
> 'Are you consulting your own feelings in the present case, or do you imagine that you are gratifying mine?'
>
> 'Both,' replied Elizabeth archly; 'for I have always seen a great similarity in the turn of our minds.—We are each of an unsocial, taciturn disposition, unwilling to speak, unless we expect to say something that will amaze the whole room, and be handed down to posterity with all the eclat of a proverb.'
>
> 'This is not a very striking resemblance of your own character, I am sure,' said he. 'How near it may be to *mine*, I cannot pretend to say.— *You* think it a faithful portrait undoubtedly.'
>
> 'I must not decide on my own performance.'
>
> He made no answer. . . . (*PP* 133–134)

Elizabeth's recent conversation with Wickham (Chapter 16) has confirmed her in her opinion of Darcy's pride. In this scene she sets out to bait him. Darcy is here even less able to discern Elizabeth's motives than he was in the previous scene. The stage is being prepared for the gross misunderstandings which lead to Darcy's first proposal and Elizabeth's refusal (Chapter 34). Soon after this encounter Darcy departs, not to meet Elizabeth again before she goes to visit her friend Charlotte and he to visit his aunt. He goes away more impressed than ever by Elizabeth's charm and wit, unaware that her opinion of him is far from favourable. For her part, in the interim, Elizabeth grasps at every bit of evidence against Darcy which is consistent with the image she has already formed of him. In this respect, she resembles Emma, who is a past master of what might be called 'selective perception'. In the scene above, Darcy's initial silence and subsequent civil responses are motivated by politeness, but also by a stronger feeling of which Elizabeth is unaware and the reader unsure. For example, the reader cannot be certain how to interpret Darcy's willingness to say whatever Elizabeth would like him to. Perhaps, Darcy is just matching Elizabeth in her facetiousness, but it is also possible that his 'willingness' is an indication of his growing interest in Elizabeth. Most of the remarks in this scene are marked in such a complex manner that intentions and responses are left unclear. Consequently, it is difficult to determine with certainty what each of the parties means to say, or what significance they assign to what they hear.

As suggested above, this method of presentation is a departure from what the author has done previously. In *Northanger Abbey* and *Sense and Sensibility*, intentions and responses are readily deduced from the immediate context. Complete understanding among the participants is infrequent, but the direction of the misunderstandings is clearly defined. In the Darcy–Elizabeth scenes such clarity is absent. Conversation as a social activity takes place, and none of the rules for correct behaviour are broken; but as subsequent events confirm, no real understanding between those involved occurs. The smiles, the silences, and the surprised reactions which are features of these encounters contribute to the ambiguities. Such ambiguities are not absent from the novels which were to follow; however, in none of the other novels is the development of the action so dependent upon them.[20] For the first time, Jane Austen succeeds in integrating the local and the structural ironies. In *Northanger Abbey* local ironies are developed at the expense of the larger ironic pattern in the plot's structure. In *Sense and Sensibility* the structural ironies seem forced. In *Pride and Prejudice* Jane Austen continues to use to some extent techniques of presentation which she has employed earlier. She seldom uses an inside view, but whenever she does, it has the same function as in the other novels.[21] In her handling of the dialogue of the secondary characters, for instance in the first chapter, the author's method is similar—if more complex and more frequently employed—to what she had done previously. But in her treatment of the two characters who are the focus of attention throughout most of the novel, and in the overall conception of the narrative, she also explores new possibilities of presentation. The path of exploration and experimentation continues in *Mansfield Park*.[22]

In the last chapter, I considered Jane Austen's method of dramatizing the moral conflicts which govern the course of the action in *Mansfield Park*. She utilizes the symbolic implications of the key episodes to direct attention to the novel's central themes. In addition to trying out this new method in narrative presentation, Jane Austen continues to employ methods familiar from the earlier novels. Her means of developing the local ironies in the inside views and in many of the dramatic scenes closely resembles what she has done before. Through inside views the reader is shown how the heroine of *Mansfield Park* examines her own feelings and considers or reconsiders judgements she has made about others or about herself.

To this nest of comforts Fanny now walked down to try its influence on an agitated, doubting spirit—to see if by looking at Edmund's profile she could catch his counsel, or by giving air to her geraniums she might inhale a breeze of mental strength herself. But she had more than fears of her own perseverance to remove; she had begun to feel undecided as to what she *ought to do*; and as she walked round the room her doubts were increasing. Was she *right* in refusing what was so warmly asked, so strongly wished for? What might be so essential to a scheme on which some of those to whom she owed the greatest complaisance, had set their hearts? Was it not ill-nature—selfishness—and a fear of exposing herself? And would Edmund's judgment, would his persuasion of Sir Thomas's disapprobation of the whole, be enough to justify her in a determined denial in spite of all the rest? It would be so horrible to her to act, that she was inclined to suspect the truth and purity of her own scruples, and as she looked around her, the claims of her cousins to being obliged, were strengthened by the sight of present upon present that she had received from them. The table between the windows was covered with workboxes and netting-boxes, which had been given her at different times, principally by Tom; and she grew bewildered as to the amount of debt which all these kind rememberances produced. (*MP* 174)

The implicit and explicit parallels of this passage reflect the heroine's efforts to think carefully and rationally at this moment of stress. She tries to examine her own feelings as well as to consider those of others; however, she is only too conscious of the emotions which have been called forth by the request that she accept a role in the play. She senses that it would be wrong, but at the same time she realizes that she is in no position to judge the situation objectively. From the beginning Fanny has had grave doubts as to the propriety of putting on the play. Subsequent events have given her no reason to alter her opinion, but the preparations for the play have forced Fanny to recognize that her opposition has been motivated in part of her jealousy of the growing intimacy of the relationship between Mary Crawford and Edmund. In the passage above, Fanny is not yet capable of admitting this even to herself. The conflicts in her mind are still at a more general level, and, for the moment, she comes to no decision. When Fanny does give in finally to Edmund's request, she is motivated primarily by the need to demonstrate to herself that she is not allowing her emotions to govern her behaviour. The reader is never in as much doubt as Fanny as to how the heroine should act. It is readily apparent, for example, that Fanny's eventual submission to group pressure is a mistake, for it contradicts the very principles which have guided Fanny up to now in her judgement of her own conduct as well as that of others. Fanny's lack of self-assurance leads her into error. In the inside view cited above, the reader is more certain than Fanny is about the correctness of the heroine's inclinations, for her thoughts are not treated ironically. Moreover, here as elsewhere, Fanny's objections to the play are consistently supported by the narrator. But Fanny is far less clear-sighted than Elinor Dashwood, and, as a consequence, she finds it increasingly difficult to distinguish emotion from reason. Fanny appears to be confronted by an insoluble conflict. Unsure what to do, at first she does nothing. Her hesitancy but not her moral integrity is mocked. This is not even placed in question when she finally succumbs to the circumstances which temporarily blur her perception of her own sense of values.

Jane Austen's use of dramatic scenes in *Mansfield Park* also recalls the method used, for example, in the second chapter of *Sense and Sensibility* and the first chapter in *Pride and Prejudice*. Upon Sir Thomas' unexpected return and his discovery that the situation at Mansfield Park has got out of hand during his absence, he turns to Mrs Norris for an explanation.

Mrs Norris was a little confounded, and as nearly being silenced as ever she had been in her life; for she was ashamed to confess having never seen any of the impropriety which was so glaring to Sir Thomas, and would not have admitted that her influence was insufficient, that she might have talked in vain. Her only resource was to get out of the subject as fast as possible, and turn the current of Sir Thomas's ideas into a happier channel. She had a great deal to insinuate in her own praise as to *general* attention to the interest and comfort of the family, much exertion and many sacrifices to glance at in the form of hurried walks and sudden removals from her own fireside, and many excellent hints of distrust and economy to Lady Bertram and Edmund to detail, whereby a most considerable saving had always arisen, and more than one bad servant had been detected. But her chief strength lay in Sotherton. Her greatest support and glory was in having formed the connection with the Rushworths. *There* she was impregnable. She took to herself all the credit of bringing Mr Rushworth's admiration of Maria to any effect. 'If I had not been active,' said she, 'and made a point of being introduced to his mother, and then prevailed on my sister to pay the first visit, I am certain as I sit here, that nothing would have come of it—for

Mr Rushworth is the sort of amiable modest young man who wants a great deal of encouragement, and there were girls enough on the catch for him if we had been idle. But I left no stone unturned. I was ready to move heaven and earth to persuade my sister, and at last I did persuade her. You know the distance to Sotherton; it was the middle of winter, and the roads almost impassable, but I did persuade her.'

'I know how great, how justly great your influence is with Lady Bertram and her children, and am the more concerned that it should not have been'—

'My dear Sir Thomas, if you had seen the state of the roads *that* day! I thought we should never have got through them, though we had the four horses of course; and poor coachman would attend us, out of his great love and kindness, though he was hardly able to sit on the box on account of the rheumatism which I had been doctoring him for, ever since Michaelmas, I cured him at last; but he was very bad all the winter—and this was such a day, I could not help going to him up in his room before we set off to advise him not to venture: he was putting on his wig—so I said, "Coachman, you had much better not go, your Lady and I shall be very safe; you know how steady Stephen is, and Charles has been upon the leaders so often now, that I am sure there is no fear." But, however, I soon found it would not do; he was bent upon going, and as I hate to be worrying and officious, I said no more; but my heart quite ached for him at every jolt, and when we got into the rough lanes about Stoke, where what with frost and snow upon beds of stones, it was worse than any thing you can imagine, I was quite in agony about him. And then the poor horses too!—To see them straining away! You know how I always feel for the horses. And when we got to the bottom of Sandcroft Hill, what do you think I did? You will laugh at me—but I got out and walked up. I did indeed. It might not be saving them much, but it was something, and I could not bear to sit at my ease, and be dragged up at the expense of those noble animals. I caught a dreadful cold, but *that* I did not regard. My object was accomplished with the visit.'

'I hope we shall always think the acquaintance worth any trouble that might be taken to establish it. There is nothing very striking in Mr Rushworth's manners, but I was pleased last night with what appeared to be his opinion on *one* subject—his decided preference of a quiet family-party to the bustle and confusion of acting. He seemed to feel exactly as one could wish.'

'Yes, indeed,—and the more you know of him, the better you will like him. He is not a shining character, but he has a thousand good qualities! and is so disposed to look upon you, that I am quite laughed at about it, for every body considers it as my doing. "Upon my word, Mrs Norris," said Mrs Grant, the other day, "If Mr Rushworth were a son of your own he could not hold Sir Thomas in greater respect."'

Sir Thomas gave up the point, foiled by her evasions, disarmed by her flattery; and was obliged to rest satisfied with the conviction that where the present pleasure of those she loved was at stake, her kindness did sometimes overpower her judgment. (*MP* 204–206)

As in similar scenes in the other novels, the irony in this scene operates at three levels: Mrs Norris's response, Sir Thomas's response, and the reader's response to the situation portrayed. Neither of the participants in this conversation comprehends completely what is happening, though Mrs Norris dominates. Sir Thomas is at a particular disadvantage, since he is not in a position to identify correctly the motives behind Mrs Norris's remarks. By contrast, the narrator informs the reader at the beginning of this scene as to what it is that motivates Mrs Norris's evasiveness. Neither the reader nor Sir Thomas is in a position to accept Mrs Norris's utterances at face value, that is to assign to them the interpretation which she has intended. Presumably, she intends to evoke 'praise' or at least 'gratitude', but she misjudges her audience and chooses a totally inappropriate situation in which to gain such recognition. Moreover, what she is saying has actually very little to do with what she is thinking under the present circumstances. In other words, her exercise in self-praise is motivated partly by a desire for recognition, but even more strongly by a desire to avoid exposure of her negligence. Recent events at Mansfield Park require an explanation, and Sir Thomas expects one. He is not in the mood to listen to a recitation of everything Mrs Norris has done for his family and Mansfield Park during his absence. He is much more concerned about what has been left undone. Therefore, the content of what Mrs Norris has to say influences Sir Thomas only to the extent that it convinces him that she will never get back to answering the question. Contrary to her intention, Mrs Norris produces resignation and incomprehension in her listener. The motives Sir Thomas attributes to Mrs Norris at the end of the passage indicate how limited his insight into her character is. From his position of superior knowledge gained from the experience of the text up to this point and the ironic perspective established by the narrator in this scene, the reader is less taken in than Sir Thomas is by Mrs Norris's awkward efforts to politely change the subject.

In *Emma* the dramatic scenes provide the reader with an opportunity to witness how Emma transforms her ideas into action and to examine Emma's opinions of other characters in the light of their behaviour in such scenes. Having just received a written proposal of marriage, Harriet turns to Emma for advice.

'Yes. But what shall I say? Dear Miss Woodhouse, do advise me.'

'Oh, no, no! the letter had much better be all your own. You will express yourself very properly, I am sure. There is no danger of your not being intelligible, which is the first thing. Your meaning must be unequivocal; no doubts or demurs: and such expressions of gratitude and concern for the pain you are inflicting as propriety requires, will present themselves unbidden to *your* mind, I am persuaded. *You* need not be prompted to write with the appearance of sorrow for his disappointment.'

'You think I ought to refuse him then,' said Harriet, looking down.

'Ought to refuse him! My dear Harriet, what do you mean? Are you in any doubt as to that? I thought—but I beg your pardon, perhaps I have been under a mistake. I certainly have been misunderstanding you, if you feel in doubt as to the *purport* of your answer. I had imagined you were consulting me only as to the wording of it.'

Harriet was silent. With a little reserve of manner, Emma continued:

'You mean to return a favourable answer, I collect.'

'No, I do not; that is, I do not mean—What shall I do? What would you advise me to do? Pray, dear Miss Woodhouse, tell me what I ought to do?

'I shall not give you any advice, Harriet. I will have nothing to do with it. This is a point you must settle with your own feelings.'

'I had no notion that he liked me so very much,' said Harriet, contemplating the letter. For a little while Emma perservered in her silence; but beginning to apprehend the bewitching flattery of that letter might be too powerful, she thought it best to say, 'I lay it down as a general rule, Harriet, that if a woman *doubts* as to whether she should accept a man or not, she certainly ought to refuse him. If she can hesitate as to "Yes," she ought to say "No" directly. It is not a state to be safely entered into with doubtful feelings, with half a heart. I thought it my duty as a friend, and older than yourself, to say this much to you. But do not imagine that I want to influence you.'

'Oh! no, I am sure you are a great deal too kind to—but if you would just advise me what I had best do—No, no, I do not mean that—As you say, one's mind ought to be quite made up—One should not be hesitating—It is a very serious thing,—It will be safer to say "No", perhaps.—Do you think I had better say "No?"'

'Not for the world,' said Emma, smiling graciously, 'would I advise you either way. You must be the best judge of your own happiness. If you prefer Mr Martin to every other person; if you think him the most agreeable man you have ever been in company with, why should you hesitate? You blush, Harriet.— Does any body else occur to you at this moment under such a definition? Harriet, do not deceive yourself; do not be run away with by gratitude and compassion. At this moment whom are you thinking of?'

The symptoms were favourable.—Instead of answering, Harriet turned away confused, and stood thoughtfully by the fire; and though the letter was still in her hand, it was now mechanically twisted about without regard. Emma waited the result with impatience, but not without strong hopes. At last, with some hesitation, Harriet said—

'Miss Woodhouse, as you will not give me an opinion, I must do as well as I can by myself; and I have now quite determined, and really almost made up my mind—to refuse Mr Martin. Do you think I am right?' (*E* 78–80)

Emma is no less careful in her choice of words than Mrs Dashwood is in *Sense and Sensibility*. Emma is in total control of the situation. Like Mr Dashwood, Harriet is led cautiously to make the right decision while remaining completely unaware of the fact that her mind is being made up for her. Harriet fails to perceive either of Emma's true motives. Emma wants to persuade Harriet to make the correct decision, and at the same time give her the impression that she has made the decision on her own. Emma's real intentions are highlighted by the narrator's comments.

> Harriet was silent. With a little reserve of manner, Emma continued; . . .

> For a little while Emma perservered in her silence; but beginning to apprehend the bewitching flattery of that letter might be too powerful, she thought it best to say, . . .

> The symptoms were favourable . . . Emma waited the result with impatience, but not without strong hopes.

These comments confirm what is already implicit in Emma's remarks: the heroine has no intention of allowing Harriet to arrive at a decision without benefiting from the advice of her mentor. Emma considers the situation of the moment cautiously before proceeding further in her efforts to influence her young friend. The structure of this scene resembles the structure of those scenes found in the earlier novels. The scene can be defined in terms of the reader's response, Emma's response, and Harriet's response. Harriet's reaction is exactly what Emma has anticipated. Harriet gives the reading to Emma's utterances that is intended. Emma's declarations of disinterest and her expressed desire not to interfere are accepted as such. Viewing this conversation the other way around, Harriet is in no position to anticipate Emma's responses, because of her ignorance of Emma's motives. One of the ironies of this scene is that Harriet succeeds in her plea for advice and guidance without realizing it. A second irony is the contradiction between Emma's conviction on the one hand of Harriet's exceptional talents and Emma's equally strong certainty on the other that she can direct Harriet's interests at will. The reader's response differs from that of either of the participants in this scene. He perceives a fundamental irony in the fact that neither Harriet nor Emma fully comprehends the significance of this conversation. Unlike Harriet, the reader cannot assign the desired interpretation to Emma's utterances. This is not possible, because he knows they are not an expression of what Emma actually thinks. Similarly, he recognizes that Harriet's belief that she has failed in her appeal for guidance is incorrect. Her utterances stimulate a response which goes beyond what Harriet could have anticipated.

Despite her self-confidence, Emma is capable of being misled as well as being misleading. This is brought out especially in the scenes between Emma and Frank Churchill, who has several of Emma's weaknesses, but fewer of her redeeming qualities. In the following scene, Emma speculates about who it might have been that gave Jane Fairfax a pianoforte.

'Why do you smile?' said she.

'Nay, why do you?'

'Me!—I suppose I smile for pleasure at Col. Campbell's being so rich and so liberal.—It is a handsome present.'

'Very.'

'I rather wonder that it was never made before.'

'Perhaps Miss Fairfax has never been staying here so long before.'

'Or that he did not give her the use of their own instrument—which must now be shut up in London, untouched by any body.'

'That is a grand pianoforté, and he might think it too large for Mrs Bates' house.'

'You may *say* what you chuse—but your countenance testifies that your *thoughts* on this subject are very much like mine.'

'I do not know. I rather believe you are giving me more credit for acuteness than I deserve. I smile because you smile, and shall probably suspect whatever I find you suspect; but at present I do not see what there is to question. If Col. Campbell is not the person, who can it be?'

'What do you say to Mrs Dixon?'

'Mrs Dixon! very true indeed. I had not thought of Mrs Dixon. She must know as well as her father, how acceptable an instrument would be; and perhaps the mode of it, the mystery, the

surprize, is more like a young woman's scheme than an elderly
man's. It is Mrs Dixon I dare say. I told you that your suspicions
would guide mine.'

'If so, you must extend your suspicions and comprehend *Mr*
Dixon in them.' (*E* 225–226)

Frank Churchill encourages Emma in her fanciful speculations, though he knows she is wrong. In his responses
Churchill gives Emma the impression that he is being guided
by the logic of her argument. This is of course the same role

which Emma has already defined for herself in her relationship to Harriet. Churchill appears to be in agreement with
Emma's suppositions, and this is how she interprets his response to what she has to say; however, in reality his remarks
neither reflect what he is actually thinking, nor anticipate how
he will act subsequently. But, for the moment, the reader is
hardly in a better position than Emma to perceive this. In
judging Emma's behaviour in this scene, the reader has less
difficulty, for her conduct follows a well-established pattern.
As so often in the past, Emma's reasoning is not based on a
consideration of the facts but on a preconceived notion,
whose relationship to an objective reality is in inverse proportion to the intensity of Emma's interest in the matter.
Harriet accepts the logic of Emma's arguments, because
Harriet is too naïve and too stupid to see through it. Knightley's response is much more circumspect. He warns Emma
repeatedly of the dangers of her over-active imagination,
pointing out that her speculations can lead to no good.
Frank Churchill's response raises questions which for the
time being remain unanswered. He appears a little too ready
to encourage Emma in her speculations, but the reader is
left to guess at what might lie behind Churchill's attitude.
Churchill's motives are far from clear. He might be just
indulging in flattery, or he might have a more sinister aim in
mind. On the surface this dialogue seems to function smoothly,
and Emma is totally unaware that something considerably less
than complete mutual understanding has taken place. She
fails to realize that she is being manipulated in much the same
manner which she employs in directing Harriet's interests.

Her utterances are not understood the way she assumes because, although Churchill appears to give them the desired interpretation, his words belie his thoughts. As in the Elizabeth Bennet–Darcy scenes in *Pride and Prejudice*, the reader has to wait for further developments in the action before assigning a final interpretation to this conversation between Emma and Frank Churchill.

One of the features which distinguishes *Emma* from Jane Austen's other novels is the fact that the heroine's romance makes up a comparatively small part of the story. Quite early all of Jane Austen's other heroines—with the qualified exception of Elizabeth—know whom it is that they would like to marry, and from this point on an important element in the plot is the overcoming of the hindrances that stand between the heroine's aspirations and perfect happiness. In *Emma* the situation is different. Neither Emma nor Knightley seriously entertains the idea of their marriage until quite late in the course of the action. In the following exchange, both of them move a step closer to a recognition of their common destiny.

'Whom are you going to dance with?' asked Mr Knightley.

She hesitated a moment, and then replied, 'With you, if you will ask me.'

'Will you?' said he, offering his hand.

'Indeed I will. You have shown you can dance, and you know we are not really so much brother and sister as to make it at all improper.'

'Brother and sister! no, indeed.' (*E* 327–328)

Knightley and Emma become half conscious of a possibility that neither of them has articulated before. Their polite conversation brings about a moment of self-recognition. Each of them discovers that he has said more than he intended. There is no effort by Emma or Knightley to direct the conversation. The responses are spontaneous and free of any ulterior motive. They are suggestive of the long-standing friendship which the speakers share. This scene represents the beginning of Knightley's re-examination of his own feelings towards Emma. As the story progresses, the emotions awakened here are aggravated by Emma's apparent interest in Frank Churchill. The process of change which Knightley begins to undergo at this point, however, is kept at some distance from the reader. Since the story continues to be presented from Emma's point of view, the reader continues to see Knightley in his function as guide and mentor rather than as an unhappy potential lover. Knightley frequently finds it necessary to reprimand Emma for her ill-considered behaviour, and the feelings aroused in the scene quoted above do not distract him from carrying out what he considers to be his duty. Whenever it is necessary to remonstrate with Emma, Knightley refuses to allow his pupil to ignore the full meaning of his remarks.

'Emma, I must once more speak to you as I have been used to do: a privilege rather endured than allowed, perhaps, but I must still use it. I cannot see you acting wrong, without remonstrance. How could you be so unfeeling to Miss Bates? How could you be so insolent in your wit to a woman of her character, age, and situation?—Emma, I had not thought it possible.'

Emma recollected, blushed, was sorry, but tried to laugh it off. 'Nay, how could I help saying what I did?—Nobody could have helped it. It was not so very bad. I dare say she did not understand me.'

'I assure you she did. She felt your full meaning. She has talked of it since. I wish you could have heard how she talked of it—with what candour and generosity. I wish you could have heard her honouring your forbearance, in being able to pay her such attentions, as she was for ever receiving from yourself and your father, when her society must be so irksome.'

'Oh!' cried Emma, 'I know there is not a better creature in the world: but you must allow, that what is good and what is ridiculous are most unfortunately blended in her.'

'They are blended,' said he, 'I acknowledge; and were she prosperous, I could allow much for the occasional prevalence of the ridiculous over the good. Were she a woman of fortune, I would leave every harmless absurdity take its chance, I would not quarrel with you for any liberties of manner. Were she your equal in situation—but, Emma, consider how far this is from being the case. . . .' (*E* 367–368)

Emma is too intelligent and has known Knightley too long to doubt the validity of his remarks; nevertheless, she would like to avoid accepting the truth if possible. Her mentor does not allow her this alternative. Knightley knows his audience, and he has no reason to doubt that his listener is capable of assigning the correct interpretation to his remarks if he does not allow her to find excuses for her behaviour. Knightley controls the conversation, but unlike Mr Bennet, Mrs Dashwood or other manipulators in Jane Austen's fiction, his object is not to mislead but to guide his listener. Like Mrs Norris in *Mansfield Park*, Emma sets out to avoid the truth at all costs; however, her mentor is more perceptive than Sir Thomas Bertram. Knightley knows Emma far too well to be taken in by her attempt to downplay the significance of the incident. Her defensive remarks fail in their intended effect. In the end Emma is compelled to admit that Knightley is completely justified in his harsh criticism.

The dramatic scenes are the reader's main source of information about the thoughts and attitudes of all the other characters apart from Emma. As in *Mansfield Park*, the characters are brought together at intervals by the author in order to reveal their attitudes towards one another as well as their general moral and social attitudes. The symbolic suggestiveness of these episodes is less obvious than in *Mansfield Park*, but their function is the same—the relation of external scene to states of mind.[23] In the last third of the novel, there are two important episodes of this kind: the picnic at Donwell Abbey and the one on the following day at Box Hill. At the former each of the characters goes his own way, though they have supposedly come together to share a pleasant afternoon. Their separateness on this occasion reflects a divergence in their interests and preoccupations. Emma is struck by the true gentility of Donwell Abbey and the idyllic beauty of the Martin's Abbey Hill Farm. These images contrast sharply in her mind with her own previous opinion of the Martin family, and with what appears to her the impropriety of Frank Churchill's and Jane Fairfax's behaviour on this particular day. Jane Fairfax leaves early and Frank Churchill arrives late, and neither of them during the time that they are present makes an effort to become involved with the others. The conflicts implicit in this scene come more out into the open the next day at Box Hill. Once again, there is only an apparent unity among those present. Emma and Frank Churchill indulge in their own whims, ignoring the feelings of everyone else. For a time, Emma is flattered as she had been occasionally in the past by Churchill's intentions. She encourages him in his romantic raillery, and he likewise encourages her to play her dominating role among the party that has come together for a day's outing. Overcome by a certain *hubris* and giving in to temptation, Emma makes fun of Miss Bates's meandering and sometimes incoherent manner of talking about nothing in particular. The Sotherton episode in *Mansfield Park* foreshadows the conflicts that develop in the course of the novel. By contrast, the episodes at Donwell Abbey and Box Hill highlight and clarify the conflicts which have emerged in the course of the action, and they prepare the stage for the climactic phase in Emma's development from self-delusion to self-awareness. Jane Fairfax is isolated. Frank Churchill's conduct is inexcusable. Emma's manner is rude, unfeeling, and egotistical. She snubs Jane, is cruel to Miss Bates, continues to plan Harriet's future, and is still blind to Churchill's true character and Knightley's feelings for her. These scenes, like the action of the novel as a whole, are organized about what Emma does, says and thinks. Her inclination to reshape her little world to conform to her preconceptions and to ignore whatever does not fit into this image evoke the author's scathing irony.

Anne Elliot is also an object of Jane Austen's irony, but the implied criticism is much more restrained, for Anne's weaknesses are much more understandable and excusable considering the circumstances in which she finds herself. The harsher thrusts of the author's irony in *Persuasion* are reserved for the secondary characters. The further they deviate in their conduct from the ideal embodied in Anne the more unremittingly they are subjected to Jane Austen's irony. Apart from Wentworth, none of the characters is left untouched. The most obvious objects of irony are the members of Anne's immediate family: Mary Musgrove, Elizabeth and

Sir Walter Elliot. These characters share what is referred to as 'the Elliot pride' (*P* 111), that is, a total preoccupation with oneself and one's appearance. Years of marriage and children apparently have altered Mary, for she differs in some respects from Sir Walter and Elizabeth. But it is questionable whether or not Mary has been 'improved' by her separation from the family estate.

Though better endowed than the elder sister, Mary had not Anne's understanding, or temper. While well, happy, and properly attended to, she had great good humour and excellent spirits; but any indisposition sunk her completely; she had no resources for solitude; and inheriting a considerable share of the Elliot self-importance, was very prone to add to every other distress that of fancying herself neglected and ill-used. In person, she was inferior to both sisters, and had even in her bloom, only reached the dignity of being 'a fine girl.' She was now lying on the faded sofa of the pretty little drawing-room, the once elegant furniture of which had been gradually growing shabby, under the influence of four summers and two children; and, on Anne's appearing, greeted her with,

'So, you are come at last! I began to think I should never see you. I am so ill I can hardly speak. I have not seen a creature the whole morning!'

'I am sorry to find you so unwell,' replied Anne. 'You sent me such a good account of yourself on Thursday!'

'Yes, I made the best of it; I always do; but I was very far from well at the time; and I do not think I ever was so ill in my life as I have been all this morning—very unfit to be left alone, I am sure. Suppose I were to be seized of a sudden in some dreadful way, and not able to ring the bell! So Lady Russell would not get out. I do not think she has been in this house three times this summer.'

Anne said what was proper, and enquired after her husband.

'Oh! Charles is out shooting. I have not seen him since seven o'clock. He would go, though I told him how ill I was. He said he should not stay long; but he has never come back, and now it is almost one. I assure you, I have not seen a soul this whole long morning.'

'You have had your little boys with you?'

'Yes, as long as I could bear their noise; but they are so unmanageable that they do me more harm than good. Little Charles does not mind a word I say, and Walter is growing quite as bad.'

'Well, you will soon be better now,' replied Anne, cheerfully. 'You know I always cure you when I come. How are your neighbours at the Great House?' (*P* 64–65)

The conversation continues in this manner for some time until Anne nearly succeeds in convincing her sister that Mary is feeling far better than she imagines. The Elliot pride takes a distinctive form in Mary. She has the neurotic need to fill the emotional void in her life with the attentions and sympathies of others. Jane Austen is always critical of characters who over-indulge their feelings; and, in this instance, where there is actually no reason for Mary to be emotionally upset, the author's irony is unrestrained. The narrator's introduction leaves no room for a misinterpretation of Mary's conduct. Her conversation with Anne illustrates Mary's characteristic preoccupation with herself. Her implicit demands for sympathy and attention evoke a reserved and not uncritical response from Anne. Mary's frequent use of the pronoun 'I' serves as a reminder that her circle of interests extends no further than her father's. The reader's response is determined by the narrator's introduction, and reinforced by Anne's objective evaluation of Mary's condition and by Mary's obvious incapacity to extend her thoughts to anyone else, except as these persons in their behaviour affect her personally. In this scene the method of presentation is simple, corresponding to the simplicity of Mary's character. Her character is fixed for the rest of the novel. The presentation of Mrs Clay is more complex. Certain flaws in her character are obvious from the beginning, but questions relating to her motives and ambitions are left open.

'They would look around them, no doubt, and *bless their good fortune*,' said Mrs Clay, for Mrs Clay was present; her father had driven her over, nothing being so much use to Mrs Clay's health as a drive to Kellynch: 'but I quite agree with my father in thinking a sailor might be a very desirable tenant. I have known a good deal of the profession; and besides their liberality, they are so neat and careful in all their ways! These *valuable* pictures of yours, Sir Walter, if you chose to leave them, would be perfectly safe.

Every thing in and about the house would be taken such excellent care of! the gardens and shrubberies would be kept in *almost as high order* as they are now. You need not be afraid, Miss Elliot, of your own sweet flower-garden's being neglected.' (*P* 48)[24]

As the daughter of John Shepherd—the man who is trying diplomatically to guide Sir Walter into accepting an unavoidable decision—Mrs Clay echoes the subservient attitude of her father, but her remarks are more obvious attempts at flattery and her motives more suspect. The explanation offered, that Mrs Clay has accompanied her father only because of the benefits to her health, puts the reader on his guard, since this explanation seems most unlikely in the context of the novel as a whole. Sir Walter is being manipulated without being in the least aware of it. Mrs Clay, John Shepherd, and Anne for very different reasons are engaged in a mutual effort to convince Sir Walter of the advantages of the step which will have to be taken in any case. The intensity with which Mrs Clay supports her father in his efforts to reason with Sir Walter reinforces the doubts concerning her motives. The italicized words are obviously not an expression of what she thinks, but a reflection of what Mrs Clay assumes her audience wants to hear. Much later in the action, Anne and Mr Elliot suspect that Mrs Clay may have designs on Sir Walter. It is quite possible that Jane Austen originally intended to develop this idea more fully. Mrs Clay's first appearance in the narrative anticipates such a sub-plot; however, this theme never takes on the dimensions of a serious threat to Sir Walter's placid contentment with himself. But for the time being, the reader remains less certain about Mrs Clay's character than he is about Mary Musgrove's when she is introduced. The narrator shares less information with the reader, so that the question as to whether Mrs Clay is primarily interested in serving her father's interests or in forwarding her own is left unanswered.

The presentation of Sir Walter's character is unambiguous and direct. There is nothing in his personality which would lend itself readily to a more complex treatment. Like his daughter Mary's, Sir Walter's character is fixed when he is introduced, and he behaves accordingly thereafter. In one paragraph, Jane Austen gives the reader Sir Walter's full character, echoing his own rigidly formal syntax while doing so.

Vanity was the beginning and the end of Sir Walter Elliot's character; vanity of person and situation. He had been remarkably handsome in his youth; and, at fifty-four, was still a very fine man. Few women could think more of their personal appearance than he did; nor could the valet of any newly made lord be more delighted with the place he held in society. He considered the blessing of beauty as inferior only to the blessing of a baronetcy; and the Sir Walter Elliot, who united these gifts, was the constant object of his warmest respect and devotion. (*P* 36)

The absoluteness and formality of this passage seems unfair; however, the course of events bears out the narrator's initial harsh judgement. There are no subtle nuances in Sir Walter's personality, any more than there are in his rhetoric. The narrator's prejudices are self-evident, but the reader is soon given reason to share them. In the following passage, Sir Walter comments on the naval profession.

'Yes; it is in two points offensive to me; I have two strong grounds of objection to it. First as being the means of bringing persons of obscure birth into undue distinction, and raising men to honours which their fathers and grandfathers never dreamt of; and secondly, as it cuts up a man's youth and vigour most horribly; a sailor grows older sooner than any other man; I have observed it all my life. A man is in greater danger in the navy of being insulted by the rise of one whose father, his father might not have distained to speak to, and of becoming prematurely an object of disgust himself, than in any other line.' (*P* 49)

In its presumptuousness and its studied parallels, this passage reads like a parody of the Johnsonian manner. It reflects Sir Walter's vain, supercilious attitude towards life. He is not trying to hide anything; he is simply not capable of comprehending an image of a man that deviates from his own ideal. The implicit and explicit parallels contribute to the formality of the passage. It is a formality achieved not through any special effort of the moment, but from long years of habitually seeking the proper words appropriate to the occasion and one's station in life. Sir Walter's acquaintances have presumably long since become accustomed to his manner of speaking, so that his performance on this occasion does nothing more than meet with their expectations. For the reader, however, such remarks serve only to confirm what the narrator has already suggested: Sir Walter is a very vain and foolish gentleman, whose formal eloquence reflects a certain superficial perfection in his social behaviour.

Anne is the exception in the family. The insensitivity and egotism of her father and two sisters contrast markedly with Anne's hesitance to place her own interests before those of others and her unwillingness to give priority to social values over values of the heart. When Louisa becomes engaged to Captain Benwick, Anne is elated by the possibility that Wentworth is no longer attached; but, at the same time, she is concerned as to whether or not Wentworth has lost Benwick's friendship because of the engagement. Like Fanny Price in *Mansfield Park*, Anne is isolated throughout much of the action. It is a psychological rather than a physical isolation, for Anne is always a member of a group at Kellynch Hall, Uppercross, Lyme or Bath. Anne is much more active than Fanny, frequently taking the initiative while others are still wondering what should be done; nevertheless, it is Anne's mental life which is the focus of the reader's attention: her observations and evaluations of the behaviour of the other characters as well as her critical examination of her own conduct and feelings. For this reason, the author makes considerable use of inside views. A large part of the narrative is devoted to Anne's analyses of what she observes and what she feels. As has been shown above, inside views are employed to some extent in all of Jane Austen's novels. In *Northanger Abbey* and *Emma*, they are used to reveal the heroine's inability to distinguish fact from fiction; in *Sense and Sensibility* and *Mansfield Park*, to show the heroine's right-mindedness. Only in *Pride and Prejudice* are inside views avoided for the most part, for the insights they would provide into the heroine's character would undercut the ambiguities surrounding the relationship between Elizabeth and Darcy. In *Persuasion* the inside views have a much broader function. They are employed not only to reveal Anne's ability to judge others as well as herself, but also to show the quality of Anne's mind.

> They knew not each other's opinion, either its constancy or its change, on the leading point in Anne's conduct, for the subject was never alluded to,—but Anne at seven and twenty, thought very differently from what she had been made to think at nineteen.—She did not blame Lady Russell, she did not blame herself for having been guided by her; but she felt that were any young person, in similar circumstances, to apply counsel, they would never receive any of such certain immediate wretchedness, such uncertain future good—She was persuaded that under every disadvantage of disapprobation at home, and every anxiety attending his profession, all their probable fears, delays and disappointments, she should yet have been a happier woman in maintaining the engagement, than she had been in the sacrifice of it; and this, she fully believed, had the usual share, had even more than a usual share of all such solicitudes and suspense been theirs, without reference to the actual results of the case, which as it happened, would have bestowed earlier prosperity than could be reasonably calculated on. All his sanguine expectations, all his confidence had been justified. His genius and ardour had seemed to foresee and to command his prosperous path. (*P* 57–58)

The complexity of the sentence structure in this passage reflects the fineness of the discriminations which Anne is making.[25] The implicit and explicit parallels indicate Anne's attempt to think rationally and logically about her own past conduct. The passage is without irony. The reader is expected to perceive the correctness of Anne's thinking. With the aid of passages like this, the reader comes to realize that Anne is the best guide in the evaluation of characters and events. There is never any doubt that wherever values come into conflict Anne's are to be preferred.

Other opportunities of making her observations could not fail to occur. Anne had soon been in company with all the four together often enough to have an opinion, though too wise to acknowledge as much at home, where she knew it would have satisfied neither husband or wife; for while she considered Louisa to be rather the favourite, she could not but think, as far as she might dare to judge from memory and experience, that Captain Wentworth was not in love with either. They were more in love with him; yet there it was not love. It was a little fever of admiration; but it might, probably must, end in love with some. Charles Hayter seemed aware of being slighted, and yet Henrietta had sometimes the air of being divided between them. Anne longed for the power of representing to them all what they were about, and of pointing out some of the evils they were exposing themselves to. She did not attribute guile to any. It was the highest satisfaction to her, to believe Captain Wentworth not in the least aware of the pain he was occasioning. There was no triumph, no pitiful triumph in his manner. He had, probably, never heard, and never thought of any claims of Charles Hayter. He was only wrong in accepting the attentions—(for accepting must be the word) of two young women at once. (*P* 105)

The parallelism of this passage once again suggests Anne's careful ordering of her thoughts; however, in this instance, there is a hint of irony. In returning in her thoughts to her own earlier romance with Wentworth, Anne becomes less objective than she realizes. If at one level she feels it is wrong for Wentworth to accept the attentions of both young ladies, at another level she feels it is wrong for him to encourage either one of them. It is doubtful that Anne is conscious of such a selfish motive. Out of context it is difficult to determine whether or not such a motive is implied. The narrator is silent; there is no intermediary between the reader and Anne's thoughts. But in the context of the novel as a whole, it is apparent that Wentworth is always in the forefront of Anne's mind, and that she views everything as it relates to him and as it might relate to her as well. Anne's attitudes are at times less clearly defined than has often been claimed. The ambiguity is achieved by reducing the distance between the reader and the heroine.

The sources of Jane Austen's irony are multifarious but not arbitrary. The ironic perspective is determined by a system of norms and values—a fixed set of priorities— implicit in all of the novels. These values are usually not made explicit, but they constitute the standard by which conduct and character are judged. The author exploits the possibilities of inside views and dramatic scenes in order to delineate the nature of human interactions in her fictional world and to place her characters and their conduct within a moral frame of reference. Much of the structural as well as the local irony derives from the inability of the characters to communicate at the same level. Although on the surface communication appears to function smoothly, this apparent harmony is belied by the fact that as a rule one of the participants—and occasionally both of them—fail to fully comprehend the import of what has been said. From his perspective of superior knowledge, the reader is in a better position to recognize the uncertainties, misunderstandings and more serious problems which emerge from these dramatic scenes, though he, too, is frequently forced to reassess what he has thought in the light of subsequent events, because the motivation of some of the characters as well as the underlying moral conflicts in these dramatic scenes often become clear only in retrospect.

In Jane Austen's fiction, there is a general tendency for conflicts to originate in the dramatic scenes and to be clarified in the inside views, especially in *Sense and Sensibility*, *Mansfield Park* and *Persuasion*. As a consequence, the reader's comprehension of what is happening is strongly influenced by what he learns from the views into the heroine's mental life. The function of the inside views is perhaps best illustrated by *Pride and Prejudice*, where they are rarely introduced. As in the other novels, the central conflicts originate in the dramatic scenes; however, since the reader has few opportunities to examine Elizabeth's thoughts about what she experiences, he has to rely more or less on his own resources in interpreting the significance of these scenes. The action turns on the resulting ambiguities. In the other novels, the inside views provide the reader with the guidance missing in *Pride and Prejudice*. Of course, not all of the heroines are equally reliable guides. If the narrator offers little support for the heroine's views, the reader is likely to consider them with more circumspection. It does not take long for the reader to discover that he can depend more on Anne's or Elinor's perceptions than on Emma's or Catherine's. The reader's relation to inside views differs from his relation to the dramatic scenes. Whereas in the dramatic scenes the reader may be misled even though none of the participants has misunderstood what has happened—to cite the most extreme alternative—this is not possible in the inside views. Assuming that misunderstanding occurs—and it usually does—either the reader along with the heroine misconstrues what the heroine has experienced, or the heroine errs and the reader perceives her error because of the advantage of his perspective.

Both the inside views and the dramatic scenes focus attention on the difficulties individuals have in communicating with one another. As the stories progress, it becomes evident that these difficulties are not arbitrary but arise from widely divergent and conflicting values. Most of the characters succeed in maintaining at least the appearance of polite conversation. The few who fail in this respect, such as John Thorpe, Lucy Steele and Mr Collins, are all portrayed as being ridiculous. The fundamental problem lies elsewhere—and it is not always the same, though it is always an indication of moral weakness. Self-interest, moral blindness and insensitivity are just some of the reasons why characters try to mislead and refuse to be open and frank. The ideal of mutual understanding is a basic theme running through all the novels, and it is given particular prominence in *Pride and Prejudice*, *Emma* and *Persuasion*. Like many of the characters, the reader is guided and manipulated throughout the course of each of the novels until he gains that understanding of character and conduct, and the system of values by which these are judged, which the narrator has had from the beginning, and which—with the qualified exception of *Northanger Abbey*—has determined the structure of the whole.

III

Jane Austen's Sense of Ending

This chapter examines the means with which Jane Austen brings her stories to an end for the light they throw on the author's relation to her texts. The conclusions to all the novels bear a certain resemblance to one another; they all end, more or less, with a conventional summary of the events which take place after the climactic point in the narrative has been reached.[1] *Persuasion* and *Northanger Abbey* most obviously stand apart from the other novels in this respect. The open ending of *Persuasion* suggests that Jane Austen was entering a new phase in her artistic development;[2] *Northanger Abbey* ends with the parody of Mrs Radcliffe's conclusion to *The Mysteries of Udolpho*.[3] But there is considerable variation in Jane Austen's methods of concluding the other. novels as well. The ending of *Sense and Sensibility* reflects both the didactic structure of the whole and certain technical difficulties which the author was later able to avoid. *Emma* goes on almost too long after the climax has been reached.[4] The resolution to *Pride and Prejudice* is the best prepared for, and it completes the symmetrical pattern which has been built up.[5] The conclusion of *Mansfield Park* is the formal ending to a story about a number of concerns besides the fate of the heroine. The differences in the conclusions are not just a question of content; they are above all formal differences. Confronted with similar problems at the end of each of her novels Jane Austen makes use of different possibilities for resolving them. In the process she comes closer to revealing herself and her attitude towards her subject matter than at any other point in the narratives.

In this respect *Sense and Sensibility* is the most revealing, because the author is more direct and less consistently successful than she is elsewhere. Some of the technical problems of presentation remain unresolved. In this novel Jane Austen portrays two stories of unrequited love that in outline are very similar; however, they differ in two important points: the attitudes of the two young ladies to their situations and the outcome of the two affairs. Marianne responds by giving herself up to her feelings and nearly dying of the illness contracted as a consequence of her disappointment in love. Although Elinor is equally frustrated in her love, she refuses to allow her emotions to interfere with what her good sense tells her is proper. That Elinor's response rather than Marianne's is the correct one is underscored in three ways. First, Elinor does not follow her sister's precedent and become physically ill. Secondly, contrary to her own expectations, Elinor does eventually marry the man she has fallen in love with. And finally, Marianne comes to realize that she has been in error all along and that she should have long since recognized in her sister an example of how she should have reacted and made an effort to come to terms with her situation instead of giving in to it. The problems in working out a conclusion to *Sense and Sensibility*, then, include bringing Elinor and Edward together, rendering an enlightened and reformed Marianne, and reaffirming the correctness of Elinor's behaviour throughout the course of the action.

To solve the first of these problems Jane Austen relies on the awkward device of 'mistaken identities'.[6] The second of these problems is more complex. Marianne is supposed to realize where she has erred in the past and to gain some insight into what her sister has endured and how she has held up under the strain; furthermore, Marianne needs to draw the logical conclusions for her own future behaviour from what she observes in her sister's, and, in the end, to act according to this newly gained knowledge. Jane Austen deals with this problem by keeping Marianne at some distance from the reader, making it impossible for him to follow the stages in Marianne's development which transform her from a self-indulgent, spontaneous and emotional young lady into a mirror-image of Elinor's rationality, ready and willing to marry Colonel Brandon. The third problem is the easiest to deal with, since it involves no more than a continuation of what is implicit from the beginning in the plot structure of the novel and the predominance of Elinor's perspective throughout the narrative. Even though the angle of vision shifts in the last chapters from Elinor to the author, nothing is introduced to undercut the general impression that Elinor has behaved in an exemplary manner and that her judgements of the behaviour of others have been wellfounded. On the contrary, Elinor's interpretation of Marianne's behaviour and her own is clearly consistent with the author's. A closer look at some passages near the end of *Sense and Sensibility* should reveal more about Jane Austen's method of dealing with these and related problems.

Near the end of Chapter 48 Edward Ferrars arrives un-expectedly. Elinor, her mother and her sisters prepare to welcome the man who preferred to marry Lucy Steele rather than Elinor—or so the Dashwoods have been led to believe.

Not a syllable passed aloud. They all waited in silence for the appearance of their visitor. His footsteps were heard along the gravel path; in a moment he was in the passage; and in another, he was before them.

His countenance, as he entered the room, was too happy, even for Elinor, as if fearful of his reception, and conscious that he merited no kind one. Mrs Dashwood, however, conforming, as she trusted, to the wishes of that daughter, by whom she then meant in the warmth of her heart to be guided in everything, met him with a look of forced complacency, gave him her hand, and wished him joy.

He coloured, and stammered out an unintelligible reply. Elinor's lips had moved with her mother's, and when the moment of action was over, she wished that she had shaken hands with him too. But it was then too late, and with a countenance meaning to be open, she sat down again and talked of the weather.

Marianne had retreated as much as possible out of sight, to conceal her distress; and Margaret, understanding some part, but not the whole, of the case, thought it incumbent on her to be dignified, and therefore took a seat as far from him as she could, and maintained a strict silence.

When Elinor had ceased to rejoice in the dryness of the season, a very awful pause took place. It was put to an end to by Mrs Dashwood, who felt obliged to hope that he had left Mrs Ferrars very well. In a hurried manner, he replied in the affirmative.

Another pause.

Elinor, resolving to exert herself, though fearing the sound of her own voice, now said,

'Is Mrs Ferrars at Longstaple?'

'At Longstaple!' he replied, with an air of surprise—'No, my mother is in town.'

'I meant,' said Elinor, taking up some work from the table, 'to inquire after Mrs *Edward* Ferrars.'

She dared not look up;—but her mother and Marianne both turned their eyes on him. He coloured, seemed perplexed, looked doubtingly, and after some hesitation, said,

'Perhaps you mean—my brother—you mean Mrs—Mrs *Robert* Ferrars.'

'Mrs Robert Ferrars!'—was repeated by Marianne and her mother, in an accent of the utmost amazement;—and though Elinor could not speak, even *her* eyes were fixed on him with the same impatient wonder. He rose from his seat and walked to the window, apparently from not knowing what to do; took up a pair of scissars that lay there, and while spoiling both them and their sheath by cutting the latter to pieces as he spoke, said, in a hurried voice,

'Perhaps you do not know—you may not have heard that my brother is lately married to—to the youngest—to Miss Lucy Steele.'

His words were echoed with unspeakable astonishment by all but Elinor, who sat with her head leaning over her work, in a state of such agitation as made her hardly know where she was.

'Yes,' said he, 'they were married last week, and are now at Dawlish.'

Elinor could sit no longer. She almost ran out of the room, and as soon as the door was closed, burst into tears of joy, which at first she thought would never cease. (*SS* 348–350)

These paragraphs record the moment when Elinor suddenly realizes that, contrary to rumour, Edward is still unmarried and that there are no longer any obstacles standing between her and her aspirations. This scene divides into three parts. The first part concerns Edward's arrival and the formalities of exchanging greetings and establishing the context within which social intercourse usually takes place—although the conversation founders in the awkwardness of the moment before it has had a chance to get started. This awkwardness derives from misunderstandings on both sides. Edward Ferrars arrives feeling guilty about his past behaviour, but he is not guilty of the one deed ascribed to him by the others in the room: he is not yet married. The second part of this scene begins when there is nothing more to say. This embarrassing silence is broken by Mrs Dashwood's inquiry concerning 'Mrs Ferrars', which, in turn, leads to the confusion that eventually brings all those present to an awareness of the truth. Like Colonel Brandon in an earlier episode in which he asks Elinor to inform Edward that he is about to come into possession of a living, Mrs Dashwood also places her daughter in a situation in which she has to disregard her own feelings in her desire to help others.[7] Elinor has no reason to suspect that she in fact will gain more than anyone else from her initiative. Her inquiries mark the beginning of the third part of the scene. I draw attention to its three-part structure in order to show how Jane Austen manipulates the point of view at this crucial stage of the action.

In the course of this scene, the perspective shifts from the middle distance to a close-up, then back again to the all-encompassing, omniscient perspective of the author. At this point in the narrative, a knowledge of literary convention leads the reader to anticipate the reappearance of Edward Ferrars and the happy resolution to the plot. However, what the narrator has to relate lends little support to this assumption; it is simply an unmediated record of Elinor's thoughts.

> He stopt at their gate. It was a gentleman, it was Colonel Brandon himself. Now she should hear more; and she trembled in expectation of it. But—it was *not* Colonel Brandon—neither his air—nor his height. Were it possible, she would say it must be Edward. She looked again. He had just dismounted;—she could not be mistaken;—it *was* Edward. (*SS* 348)

The narrator's limited omniscience is evident here as elsewhere, and his lack of knowledge contributes to the suspense of the climax. The reader follows Elinor in her train of thought from a state of ignorance as to who is approaching to the realization—arrived at slowly and by degrees—that it is Edward. Her desire for information concerning recent events is now likely to be fulfilled in an unexpected and perhaps painful manner. Elinor's thoughts serve as an introduction to the climactic scene. Up to this point the reader's expectation of a happy ending has been based primarily on his familiarity with how novels characteristically end. This largely because of the restrictions the narrator has imposed on the reader's knowledge. Such restrictions are unnecessary at this stage; therefore, the middle perspective employed throughout most of the text can be dispensed with, which is precisely what occurs at the end of this scene. In the second part of the scene, the author moves in for a close-up, dramatizing the turning point in the action. The dialogue is limited to Mrs Dashwood's and Elinor's questions and Edward's responses. The dramatic confrontation of the two central figures is not developed at length as it is later in *Pride and Prejudice* and *Emma*, where there are no third parties present either to inhibit or stimulate conversation.[8] In part this may be due to the differences in the personalities of the main characters. Such a scene involving Elinor might be inherently of less interest than a similar scene involving Emma or Elizabeth. But at least in part the absence of a dramatic confrontation is due to Jane Austen's tendency throughout *Sense and Sensibility* to avoid the direct presentation of some of the more problematical aspects of the story and the characters that are a part of it. Nowhere is this tendency more evident than in the concluding pages of the novel, where Jane Austen avoids the direct representation of an Elinor whose behaviour is no longer completely governed by reason, an embarrassed Edward awkwardly proposing for the second time (this time to Elinor), or a Marianne being brought to her senses by the lesson to be learned through the observation of her sister— to mention only the most obvious omissions. Elinor's departure in the third part of the scene quoted above is a good illustration of this tendency. Her exit eliminates the problem of portraying an Elinor overwrought with emotion. The

H

absence of a direct representation of Elinor's emotional state at this stage does not derive from any limitations imposed on the narrator's range of vision, because at this point in the narrative the author intervenes to relate not only the remainder of this scene but also the rest of the novel from her angle of vision.

In the first part, then, the narrator is placed at an intermediate distance between the events being portrayed and the reader, where he serves to guide the reader into an acceptance of what is being presented. The reader is given no cause to doubt the narrator's view and interpretation of the action apart from the awareness that there are limits to the narrator's knowledge as well as his own. The reader needs less guidance in the second part, since the significance of the dramatic exchange is readily apparent. As a consequence the narrator's comments simply confirm what the reader has learned to expect from Elinor and the others. In the third part the manipulation of the reader is once again more obvious. The author intervenes to render the remainder of this scene as well as what follows in the final two chapters from her perspective. The reader is distanced from the action and his attention focused on Elinor's departure. The response of the other characters to their newly gained knowledge of the situation is not mentioned until the next chapter. It begins:

Unaccountable, however, as the circumstances of his release might appear to the whole family, it was certain that Edward was free: and to what purpose that freedom would be employed was easily predetermined by all;—for after experiencing the blessings of *one* imprudent engagement, contracted without his mother's consent, as he had already done for more than four years, nothing less could be expected of him in the failure of *that*, than the immediate contraction of another.

His errand at Barton, in fact, was a simple one. It was only to ask Elinor to marry him;—and considering that he was not altogether inexperienced in such a question, it might be strange that he should feel so uncomfortable in the present case as he really did, so much in need of encouragement and fresh air.

How soon he had walked himself into the proper resolution, however, how soon an opportunity of exercising it occurred, in what manner he expressed himself, and how he was received, need not be particularly told. This only need be said:—that when they all sat down to table at four o'clock, about three hours after his arrival, he had secured his lady, engaged her mother's consent, and was not only in the rapturous profession of the lover, but in the reality of reason and truth, one of the happiest of men. (*SS* 351)

This passage is in some respects typical of Jane Austen's method of ending all her novels; however, it also suggests the central unresolved problem of *Sense and Sensibility*. The authorial voice, the level of generality and the summary manner are characteristic of all Jane Austen's conclusions. In addition, the irony of this particular passage anticipates the opening sentence of *Pride and Prejudice*: the opposite of what is being asserted would in fact be consistent with our experience of the 'real' world. A young man who has just broken off a long engagement in which he had become disillusioned and disinterested is very unlikely to become engaged again immediately. This reversal of the predictable course of events serves as a reminder that we are reading a comedy, that is, a fiction set in a realm where the impossible or at least the unlikely can happen. Missing from this passage and not treated at all adequately in the final chapters are the implications and consequences of the moral themes central to the plot and given such prominence throughout most of the novel. In *Sense and Sensibility* Jane Austen fails to maintain consistently the delicate balance between the comic and serious aspects of her story. She handicaps herself in choosing to oppose Elinor and Marianne diametrically. Nowhere are the difficulties inherent in this choice more evident than in the novel's conclusion. Both Elinor and Marianne undergo a transformation whereby each is forced to make some compromises with the inflexible attitudes she has held previously. They do not exchange roles, but they move closer together in their thinking, each having reordered her priorities in her own way. In the novels that follow Jane Austen works out various alternatives to the rigid parallel structure of *Sense and Sensibility*. In *Pride and Prejudice* moral themes are subordinated to the comic and dramatic conflict between Elizabeth and Darcy. In *Mansfield Park, Emma* and *Persuasion* the reader's attention is directed repeatedly to the context of moral seriousness within which the stories unfold, but the author works with more subtle shadings of character, with the result that she is not again confronted with the problem of completely transforming someone in the last few pages of the novel, as she has to do in her portrayal of Marianne.

A comparison of the end of *Sense and Sensibility* with the concluding chapters of *Pride and Prejudice* reveals some of the major ways the author has improved in her ability to work out the exigencies of the plot. At first glance the subject matter of the two novels appears very similar; but the plot of *Pride and Prejudice* is based in character while the plot of *Sense and Sensibility* is based on an idea. As a consequence the resolution of *Pride and Prejudice* derives from the behaviour of individuals, and, in contrast, the resolution of *Sense and Sensibility* derives from an abstract notion of proper moral behaviour and the lesson to be learned from misbehaviour. Further, the actual means Jane Austen uses to work out her conclusion are different.

'Let me thank you again and again, in the name of all my family, for that generous compassion which induced you to take so much trouble, and bear so many mortifications, for the sake of discovering them.'

'If you *will* thank me,' he replied, 'let it be for yourself alone. That the wish of giving happiness to you, might add force to the other inducements which led me on, I shall not attempt to deny. But your *family* owe me nothing. Much as I respect them, I believe I thought only of *you*.'

Elizabeth was too much embarrassed to say a word. After a short pause, her companion added, 'You are too generous to trifle with me. If your feelings are still what they were last April, tell me so at once. *My* affections and wishes are unchanged, but one word from you will silence me on this subject for ever.'

Elizabeth feeling all the more than common awkwardness and anxiety of his situation, now forced herself to speak; and immediately, though not very fluently, gave him to understand, that her sentiments had undergone so material a change, since the period to which he alluded, as to make her receive with gratitude and pleasure, his present assurances. The happiness which this reply produced, was such as he had probably never felt before; and he expressed himself on the occasion as sensibly and as warmly as a man violently in love can be supposed to do. (*PP* 375)

Here Jane Austen portrays what is omitted from *Sense and Sensibility*. Although she does not relate everything that was actually said, the author does record the stages by which Elizabeth and Darcy gradually gain the necessary knowledge of one another's feelings to live happily ever after. Circumstances 'force' Elizabeth to speak just as Elinor is forced to take the initiative in the scene discussed above. The difference in the method used in the two scenes is revealing. In *Sense and Sensibility* Elinor's mother serves as the catalyst, causing the awkward situation in which Elinor feels compelled to act. In this scene from *Pride and Prejudice*, there is no third party present to create such a situation. At this point in the narrative, as throughout *Pride and Prejudice*, the main problems stem from the central characters and the dramatic conflict— as yet unresolved—that has developed between them. Elizabeth and Darcy learn to recognize that they were very much in error in their initial impressions of one another, but the process by which Darcy arrives at a revaluation of Elizabeth's character is kept at a much greater distance than the similar process which Elizabeth undergoes. Throughout the novel the reader has little direct access to Darcy's thoughts and feelings and little opportunity to observe the fundamental changes in Darcy's thinking that lead to this meeting with Elizabeth. It is the culmination of the long sequence of dramatic confrontations between Darcy and Elizabeth, and, like the others, is presented for the most part in terms of Elizabeth's responses to the situation. This point of view reinforces the initial impression that Darcy's behaviour is unmotivated in much the same sense that Marianne's decision to marry Colonel Brandon is unconvincing; however, as Brower has shown, this reversal in Darcy's attitude is carefully prepared for.[9] The apparent problem lies in the fact that Darcy's revaluation of Elizabeth is a gradual process which occurs almost entirely beyond Elizabeth's, and hence beyond the reader's, range of vision. The reader catches glimpses of Darcy's mental life before the climactic scene; therefore, it is only in retrospect that a second, more favourable interpretation can be ascribed to Darcy's behaviour in his dramatic exchanges with Elizabeth. As it becomes obvious that the heroine's hopes are about to be realized, the point of view shifts from the narrator to the author. The restrictions imposed by the limited omniscience of the narrator are no longer necessary. The action and the consequences of the action in this novel are raised to a new plane of perception. The insights gained by Elizabeth and Darcy as well as the reader in this scene serve as a kind of release which in the remainder of the chapter is mirrored in the intimacy and freedom with which Darcy and Elizabeth talk with each other. For the reader as for Elizabeth the uncertainties concerning Darcy's character dissolve and the apparent hindrances to a marriage between Darcy and Elizabeth vanish.

In contrast to her method in *Sense and Sensibility* and *Pride and Prejudice*, in working out the conclusion to *Mansfield Park* Jane Austen uses summary rather than dramatic scene. She avoids the intermediate distance employed in the portrayal of Edward's unexpected arrival in *Sense and Sensibility* and also the close-up used when Darcy proposes to Elizabeth for the second time. There are three interrelated reasons for this change in method. First of all, the subject matter of *Mansfield Park* requires a more complex treatment than that of *Sense and Sensibility* or *Pride and Prejudice*.[10] On the one hand the author wants to bring her story to an end; on the other hand she wants to place the behaviour of all the major characters in proper moral perspective. Secondly, neither Fanny nor Edmund is all that lively or interesting. A dramatization of the climactic scene between them would at the very least be problematical. They lack the quick wit and superficial charm of Mary and Henry Crawford, who serve as contrast, and as an indirect reminder that there are values which are much more important than those evinced in the Crawfords' conduct. Fanny's moral steadfastness and her rather unimaginative response to the world around her are of intentional creations of the author, but they are not qualities which lend themselves readily to dramatic presentation. Finally, a summary method allows Jane Austen to establish an intimate bond between herself and the reader.

Let other pens dwell on guilt and misery, I quit such odious subjects as soon as I can, impatient to restore every body, not greatly in fault themselves, to tolerable comfort, and to have done with all the rest.

My Fanny indeed at this very time, I have the satisfaction of knowing, must have been happy in spite of every thing. She must have been a happy creature in spite of all that she felt or thought she felt, for the distress of those around her. She had sources of delight that must force their way. She was returned to Mansfield Park, she was useful, she was beloved; she was safe from Mr Crawford, and when Sir Thomas came back she had every proof that could be given in his then melancholy state of spirits, of his perfect approbation and increased regard; and happy as all this must make her, she would still have been happy without any of it, for Edmund was no longer the dupe of Miss Crawford. (*MP* 446)

I purposely abstain from dates on this occasion, that every one may be at liberty to fix their own, aware that the cure of unconquerable passions, and the transfer of unchanging attachments, must vary much as to time in different people.—I only intreat every body to believe that exactly at the time when it was quite natural that it should be so, and not a week earlier, Edmund did cease to care about Miss Crawford, and became as anxious to marry Fanny, as Fanny herself could desire. (*MP* 454)

Since the reader's dominant impression of *Mansfield Park* is one of moral seriousness, the playfulness of these two passages—taken out of context—seems inconsistent with the novel's main themes. Such a modern interpretation glosses over the fact that wherever beliefs or moral convictions can be taken for granted they need not always be treated seriously. There is no question but that such convictions are central to the novel. If it were not so long, it would be useful to quote the entire final chapter, whose length reflects the author's desire to review all the significant consequences of past behaviour. This chapter as well as the novel as a whole is based on the assumption that the reader shares the author's moral views, an assumption that makes *Mansfield Park* less readily accessible to the modern reading audience than any of Jane Austen's other novels. Within his own moral frame of reference, the modern reader is likely to assign a significance quite different from Jane Austen's to the abandonment of a chapel into disuse, the improvement of an estate, or the private performance of a play. Jane Austen's frame of reference is already implied in the opening paragraphs of the novel and gradually becomes more fully developed in the course of the action.

Jane Austen begins her story by introducing the three Ward sisters, who long before the story opens married to become Lady Bertram, Mrs Norris and Mrs Price. Although the circumstances surrounding each of these marriages is only hinted at, in each instance the motives behind the decision to marry seem to have been highly questionable. Apparently, it was not so much errors of the heart which were involved but errors of judgement. The sisters seem to have been no more able in their youth than in later life to differentiate properly among material, social and moral values. None of them ever achieves a sense of priorities which would enable her to serve as a moral guide to the next generation. Fanny's mother, Mrs Price, is so preoccupied with the material concerns brought on by a large family and a ne'er-do-well husband that she loses sight of any other values. Early in life Lady Bertram was attractive and fortunate enough to achieve the material and social comforts she needed to cease reflecting about anything at all. Mrs Norris's fate lies somewhere in between that of her two sisters. Without ever quite achieving the material and social success of Lady Bertram, Mrs Norris comes close enough to it to spend most of her waking hours thinking about social and, especially, material matters. What is missing in all three of the sisters is a moral centre. They are members of the older generation, and like other members of this group they are kept in the background for long stretches of the narrative. With the exception of Mrs Norris, they never dominate a scene. Nevertheless, Lady Bertram, Mrs Norris and Mrs Price are one of the main means Jane Austen employs to establish the moral context in which the action takes place. They function as points for reference and comparison. This function is perhaps most obvious when Sir Thomas sends Fanny for an extended visit to her mother in the hope that from this experience Fanny will gain more insight into the advantages of a marriage with Henry Crawford. The insights she gains, however, only confirm her conviction that such a marriage would be an error. For the reader the situation of Fanny's mother is an example of what such errors in judgement may lead to. It would be an oversimplification to suggest that Lady Bertram, Mrs Norris and Mrs Price represent the possible fates of the young ladies who come together at Mansfield Park; however, like the younger generation, these three sisters at a critical point in their lives were confronted with a moral challenge, a challenge which they failed to come to terms with, either because of an inability to comprehend the moral implications of their situations or because of an indifference of the moral consequences of their choices.

A second theme closely related to that of learning to distinguish among material, social and moral values concerns the responsibility of the older generation to take an active interest in the education of the next generation. From what has already been said of Lady Bertram, Mrs Norris and Mrs Price, it is evidence that they could not exert a proper moral and educational influence. With Sir Thomas Bertram it is less a question of competence than commitment, as he comes to realize himself.

Here had been grievous mismanagement; but, bad as it was, he gradually grew to feel that it had not been the most direful mistake in his plan of education. Something must have been wanting *within*, or time would have worn away much of its ill effect. He feared that principle, active principle, had been wanting, that they had never been properly taught to govern their inclinations and tempers, by that sense of duty which can alone suffice. They had been instructed theoretically in their religion, but never required to bring it into daily practice. To be distinguished for elegance and accomplishments—the authorised object of their youth—could have no useful influence that way, no moral effect on the mind. He had meant them to be good, but his cares had been directed to the understanding of manners, not the disposition; and of the necessity of self-denial and humility, he feared they had never heard from any lips that could profit them. (*MP* 448)

This passage reveals the insight Sir Thomas has gained into the errors he made in the education of his children. Their moral failings reflect his own previous blindness. The passage is as close as the author comes to making an explicit statement. This record of Sir Thomas' thoughts—an evaluation of his children's conduct and a criticism of his own response to it—is untinged by any irony. The author clearly agrees with the harsh judgement Sir Thomas passes on himself and his progeny.

In contrast to those of *Sense and Sensibility*, none of the principals serves here as a spokesman for the author's views. Where necessary the narrator is given this function. The author prefers to develop her moral themes through implied contrasts and comparisons of behaviour, situation and setting. The reader is expected to recognize their moral significance without its being stated. If he fails in this respect, the final chapter as well as the plot structure of the whole novel may seem arbitrary or even forced. In the last chapter Jane Austen assumes that she shares with the reader not only a knowledge of what has happened but also an awareness of its significance for each of the individuals involved. As in *Pride and Prejudice* and *Sense and Sensibility*, the angle of vision shifts from the narrator to the author, who comments at least in passing on all of the characters, placing their behaviour and its consequences in the harsh critical light of her moral frame of reference. Some characters require little further comment, most notably Lady Bertram and Mrs Norris.

Selfishly dear as she had long been to Lady Bertram, she could not be parted with willingly by *her*. No happiness of son or niece could make her wish the marriage. (*MP* 456)

She was regretted by no one at Mansfield. She had never been able to attach even those she loved best, and since Mrs Rushworth's elopement, her temper had been in a state of such irritation as to make her every where tormenting. Not even Fanny had tears for aunt Norris—not even when she was gone for ever. (*MP* 450)

Neither of these characters is at any point in the action capable of comprehending anything which is not self-serving. The idea that they could have and should have exerted some moral influence on the young people never occurs to either of them. When Sir Thomas inquires of Mrs Norris why she did not prevent things from going so far, her response is incomprehension. Because of the bond of shared knowledge that Jane Austen assumes has been established between herself and the reader, the indirect and ironic perspective of the narrator is no longer needed. The course of events is known and the outcome presumably long since anticipated by the reader. As a consequence, Jane Austen intervenes in the final chapter to underline the moral significance of what has been related, using summary to bring the story quickly to its predictable conclusion.

The conclusion to *Emma* represents once again a departure from what Jane Austen has done previously. This is due to the concentration on the central figure throughout the novel and the angle of vision from which her heroine is presented. Briefly, *Sense and Sensibility* is the story of two sisters; *Pride and Prejudice* is the story of Elizabeth and Darcy; *Mansfield Park* concerns the moral education of a group of young people; and *Emma* is the story of a young woman who has 'rather too much her own way, and a disposition to think a little too well of herself' (*E* 37). From the beginning Emma's mental life is presented from the narrator's perspective of limited omniscience. The limitations imposed on the narrator's view, however, relate only to the other characters, not to Emma herself. Her essentially good nature as well as her more questionable qualities are placed in full view of the reading audience. In fact it is the reader's closeness to Emma which prevents him from always comprehending the actions of others. The reader's lack of knowledge is essential for the development of the plot.[11] The reader shares with the narrator

an ironic attitude towards the contradictions, fantasies, en-
thusiasms and attempts to be rational which are all a part of
Emma's response to her circle of acquaintance and the small
world in which she lives. This perspective partly explains
why the author continues to remain in the background even
in the final chapters. There is no need for the author to
intervene in order to correct and place Emma in a new light.
Moreover, since the moral implications of Emma's behaviour
become a major topic of her conversations with Knightley,
Jane Austen need not intrude into her narrative to direct
attention to this topic as she does, for example, in *Mansfield
Park*. This method of having the characters themselves discuss the significance of past events is used elsewhere, most
obviously in *Pride and Prejudice*; however, in the earlier
novel Elizabeth and Darcy have no cause to deal with the
moral issues in detail. Neither of them demonstrates the
willful, egotistical blindness of Emma.

The turning point in the action of *Emma* comes earlier than
in any of the other novels. The situation is motivated by the
arrival of a letter from Frank Churchill. In the ensuing
scene neither of the participants is in a position to anticipate
how the other is likely to react. For his part Knightley knows
that Emma at least for a time was playing with the notion of
being in love with Churchill. He is also conscious of the fact
that Frank Churchill encouraged Emma's interest and gave
the impression of being more than a little struck by her.
During the course of these developments, Knightley realizes
that he is jealous and that he has actually been in love with
Emma himself for years. She is unaware of his feelings; and
until she learns the contents of the letter, unaware that
Churchill was already engaged when he first came to Highbury. The passage below begins at that point in the scene
where Emma and Knightley have just finished discussing the
letter.

'And now, let me talk to you of something else. I have another
person's interest at present so much at heart, that I cannot think
any longer about Frank Churchill. Ever since I left you this
morning, Emma, my mind has been hard at work on one subject.'
The subject followed; it was plain, unaffected, gentleman-like

English, such as Mr Knightley used even to the woman he was in love with, how to be able to ask her to marry him, with out attacking the happiness of her father. Emma's answer was ready at the first word. 'While her dear father lived, any change of condition must be impossible for her. She could not quit him.' Part only of this answer, however, was admitted. The impossibility of her quitting her father, Mr Knightley felt so strongly as herself; but the inadmissibility of any other change, he could not agree to. (*E* 432–433)

In this scene the author characteristically refrains from giving the actual words of Knightley's proposal and Emma's response. Emma's inclinations are clear, but a quick acceptance would be inconsistent with what the reader has come to know of Emma and her relations to Knightley and to her father. Emma hesitates for reasons only some of which are known to Knightley. Her primary concern is indeed her father, but she is also concerned about Harriet Smith's probable reaction to an engagement between Emma and Knightley. Emma has gravely erred in encouraging Harriet to fall in love with every eligible bachelor to come along: it is inevitable that Harriet sooner or later should feel a growing attachment to Knightley. Emma of course had not anticipated this development. For a time Harriet has fancied herself in love with Knightley, and Emma assumes this is still the case. As a consequence, Knightley's proposal puts Harriet Smith and above all Mr Woodhouse in the forefront of Emma's thoughts. The author needs four further chapters to resolve the predicament that Emma finds herself in and to gather up the loose ends of her story. In these chapters Jane Austen shows that Emma may have learned the error of her ways, but that she is far from completely overcoming them. The author shows Harriet recovering her sense of proportion and directing her interests to a more suitable future husband. And, finally, Jane Austen shows Emma's father being brought around to the idea of accepting Emma's marriage.

Following the climax, Emma's conversations with Knightley take on a new character. She more readily admits error and accepts responsibility for the consequences of some of her past actions; however, she does not reach the point where she can be completely open with herself or with Knightley. Her tendency to ignore or suppress some of the objective facts with which she is confronted continues. For sixteen years Mrs Weston was Emma's governess and friend. As a consequence she was primarily responsible for Emma's upbringing. The following conversation takes place shortly after Mrs Weston has given birth to a daughter. It is suggested that it would have been 'quite a pity that any one who so well knew how to teach, should, not have their powers in exercise again.' Emma continues the point.

'She has had the advantage, you know, of practising on me,' she continued—'like La Baronne d'Almane on La Comtesse d'Ostalis, in Madame de Genlis' Adelaide and Theodore, and we shall now see her own little Adelaide educated on a more perfect plan.'

'That is,' replied Mr Knightley, 'she will indulge her even more than she did you, and believe that she does not indulge her at all. It will be the only difference.'

'Poor child!' cried Emma, 'at that rate, what will become of her?'

'Nothing very bad.—The fate of thousands. She will be disagreeable in infancy, and correct herself as she grows older. I am losing all my bitterness against spoilt children, my dearest Emma. I, who am owing all my happiness to *you*, would not it be horrible ingratitude in me to be severe on them?'

Emma laughed, and replied: 'But I had the assistance of all your endeavours to counteract the indulgence of other people. I doubt whether my own sense would have corrected me without it.'

'Do you?—I have no doubt. Nature gave you understanding:— Miss Taylor gave you principles. You must have done well. My interference was quite as likely to do harm as good. It was very natural for you to say, what right has he to lecture me?— and I am afraid very natural for you to feel that it was done in a disagreeable manner. I do not believe I did you any good. The good was all to myself, by making you an object of the tenderest affection to me. I could not think about you so much without doating on you, faults and all; and by dint of fancying so many errors, have been in love with you ever since you were thirteen at least.'

'I am sure you were of use to me,' cried Emma. 'I was very

often influenced rightly by you—oftener than I would own at the time. I am very sure you did me good. And if poor little Anna Weston is to be spoiled, it will be the greatest humanity in you to do as much for her as you have done for me, except falling in love with her when she is thirteen.' (*E* 444–445)

This scene functions in a manner similar to the inside view of Sir Thomas Bertram's thoughts quoted from the final chapter of *Mansfield Park*. In both instances the characters consider the problems involved in the education of children and the question of the older generation's responsibility in this matter. At this stage in the two novels the reader is in a position to make judgements of his own. The author agrees with Sir Thomas, and this encourages the reader to accept his views. In the scene quoted above the reader receives less guidance from the author. The light-hearted and intimate tone of the conversation, therefore, may lead the reader into accepting Knightley's comments uncritically, forgetting that Knightley is always disposed to be considerate of others' feelings and, as a man very much in love, even more inclined than usual to be kind and generous in his remarks concerning those he knows so well. Such acceptance would be an error. From his own knowledge of Emma, the reader is aware of how dangerous an indulgent attitude towards a child's upbringing may be. More often than not Emma's fundamentally good nature and positive moral tendencies are overshadowed by her egotism and lack of insight into herself and others. That she fails to cause much harm is due less to any inclination to stifle questionable impulses than to the intervention of accident or, more often, Knightley. *Emma* is a far less explicitly didactic novel than *Mansfield Park* or *Sense and Sensibility*; however, through a portrayal of a character's strengths and weaknesses, the theme of education and its consequences becomes central to the novel as a whole. The angle of vision prevents this theme from becoming explicit, since the perspective is very close to Emma's. The reader's best opportunities to gain an additional perspective are in such dramatic scenes as the one quoted above, where various characters react and respond to Emma.[12]

The next-to-last chapter returns to one of the subjects

that have been weighing on Emma's mind since Knightley proposed to her.

'I have something to tell you, Emma, some news.'

'Good or bad?' said she, quickly, looking up at his face.

'I do not know which it ought to be called.'

'Oh! good I am sure.—I see it in your countenance. You are trying not to smile.'

'I am afraid,' said he, composing his features, 'I am very much afraid, my dear Emma, that you will not smile when you hear it.'

'Indeed! but why so?—I can hardly imagine that any thing which pleases or amuses you, should not please and amuse me too.'

'There is one subject,' he replied, 'I hope but one, on which we do not think alike.' He paused a moment, again smiling, with his eyes fixed on her face. 'Does nothing occur to you?—Do not you recollect?—Harriet Smith.'

Her cheeks flushed at the name, and she felt afraid of something, though she knew not what.

'Have you heard from her yourself this morning?' cried he. 'You have, I believe, and know the whole.'

'No, I have not; I know nothing; pray tell me.'

'You are prepared for the worst, I see—and very bad it is. Harriet Smith marries Robert Martin.'

Emma gave a start, which did not seem like being prepared—and her eyes, in eager gaze, said, 'No, this is impossible!' but her lips were closed.

'It is so, indeed,' continued Mr Knightley; 'I have it from Robert Martin himself. He left me not half an hour ago.'

She was still looking at him with the most unspeakable amazement.

'You like it, Emma, as little as I had feared.—I wish our opinions were the same. But in time they will. Time you may be very sure, will make one or the other of us think differently; and, in the meanwhile, we need not talk much on the subject.'

'You mistake me, you quite mistake me,' she replied, exerting herself. It is not that such a circumstance would now make me feel unhappy, but I cannot believe it. It seems an impossibility!—You cannot mean to say, that Harriet Smith has accepted Robert Martin. You cannot mean that he has even proposed to her again—yet. You only mean, that he intends it.'

'I mean that he has done it,' answered Mr Knightley,

with smiling but determined decision, 'and been accepted.'
    'Good God!' she cried.—'Well!'—then having recourse to
her workbasket, in excuse for leaning down her face, and concealing
all the exquisite feelings of delight and entertainment which she
knew she must be expressing, she added, 'Well, now tell me
every thing; make this intelligible to me.' (*E* 452–453)

The most significant feature of this scene is Emma's desire
to conceal her sense of relief. As in the scene concerning
Frank Churchill's letter, Emma and Knightley begin this
conversation with very different kinds of knowledge. Knightley recalls how strongly Emma originally opposed the idea
that Harriet should ever marry Robert Martin. For her part
Emma realizes that one of the reasons why she hesitates to
marry Knightley is that it would mean she would once again
be responsible for Harriet's unhappiness. This in itself would
not keep her from marrying Knightley, but it is a psychological burden which she has yet to come to terms with. Jane
Austen uses this scene to tie up one of the loose threads of her
story and eliminate one of the obstacles to Emma's marriage.
But more importantly, the author uses this scene to dramatize
Emma's sense of guilt concerning her past behaviour and to
reveal the heroine's inability to be completely frank about it
with Knightley. The extent to which Emma has learned from
her experience is left open. Her feelings of guilt may not be
sufficient to enable her to resist temptation if it comes her
way. Emma's inclination to fantasy and manipulation may be
restrained by Knightley's steadying influence, but only time
will reveal whether or not Mrs Weston's daughter and the
possibility of finding an appropriate match for her will
prove too much of a temptation for Emma.

The concluding chapters of *Emma* focus less on a moral
context in which the action takes place and the gradual ad-
justments the hero and heroine make in their opinions of
one another than on the workings of Emma's mind. The com-
plexities of her thinking—including the less attractive aspects
—necessitate the complex method of presentation. In the
final chapters Emma is caught between her desire to please a
man intimately familiar with her past errors and a desire to
avoid further awkward situations. Such situations arise as a

I

rule because of Emma's desire to have matters her own way regardless of whatever rational and objective arguments there might be to oppose this idea. Knightley assumes that Emma's willfulness is a thing of the past. The reader is given good reason to doubt the validity of this assumption. Jane Austen makes use of dramatic scenes in the final chapters to record Emma's response to her new situation as the fiancée of Mr Knightley. Through the reactions of the other characters to Emma as well as through descriptions of Emma's own thoughts and gestures, the author portrays her heroine as having gained an understanding of the extent of her errors in the past but not as yet sufficient insight into her own weaknesses to avoid further error in future. It remains to be seen how much tempering influence Knightley will exert upon her. By encouraging Robert Martin to make a second proposal, Knightley without realizing it saves Emma from having to make yet another confession of her misdeeds. Whether or not such interventions will continue to be necessary from time to time is left up to the reader to decide.

Anne Elliot may not feel any more deeply than Elinor Dashwood does in *Sense and Sensibility*—to make the most extreme comparison—but the reader is brought much closer to the feelings of the heroine of *Persuasion*, and is therefore more readily able to accept them as lived experience. While Elinor sometimes seems like a principle or theoretical abstraction, Anne projects an image of a sensitive, feeling human being. This comparison suggests the distance Jane Austen has come since the composition of *Sense and Sensibility*. The different and often subtle shades of emotion that Anne experiences are the subject matter of the novel. Feelings are given a prominence in this story that they never have elsewhere in Jane Austen. In *Sense and Sensibility* Marianne is of course overwrought with emotion, and her lack of restraint brings the feelings themselves into question. This is not the case with Anne Elliot. Her emotions reflect a healthy and well-balanced attitude towards life. Such a personality does not seem capable of generating much story interest. How Jane Austen goes about creating such interest can be illustrated by her handling of the conclusion.

The turning point in the novel comes quite late. Originally, it occurred in the next-to-last chapter, but this was changed to establish a more satisfactory motive for Captain Wentworth's second proposal. The decisive moment comes when, in a conversation between Captain Harville and Anne, the subject turns to the topic of woman's 'constancy'. Wentworth overhears what is said while sitting at a nearby table and writing a letter for Captain Harville. As the reader soon learns, Wentworth interrupts what he is doing and writes a letter to Anne. The author sets the stage for the scene as follows:

Captain Harville, who had in truth been hearing none of it, now left his seat, and moved to a window; Anne seeming to watch him, though it was from thorough absence of mind, became gradually sensible that he was inviting her to join him where he stood. He looked at her with a smile, and a little motion of the head, which expressed, 'Come to me, I have something to say;' and the unaffected, easy manner which denoted the feelings of an older acquaintance than he really was, strongly enforced the invitation. She roused herself and went to him. The window at which he stood, was at the other end of the room from where the two ladies were sitting, and though nearer to Captain Wentworth's table, not very near. (*P* 235)

And a little further on, near the end of Anne's conversation with Captain Harville:

'We shall never agree upon this question'—Captain Harville was beginning to say, when a slight noise called their attention to Captain Wentworth's hitherto perfectly quiet division of the room. It was nothing more than his pen falling down, but Anne was startled at finding him nearer than she had supposed, and half inclined to suspect that the pen had only fallen because he had been occupied by them, striving to catch sounds, which yet she did not think he could have caught. (*P* 237)

And near the end of this scene:

Mrs Croft left them, and Captain Wentworth, having sealed his letter with great rapidity, was indeed ready, and had even a hurried, agitated air, which showed impatience to be gone. Anne knew not how to understand it. She had the kindest 'Good morning, God bless you,' from Captain Harville, but from him not a word, nor a look. He had passed out of the room without a look! (*P* 239)

It is revealing to compare this scene with similar scenes in the other novels. Edward proposes to Elinor after observing her sense of relief when she learns that he is not yet married; Darcy asks for Elizabeth's hand a second time after learning how she has stood up to Lady Catherine; Knightley broaches the subject after carefully studying Emma's reactions as he reveals the contents of Frank Churchill's letter. In other words, in each of these instances, the dénouement comes at an emotionally charged moment when one of the parties can no longer hold back his feelings. This is also the case in the climactic scene in *Persuasion*. What distinguishes this scene from the others is the fact that the heroine's response is postponed, the suspense prolonged and the reader left uncertain as to what has happened. The atmosphere in this scene is also highly charged with emotions; however, the principals are kept apart. The emphasis on the physical distance between the parties underlines the psychological distance between them. The recurrence of the word 'near' suggests that Anne and Wentworth are coming much closer together than Anne for the moment comprehends. At Wentworth's departure Anne is actually in no position to understand what has happened. Since this scene is presented from her angle of vision, the reader shares Anne's perplexity. While speaking with Captain Harville, Anne considers whether or not Wentworth might be able to hear what is being discussed. She realizes that her declaration of woman's constancy has a special relevance to her relationship to Wentworth, but she assumes that he cannot hear the conversation. That this assumption is incorrect is hinted at in the second passage quoted above: 'Anne was startled at finding him nearer than she supposed.' The reader may ascribe more significance than Anne does to Wentworth's behaviour at this point. It suggests an explanation for his apparently rude exit even before he returns to give Anne the crucial letter.

In this letter to Anne, Wentworth proposes for the second time. This idea of a proposal in writing is new in Jane Austen. It is the first time she uses this device, and the only time she gives the contents of a proposal verbatim.[13] It derives logically from the situation. As Wentworth puts it in his letter, 'I must speak to you by what means as are within my reach' (*P* 240). The climax answers the question implied from the beginning of the novel: not whether Anne and Wentworth will marry, but how this will come about. Like Darcy, Wentworth needs encouragement to face the possibility of a second rejection. Anne is of course unaware of this. The reader may assume more; but, since as in *Emma* the reader's perspective is very close to the heroine's, he actually knows little more than Anne at this point. For instance, he does not learn any sooner than Anne does that Wentworth's re-awakened interest in the heroine dates from her visit to Lyme, where he observed how Mr Elliot was struck by Anne's attractiveness. The reader may assume and, along with Anne, hope, and be more optimistic because of his familiarity with the conventions of the novel; however, he is hardly in a better position to predict the outcome with certainty until the decisive letter has been written. After this letter little remains to be told. The author brings the lovers together, and gives Wentworth an opportunity to declare his constancy and to explain what he has felt since his return to England. This review from Wentworth's perspective of events that have already been portrayed is accomplished quickly in a series of summary paragraphs with particular attention given to those times in the past when Anne was most uncertain as to how to interpret Wentworth's behaviour.

The last chapter functions as a coda to the story. It brings to a conventional close the tale of a love gained, lost and regained. The author enters into the narrative to parcel out some closing remarks to each of the major characters, and to share with the reader the pleasure of a happy ending.

Who can doubt what followed? When any two young people take it into their heads to marry, they are pretty sure by perse-verence to carry their point, be they ever so poor, or ever so imprudent, or ever so little likely to be necessary to each other's ultimate comfort. This may be bad morality to conclude with, but I believe it to be true; and if such parties succeed, how should a Captain Wentworth and an Anne Elliot, with the advantage of maturity of mind, consciousness of right, and one independent fortune between them, fail of bearing down every opposition? (*P* 250)

Jane Austen's reference to 'bad morality' need not be taken too seriously. In the unfolding of the plot the norms and values by which character and conduct are to be judged have been defined. Most of the individuals who enter into Anne's life are shown to fail in some respects to measure up to these standards. The consequences of such failings have been revealed in the course of the action. At this point in the narrative there is no need to evaluate the significance of past behaviour, as is the case for example in *Mansfield Park*. The author does, however, take the opportunity to make some observations which Anne would never have expressed no matter how strongly she felt them to be true.

Sir Walter indeed, though he had no affection for Anne, and no vanity flattered, to make him really happy on the occasion, was very far from thinking it a bad match for her. (*P* 251)

There was nothing less for Lady Russell to do, than admit that she had been pretty completely wrong, and to take up a new set of opinions and hopes. (*P* 251)

Such comments only confirm the opinions that the reader has long since formed of these characters. There is no need for the author to make explicit the ways in which various individuals have erred, or to point out where the older generation has failed to understand the needs of the young people. This has already been shown from Anne's perspective, a vantage point that represents a norm to which the author ascribes. Reiteration would be superfluous; hence the rapid pace of the concluding chapters.

A consideration of the conclusion to *Northanger Abbey* has been postponed until last, because this conclusion highlights some of the problems Jane Austen faced in working out the endings to all of her novels. Originally conceived in the 1790s, *Northanger Abbey* is Jane Austen's criticism of popular fiction.[14] She differentiates between good and bad fiction. The 'defence of the novel' in Chapter V is not of course a defence of all fiction.[15] It is a direct response to Maria Edgeworth's explanation in *Belinda* (1801) as to why she calls her work a 'Moral Tale' rather than a 'Novel'.[16] The objects of Jane Austen's criticism include the very popular works of Anne Radcliffe and Charlotte Smith as well as the kind of third-rate fiction typified by Isabella Thorpe's list of 'horrid novels'.[17] In Jane Austen's opinion, the former are not without merit. The same cannot be said of Isabella's favourite reading. In the conclusion to *Northanger Abbey* Jane Austen parodies three interrelated weaknesses of such novels: a lack of motivation, a moral arbitrarily imposed on the action, and a contrived resolution to the plot.

Northanger Abbey ends with the observation: 'I leave it to be settled by whomsoever it may concern, whether the tendency of this work be altogether to recommend parental tyranny, or reward filial disobedience' (*NA* 248). Here Jane Austen is mocking the common practice of tacking on a moral to the end of a story—the kind of ending found, for example, in one of Isabella's favourite novels, *The Orphan of the Rhine* (1798).

> They were blessed with numerous offspring, lovely as themselves, and presented, in the whole of their lives to the reflecting mind of the moralist, a striking instance of the imbecility of vice, and the triumphant power of virtue.[18]

Jane Austen's objection goes beyond a dissatisfaction with such an explicitly didactic close. She also objects to the failure in most instances of the authors to integrate the moral content into their narratives.[19] Another writer makes the same point in quite a different context.

> *Novels* and *Romances*, very few of them, are worth the trouble of reading; some of them perhaps do contain a few good morals, but they are not worth the finding where so much rubbish is intermixed.[20]

Jane Austen is not of course suggesting that writers of fiction should disregard the moral import of the characters and conduct which they portray; however, she believes that the moral themes should evolve logically and naturally out of the situations in which the characters have been placed.

A second criticism implied in the conclusion to *Northanger Abbey* concerns the pseudo-rational explanations introduced in the final pages of one of the two main types of Gothic fiction.[21] These explanations serve to enlighten the reader on the causes of what appear to be inexplicable, fantastic phenomena. In *The Mysteries of Udolpho* (1794), for instance, Anne Radcliffe goes on at some length to explain what in reality was behind 'the black veil' which so aroused Emily's curiosity, and to point out that it was only the strangeness of the circumstances in which the heroine found herself which prevented Emily from perceiving what was in fact in front of her: a wax figure and not the decaying skeleton of Lady Laurentini.[22] Jane Austen makes fun of such laboured rationalizations in her own explanation of the washing bills by which her heroine 'was involved in one of her most alarming adventures' (*NA* 247); and a little earlier in the next to the last chapter, where she writes: 'I leave it up to my readers' sagacity to determine how much of all this it was possible for Henry to communicate at this time to Catherine, how much he could have learnt from his father, in what points his own conjectures might assist him, and what portion must yet remain to be told in a letter from James' (*NA* 243). Jane Austen is very conscious of the open spaces in any literary text and the fact that the reader fills these in with his own imagination. In all of her novels she tends to be general rather than concrete, suggestive rather than specific.

Jane Austen's third criticism concerns the contrived manner in which many popular novels come to an end. The resolution to *Northanger Abbey* parodies such an obvious manipulation of the reader. Initially General Tilney is enthusiastically in favour of a match between his son and Catherine Morland; later he is just as violently opposed to it. The *deus ex machina* takes the form of the unexpected, but in the General's eyes very successful, marriage of his daughter.

This event so improves circumstances that the General is willing to lower his ambitions for his son and accept, if not condone, a marriage with Catherine.

To sum up, Jane Austen's implied criticism is based on a concept of motivation and the reader's expectations. As has been pointed out elsewhere, one of the objects of Jane Austen's satire in *Northanger Abbey* are those readers who, like Isabella Thorpe, uncritically consume the popular fiction of the period.[23] According to Jane Austen, action and the moral context in which action takes place should be integrated and motivated, and should establish the situation which logically leads to the story's dénouement. To the modern reader this appears obvious; however, in the light of the practices which were current around the end of the eighteenth century, it is evident that such fundamental ideas concerning the art of fiction were very often ignored. In the last decade of the eighteenth century the English novel as an art form reached its nadir. Authors and reviewers alike 'assumed that the only readers of fiction were those on the lowest intellectual level—impressionable adolescents and scatterbrained women.'[24] There were exceptions, including those mentioned by Jane Austen in Chapter V: Fanny Burney's novels *Cecilia* (1782) and *Camilla* (1796) and Maria Edgeworth's *Belinda* (1801); however, the general level was substantially lower than it was after Walter Scott and Jane Austen—to mention only the best known—had given fiction a new impetus. In criticizing the work of others, Jane Austen establishes some of the criteria by which her own work should be considered.

All of Jane Austen's novels end in marriage. But this statement is misleading, for it emphasizes the similarities when the differences are most important. It is of course true that each of the novels portrays a heroine in want of a husband; however, the choice of a partner becomes 'the occasion for a number of critical and far-reaching ethical decisions.'[25] These decisions have to be made before a resolution to the plot is possible. In *Northanger Abbey*, *Pride and Prejudice* and *Emma*, the heroines must first discover how they have deluded themselves before the narrative can progress to its logical conclusion. In the remaining three novels the situation is more complex: one or more of the characters must learn to see as clearly as Elinor, Fanny, or Anne. Until this occurs a dénouement is impossible. The proposal which marks the climax of each of these novels indicates that all of the obstacles standing in the way of marriage have been overcome or, in the case of *Emma*, are likely to be overcome soon.[26] But, more significantly, it marks the point where the heroine and her future husband realize that they have allowed other people and their own blindness to interfere with their love for each other. Marriage then becomes the formal conclusion to each of the novels. It brings to an end the ethical conflicts which have come up in the course of the narrative. The focus and the nature of these conflicts differs considerably from one novel to the next. Moreover, the relations between the reader, the narrator and the experience portrayed vary from novel to novel. These are the main reasons why Jane Austen employs different approaches in each instance to create a sense of ending. With the qualified exception of *Mansfield Park*, the turning point in all of the novels is a proposal of marriage, but the circumstances which lead up to this proposal differ in the weight they give to specific moral, social, and psychological problems.

IV

Ordering One's Priorities

Semantic Fields and the Real Point of View

This chapter examines the most significant patterns in Jane Austen's word-choices for the additional light these patterns throw on the *real point of view*, that is, on the author's attitude towards her subject matter. Words are an important guide for the reader to the moral frame of reference in Jane Austen's fictional world. It is a commonplace of Jane Austen criticism that she is an author very sure of her values;[1] nevertheless, her own moral stance and her attitudes towards middle-class life in Regency England have been the subject of considerable critical debate. The moral seriousness of her novels is no longer questioned, but her opinion of middle-class society and its sense of values has yet to be established to everyone's satisfaction.[2] There are several reasons why the specification of Jane Austen's relation to her texts has proved problematical. One aspect of the problem, the place and function of irony in Jane Austen's fiction, was discussed in the first two chapters of this study. Another concerns the changes the English language has undergone since the end of the eighteenth century.[3] In some important respects, Jane Austen's usage differs from modern usage; moreover, she at times gives a value or weight to a word that was not even common in the language of her contemporaries. A third aspect of the problem relates to the underlying assumptions of Jane Austen's *Weltanschauung*. She was not interested in being overtly didactic, but this lack of explicitness has led to some highly questionable interpretations of her texts by modern readers who fail to take sufficiently into consideration the philosophical distance between themselves and Jane Austen. And, finally, in a desire to place her work in the context of eighteenth-century thought, some critics have fallen into the error of trying to categorize Jane Austen, either by coming very close to claiming that she is an exponent of someone else's ideas, such as Shaftesbury's[4] or Burke's,[5] or by over-emphasizing the ideological aspect of the novels themselves. It is of course true that Jane Austen's attitudes are rooted in and shaped by the eighteenth century; however, this is less a matter of 'influence' than a manifestation of the general climate of opinion at the time.[6] Such excellent studies as the series of articles by Mark Schorer, Alistair M. Duckworth's *The Improvement of the Estate*, and Marilyn Butler's *Jane Austen and the War of Ideas* give too much emphasis to the ideological import of Jane Austen's fiction.[7] It is tempting to base an analysis on an idea or set of ideas, and the abstract concepts which serve as titles for three of the novels encourage such a line of interpretation as does the author's general tendency to weight her abstract words heavily. Nevertheless, it would be an error to view Jane Austen's work as 'ideological' in the sense that George Eliot's *Daniel Deronda* (1876), Goethe's *Die Wahlverwandtschaften* (1809), and André Gide's *Les Faux-monnayeurs* (1925) are novels of ideas. In a letter to James Stanier Clarke, the Prince Regent's librarian, Jane Austen writes:

I am quite honoured by your thinking me capable of drawing a clergyman as you gave me a sketch of in your note of Nov. 16th. But I assure you I am *not*. The comic part of the character I might be equal to, but not the good, the enthusiastic, the literary. Such a man's conversation must at times be on subjects of science and philosophy, of which I know nothing; or at least be occasionally abundant in quotations and allusions which a woman who, like me, knows only her mother tongue, and has read very little in that, would be totally without the power of giving. A classical education, or at any rate a very extensive acquaintance with English literature, ancient and modern, appears to me quite indispensable for the person who would do any justice to your clergyman; and I think I may boast myself to be, with all possible vanity, the most unlearned and uninformed female who ever dared to be an authoress.[8]

As Chapman has noted, Jane Austen is here guilty of what Darcy calls the indirect boast.[9] Although some critics—most notably H. W. Garrod—have taken this letter as a substantially accurate statement, it is a correct assessment neither of the author's knowledge nor of her reading habits.[10] The primary motivation behind this letter is quite clearly Jane Austen's disinclination to write the kind of novel proposed by Reverend Clarke, but the letter also suggests her conviction that wide reading is no substitute for the formal education which was at the time the exclusive privilege of gentlemen.[11] It is unlikely that she would have felt competent or even inclined to present her social, moral or religious views in a systematic and analytic manner, though these views inform all of her novels.[12] When Chapman first published his edition of Jane Austen's correspondence, it met with considerable disappointment among critics, confirming some of them in their prejudices.[13] The vivacity of *Pride and Prejudice* and its insights into human nature—not to mention the critical and intellectual comments on her times and reading— were missing.[14] But such critics overlook the fact that Jane Austen's ideological and critical premises are manifest in concrete human situations in her fiction.[15] This chapter is based on the assumption that the best way to gain an understanding of these premises is to take a close look at how language is used to evaluate character and conduct in these concrete situations. The care with which Jane Austen discriminates shades of meaning and the weight she gives to certain key words determine the reader's perception of her fictional world and its values. As David Lodge has written, Jane Austen 'puts every generation of readers to school, and in learning her own subtle and exact vocabulary of discrimination and evaluation, we submit to the authority of her vision.'[16] In what follows, I examine certain groups of words that inform the thematic structure of the novels and serve the reader as a guide to the author's system of values. But before examining these word patterns, it is first necessary to consider how words may be related to one another in the light of Semantic Field Theory.

That some words in a language are more closely related to

one another than others is obvious enough. Such terms as 'homophone', 'homonym', and 'synonym', such conventions as antonomasia, rhyme, and synecdoche, or the idea first proposed by Leibniz that a dictionary might be arranged according to meanings instead of spellings—an idea first realized in Roget's *Thesaurus of English Words and Phrases* (1852)—all indicate our awareness of formal or semantic affinities between words.[17] Nevertheless, it has only been in the twentieth century that scholars have recognized in the possible relations a word might have the basis for analysing the nature of signification in language, that is, how a society organizes its experience through language. To paraphrase Hjelmslev, in absolute isolation a word does not have any meaning; whatever meaning it signifies arises in context.[18] The difficulty, therefore, lies in the specification of the context. The context may be defined either from the point of view of *langue* or *parole*. The student of literature is of course concerned primarily with the latter, but most of the work in Semantic Field Theory deals with the former. It is based on the assumption that every lexical item of a language has a well-defined place in the system, which can be specified in terms of its relations to the other lexical items in the same semantic field.[19] This appears straightforward enough; however, the main problem is the definition of *semantic field*. Several definitions have been proposed, which can be divided into two groups: those which take into consideration extra-linguistic factors, such as the cultural context in which language is used, and those which do not.

Any consideration of Semantic Field Theory has to begin with the work of Jost Trier.[20] Although a number of precursors have been identified,[21] this area of scientific investigation first becomes more than just an idea in Trier's work.[22] He was interested primarily in how the relationships between words change over a period of time, and more specifically, how the alternative or paradigmatic choices open to the user of the language change. Sometimes a writer may have two word options to select from—the selection being determined by which features of his reference he wants to stress; at another time there may be three options to designate the same reference. Trier's emphasis on paradigmatic relations was soon challenged by Porzig, who argued that a study of syntagmatic relations is more likely to aid us in our understanding of how meaning functions.[23] 'Syntagmatic relations' refers to the fact that any word in sequence is determined to some extent by what word has preceded it.[24] The degree of influence varies considerably. The adjective *bad* may be followed by an almost unlimited number of lexical items; whereas, the adjective *rancid* can be followed by *butter* and not much else. Trier and Porzig eventually came to realize that their theories were not contradictory but complementary.[25] Both base their concept of a semantic field on the meaning-relations of words, but Porzig viewed his own approach as being more objective.

Jolles and Ipsen, among others, also challenged the objectivity of Trier's concept of a semantic field. Jolles argued that semantic fields should be limited to oppositional pairs, e.g., *father-son*, *day-night*, *life-death*, etc.[26] Ipsen proposed restricting a semantic field to those lexical items which have both semantic and formal affinities.[27] This proposal has met with little support among semanticists; however, from the point of view of literary textual analysis, it serves as a reminder that formal affinities may be used by an author to reinforce the semantic affinities of words, such as, *sense, sensible* and *sensibility*.

Approaching the problem of semantic fields from an entirely different perspective, Charles Bally has developed the concept of the *champ associatif*.[28] Unlike Trier's concept of *semantic field*, this concept is open-ended. Whereas Trier and the others mentioned above assume that the semantic field can be classified and organized in such a way that each lexical item helps to delimit its neighbours and is delimited by them,[29] Bally assumes there is no clear line of demarcation separating the field from the rest of the vocabulary.[30] This possibility is excluded by definition, for Bally is concerned with the degrees of relationship words may have to a particular key word. There is no set limit to the associations which may be perceived. Bally's concept is ill-suited to such tasks as those Trier and Porzig set for themselves, because only some of a word's associations can be determined within the system of language and without regard to extra-linguistic factors.[31] But for precisely this reason, Bally's concept provides a more satisfactory basis for the study of word-patterns in literature. In what follows, the term *semantic field* is used in the sense of Bally's *champ associatif*.[32]

Every author recreates the language for his own purposes, departing from or, in some cases, reaffirming established usage.[33] Drawing upon literary and cultural conventions, he creates relations and significances which may not have been a part of the language before. This is partly because an author omits more of the vocabulary than he uses, which gives additional significance to the words chosen. It is arguable, for example, that the word *sensible* in the system of language created by Jane Austen differs in some respects from the word *sensible* in the language at the end of the eighteenth century in England. Of the four usages which were current at the time, Jane Austen employs only two of them frequently and one of them rarely if at all.[34] As a consequence, the place and function of this word in her system differs from its place and function in the language from which she draws to create her own. This point is of interest, but by itself difficult to make use of in an analysis, since, in many instances, it is impossible to ascertain which additional usages and which additional word-choices the author rejected. As noted above, much more important for an analysis of meaning is the context, not only the immediate context of a word, but also the context of the work as a whole. The advantage of introducing the concept *semantic field* is that it makes possible a more precise specification of this context. Obviously, not all the words in a text are equally important. Most of them represent an author's more or less unconscious habits of formulating his ideas, but some words have quite consciously been chosen to influence the reader's response to the text. These words can be grouped into fields, and the relations between these fields as well as the relations among the words within each of these fields can be specified. This specification involves not only a consideration of the system of language which the author uses, but also the system of human interactions of which the language is a part. Every utterance occurs in a culturally determined *context-of-situation*, and the meaning of the utterance is the totality of its contribution to the maintenance of the patterns of life in the society in which the speaker lives and to the affirmation of the speaker's role and personality within the society.[35] In literature, it is the author who determines the *'context-of-situation'*, that is, the social and cultural frame of reference within which the action takes place, and the language functions as a means of communication.[36] Matoré has pointed out that in this system of human interactions (i.e. the social and cultural frame of reference) there are *key words (mots-clés)* and *witness words (mots-témoins)*.[37] The latter are defined as 'des éléments particulièrement importants en fonction desquels la structure lexicologique se hiérarchise et se coordonne.'[38] *Key words* refer to an 'unité lexicologique exprimant une société . . . un étre, un sentiment, une idée, vivants dans la mesure même où la société reconaît en eux idéal.'[39]

It is this second concept which is directly relevant to the present study. In Jane Austen's language, there are three interrelated semantic fields, which taken together determine the context-of-situation: 'material values', 'social values', and 'moral values'. These fields designate a hierarchy of values, and within each field single words are arranged in a definite pattern; that is, the individual word has a specific relationship to an ideal or set of ideals signified by a key word or group of key words. The reader can check his interpretation of an author's use of language against the patterns of meaning which emerge in the course of the text. In examining the language of individual characters, the reader is also able to determine how each of the characters maintains the patterns of life in the society in which he lives, and affirms his role and personality in society. The language of the individual character is viewed in the context of the ethical and critical values of the author. This frame of reference may be explicit, but it need not be. It is implicit in the system of language as a whole as it is used by the social group portrayed. One of the possible subjects for investigation is the extent to which the language of an individual might deviate and still be acceptable. The grammatical errors of Lucy Steele, the vulgarisms of John Thorpe, and the hollow rhetoric of Mr Collins raise questions of acceptability. But my focus is less on the performance of individuals than on the patterns of meaning which signify the norms and values by which character is judged. Before considering these patterns in detail, I want to emphasize the care Jane Austen takes to distinguish properly between the meanings of words and to use them correctly.

Jane Austen differentiates meaning with a preciseness which may catch the unwary reader off guard. Her concern with correct and exact usage sometimes becomes a topic of discussion in her correspondence and in the novels. In a letter to her sister Cassandra, she hesitates over the expressions *yesterday morning* and *yesterday evening*:[40] 'I called yesterday morning (ought it not in strict propriety to be termed yester-morning?) on Miss Armstrong. . . .'[41] And, earlier in the same letter: 'We all of us attended them both on Wednesday evening & last evening I suppose I must say or Martha will think Mr Peter Debary slighted.'[42] In two well-known passages in the novels, questions of definition are dealt with explicitly. Henry Tilney cannot resist the temptation to make fun of Catherine's use of 'amazingly' and 'nice'.

'I am very glad to hear it indeed, and now I shall never be ashamed of liking Udolpho myself. But I really thought before, young men despised novels amazingly.'
'It is *amazingly*; it may suggest *amazement* if they do—for they read nearly as many as women.' (*NA* 122)

And a little further on in this same scene:

'But now really do not you think Udolpho the nicest book in the world?'
'The nicest, by which I suppose you mean the neatest. That must depend upon the binding.'
'Henry,' said Miss Tilney, 'you are very impertinent. Miss Morland, he is treating you exactly as he does his sister. He is forever finding fault with me, for some incorrectness of language, and now he is taking the same liberty with you. The word "nicest," as you used it, did not suit him; and you had better change it as

soon as you can, or we shall be overpowered with Johnson and Blair all the rest of the way.'

'I am sure,' cried Catherine, 'I did not mean to say any thing wrong; but it *is* a nice book, and why should I not call it so?'

'Very true,' said Henry, 'and this is a very nice day, and we are taking a very nice walk, and you are two very nice young ladies. Oh! it is a nice word indeed!—it does for every thing. Originally perhaps it was applied only to express neatness, propriety, delicacy, or refinement;—people were nice in their dress, in their sentiments, or their choice. But now every commendation on every subject is comprised in that one word.' (*NA* 122–123)

The allusions to Samuel Johnson's *A Dictionary of the English Language* (1755) and Hugh Blair's *Lectures on Rhetoric* (1783) are reminders that by the end of the eighteenth century notions of prescriptive grammar and correct usage were well established.[43] When Emma suggests that Frank Churchill is 'an amiable young man,' Knightley comments in the ensuing conversation:

'No, Emma, your amiable young man can be amiable only in French, not in English. He may be very "amiable," have very good manners, and be very agreeable; but he can have no English delicacy towards the feelings of other people: nothing really amiable about him.' (*E* 166)

Such explicit distinctions occur less obviously elsewhere.[44]

Lucy was certainly not *elegant*, and her sister not even *genteel*. (*SS* 237)

He spoke to Elizabeth if not in terms of perfect *composure*, at least of perfect *civility*. (*PP* 272)

She did not really like her. She would be in no hurry to find fault, but she suspected that there was no *elegance*;—*ease*, but not *elegance*. (*E* 273)

Such passages are indications of Jane Austen's scale of values: *ease* ranks below *elegance*, *civility* below *composure*, and *genteel* below *elegant*. Often the immediate context of a word approaches explicit definition.[45]

'Good-humoured, unaffected girls, will not do for a man who has been used to *sensible* women. They are two distinct orders of being. You and Miss Crawford have made me too nice.' (*MP* 351)

Her manners were *open*, *easy* and *decided*, like one who had no distrust of herself, and no doubts of what to do; without any approach to coarsness, however, or any want of good humour. (*P* 74–75)

She liked his open manners, but a little less openheartedness would have made him a higher character. General *benevolence*, but not general friendship, made a man what he ought to be. (*E* 317–318)

Tom Bertram must have been thought pleasant, indeed, at any rate; he was the sort of young man to be generally liked, his *agreeableness* was of the kind to be oftener found *agreeable* than some endowments of a higher stamp, for he had *easy* manners, excellent spirits, a large acquaintance, and a great deal to say; . . . (*MP* 80)

As these passages suggest, Jane Austen places her words very carefully. She takes advantage of the possibilities of juxta-position and the immediate context to reinforce and clarify what she 'means' with a particular word. Moreover, the basic meaning given a word in one context is the meaning it continues to have throughout the text. There is some variation and extension of meaning, depending upon the context and who uses the word, but the core meaning remains the same. There are some exceptions. A few words are used in more than one sense, but in such cases the author is generally careful to avoid ambiguities by restricting possible interpretations of the word in context. This consistency in her usage is a manifestation of Jane Austen's desire to avoid confusion or imprecision. It enables her to make her scale of values implicit and avoids the necessity of being openly didactic in its presentation. These values underlie her choice of words in all of the novels. In turning to an examination of the semantic fields in these novels, it is important to keep in mind the author's concern for precise distinctions and definitions, for these serve the reader as a guide to the standard by which character and conduct are evaluated. The first semantic field to be considered refers to *material values*.

Elizabeth Bennet is shocked when she learns that Charlotte Lucas has accepted Mr Collins' proposal of marriage. Elizabeth cannot comprehend how Charlotte could allow the material advantages of the marriage to blind her to the fact that Mr Collins is a foolish and egotistical individual. She views Charlotte's decision as the end of their intimate friendship: in future some matters will no longer enter into their conversation. Elizabeth's attitude in this situation foreshadows her own rejection of Darcy's first proposal.[46] The most interesting question raised by Charlotte's decision is the author's attitude towards it. The answer is less simple than some critics have suggested. In a letter to her niece, Fanny Knight, Jane Austen writes, 'Single Women have a dreadful propensity for being poor—which is one very strong argument in favour of Matrimony.'[47] Moreover, Charlotte has reached the 'dangerous age' of twenty-seven, which makes her more vulnerable to temptation.[48] Her situation is more desperate than it might have been a few years earlier. Furthermore, it could be argued that an autobiographical element is touched on in this incident, for Jane Austen, together with her mother and Cassandra, had to learn to manage on increasingly modest means after her father's death.[49] This line of interpretation suggests an explanation for the prominence given the financial circumstances of each of the heroines and their families as well as those possible suitors who enter onto the scene; nevertheless, it accounts for less than it ignores. On the one hand, it is correct to say that various economic factors significantly affect the lives of almost all of the characters.[50] On the other hand, it is incorrect to assume that in the author's opinion material values should be given priority over other values.[51] On the contrary, all the characters who allow their material interests to prevail over any other consideration are presented in a negative light. The vulgar economic realities of the society Jane Austen portrays are facts which the individual should be able to come to terms with without compromising his or her moral integrity. Jane

Austen does not reject this society *in toto*, but she refuses to accept material values as a basis or justification for conduct.[52]

I use the term *material values* instead of *materialism* to avoid the political connotations of the latter. It is hardly surprising that in recent years translations of Jane Austen's novels with extensive annotations have been brought out in the Soviet Union,[53] nor that some critics have tried to categorize Jane Austen as a 'Marxist before Marx'; however, to interpret the novels as an exposé of the economic basis of social behaviour is to misconstrue the general direction of Jane Austen's thought.[54] Jane Austen's social criticism as well as her interest in the material welfare of her characters is not politically motivated. The political situation was taken for granted. In Butler's words, she is not a 'sycophant of wealth or rank, and she does not deal intimately with—or apparently much like—the great aristocracy. The class she deals with has local not national importance: in eighteenth-century terms, she is a Tory rather than a Whig.'[55]

For practically the first time in the history of the English novel, material values are shown to be closely intertwined with social and moral values. Fielding has already portrayed the individual who has to cope with the corrupt and vicious forces of a vulgar society. And no one could be more acquisitive than Defoe's characters are in their different ways. Nor was Jane Austen the first to show a woman being materially rewarded for being 'good' (*Pamela* 1740)—or, if we follow Fielding's cynical interpretation, rewarded for being clever, or disinherited for not being so (*Clarissa* 1747–1748). Nor was she the first to portray young ladies setting their sights and ambitions above their station in life. Nevertheless, no major English author before Jane Austen shows material considerations to be such a significant factor in the determination of a young woman's future. Anne Elliot is dissuaded from marrying Wentworth because he has no fortune and his future is uncertain. Fanny Price has no material prospects whatsoever, for she has neither social status nor financial expectations. The early death of their father appears to eliminate whatever chances Elinor and Marianne might have had of marrying well. Their half-brother inherits Norland, and the Dashwood sisters along with their mother are left to make do as well as they can in their new situation of comparative poverty. Similarly, in *Pride and Prejudice*, the entailment of the estate reduces the prospects of the five Bennet daughters. In light of the modest dowries which each of them can anticipate, Mrs Bennet's marital ambitions for her daughters are not only lacking in propriety but also totally unrealistic. At the beginning of *Pride and Prejudice* and *Sense and Sensibility*, Elizabeth and Jane Bennet and Marianne and Elinor Dashwood are placed in situations in which they can only look forward to learning to get by on less than they have been accustomed to.

The point is important, for it focuses attention on the fact that the circumstances in which each of these young women finds herself put psychological and social pressure on her to marry. Fanny's situation differs from the rest in that from the beginning she enjoys the privileges of the gentry only to a limited extent and only because of Sir Thomas Bertram's generosity. Catherine Morland's fate is unique among Jane Austen's heroines, since it is less affected by her actual material and social circumstances than by what is erroneously reported to General Tilney concerning them. In *Persuasion* we have a reversal of the situation in *Pride and Prejudice* and *Sense and Sensibility*. It is Wentworth whose future appears so uncertain; however, as the novel opens, this uncertainty is a thing of the past. He has since gained the fortune which makes him an 'eligible bachelor'. Only in *Emma* are material concerns of little relevance to the progress of Emma and Knightley's relationship. But in this novel the heroine's interference in other people's lives and her attitude towards various individuals is in large part determined by their economic position in comparison to her own.[56]

But the emphasis on material values goes beyond their effect on the destinies of the heroines. Practically every aspect of life in Jane Austen's fictional world is imbued with what might be called an 'economic sensibility': a tendency to give weight to the economic aspect of such matters as matrimony or a profession, and to use the vocabulary of the counting house in areas of experience and judgement which would not necessarily require it.[57] Whenever a new character is introduced, as a rule, his or her economic status is quickly established. The relative economic status of each of the heroines and their families is set down in the first few pages of the narrative. In *Sense and Sensibility*, *Pride and Prejudice*, and, in a less obvious manner, *Mansfield Park*, it is the heroine's economic circumstances which sets the plot in motion. Lord David Cecil has observed that in Jane Austen's fiction, 'it was wrong to marry for money, but silly to marry without it.'[58] This comment captures the essence of Charlotte Lucas' dilemma and Elizabeth's response; the first half of this aphorism suggesting Elizabeth's judgement of Charlotte's motives, and the second half presumably not far from Charlotte's own rationalization of her motives. Developing Cecil's point, one could argue that in Jane Austen's opinion it is wrong to ignore the economic realities of one's situation, and it is just as wrong to place the economic facts of life above all others.

The fundamental restructuring of society brought about by the industrial revolution was just beginning to affect life in the country village near the end of the eighteenth century. Society was becoming increasingly fluid, and upward as well as downward mobility on the social scale was becoming more and more a matter of economics. These social facts generate many of the conflicts faced by Jane Austen's characters. Darcy is a landowner, and his family has been established for many generations, but his friend Bingley is looking for an estate to purchase after having inherited a hundred thousand pounds.[59] Charlotte's father, Sir William Lucas, has risen from trade to a knighthood. Sir Walter Elliot belongs to a landed family which was raised to a baronetcy during the Restoration, but his income will not support his position; as a consequence, he is forced to rent Kellynch Hall to an admiral who, like Wentworth, has made his fortune at sea. The future owner of Kellynch Hall, Mr William Walter Elliot, attempts to secure his financial independence by marrying a rich woman of inferior birth. As these examples suggest, money and property are the keys to the privileges, comforts, and prestige of the country gentry. Most of Jane

Austen's characters do not enjoy all the advantages of this class, but they live close enough to them to know their value. The degree of interest in matters of money, property, and social status varies considerably. Such dissimilar characters as Mrs Norris, Sir Walter Elliot, Mrs Allen, General Tilney, and Mrs Price seem to be obsessed in their different ways with such matters, but (though Marianne for a time approaches indifference) none of the characters is completely indifferent to them.

Since the heroine is the focus of the reader's interest in all the novels, it is easy to overlook the very practical problems concerning a profession and a steady income which confront most of the young men. Darcy, Bingley, Knightley, Rushworth and Henry Crawford are financially independent. Whatever faults they may have, they fulfill not only Mrs Bennet's criteria but also the criteria of the society in which they live for 'eligibility'. However, these gentlemen belong to a minority in that they are not faced with the problem of having to find a reliable source of income. Without an income one cannot marry, and without a fortune one cannot marry well. Since the theme of marriage is central to all of the novels, it is hardly surprising that questions of a profession and financial security are recurrent topics of conversation and concern. In Jane Austen's world there are not very many career options open to a young gentleman. She concentrates on the two professions she knows best: the clergy and the navy.[60] Willoughby and William Elliot try to get around the problem of an occupation by becoming engaged to wealthy young women, but the decision turns out to have been an unfortunate one in both cases. Wickham's situation is more complex. He makes three or four half-hearted attempts to take up a profession, but fails in all of these efforts. When he runs off with Lydia Bennet, he has no intention of marrying her. His primary motive is to escape his creditors, and he takes Lydia along as a companion in flight. Later, in London, Darcy 'persuades' Wickham to marry Lydia by settling Wickham's debts and arranging a secure source of income for Lydia and Wickham. Wickham's problem is thus solved in a manner which he could not have anticipated. Long before this incident in *Pride and Prejudice*, Wickham complains to Elizabeth that he had wanted to go into the clergy, but Darcy's unwillingness to give him a living, which he had been promised by Darcy's father, forced Wickham to seek a career as an officer (cf. *PP* 122–127). Although Wickham's revelation happens to be false, it highlights the dilemma in which Charles Hayter, Edmund Bertram, Edward Ferrars, Mr Elton, Mr Collins, and Henry Tilney all find themselves at a crucial stage in their lives. Having chosen the clerical profession, they have to gain a living. This usually involves waiting, sometimes for years. Someone has to die or retire before a living becomes available, and then the intervention of some influential personage such as Colonel Brandon or Lady Catherine is as a rule necessary if the income of the living is sufficiently large to support a clergyman and his family. In other words, for these young men the acquisition of a living is a prerequisite to marriage. Mr Collins is extremely fortunate in acquiring one so soon, and, not long after he has become settled in his new situation, he sets out for Longbourn in search of a wife. Edward Ferrar's fate is more typical: a long period of waiting with little certainty as to what the future may bring. The emphasis on the economic aspect of the clerical profession is not accidental. The destinies not only of these young men but also of several of the young ladies depend upon the financial security which one of these livings represents. But it would be an error to assume that the author views the clerical profession as a means of making money just like any other. She is aware of the economic realities of the situations of young men like Edward; however, she has little sympathy for those who go into the profession without a sense of religious commitment. This comes out most clearly in *Mansfield Park*, but it is also implied in the harsh critical light in which Mr Collins and Mr Elton are portrayed.

Whenever a young man enters upon the scene in this novel, it is not long before the question of his 'eligibility' has been clarified. Since Marianne has already been distracted by the romantic circumstances surrounding her first acquaintance with Willoughby and readily impressed by the 'shooting jacket' he was wearing, it is left up to her sister to make the necessary inquiries.

'But who is he?' said Elinor. 'Where does he come from? Has he a house at Allenham?'

On this point Sir John could give more certain intelligence; and he told them that Mr Willoughby had no property of his own in the country; that he resided there only while he was visiting the old lady at Allenham Court, to whom he was related, and whose possessions he was to inherit; adding, 'Yes, yes, he is very well worth catching, I can tell you, Miss Dashwood; he has a pretty little estate of his own in Somersetshire besides; ... (*SS* 76)

The key words are: *property, possessions, inherit, wealth,* and *estate.* The narrator settles the question more succinctly when Henry Crawford and his sister are introduced in *Mansfield Park.*

Such was the state of affairs in the month of July, and Fanny had just reached her eighteenth year, when the society of the village received an addition in the brother and sister of Mrs Grant, a Mr and Miss Crawford, the children of her mother by a second marriage. They were young people of fortune. The son had a good estate in Norfolk, the daughter twenty thousand pounds. (*MP* 73)

The key words here are: *estate, fortune,* and *twenty thousand pounds.* And in the same novel, even before he is named, Mr Rushworth's credentials are established—at least in Mrs Norris' thoughts.

'If poor Sir Thomas were fated never to return, it would be peculiarly consoling to see their dear Maria well married,' she very often thought; always when they were in the company of men of fortune, and particularly on the introduction of a young man who had recently succeeded to one of the largest estates and finest places in the country. (*MP* 71–72)

Estate and *fortune* are again the key words. In *Persuasion* it is a question from Captain Wentworth which leads to a revelation of the necessary facts concerning Mr Elliot. It is only following the climax of the novel that the reader understands Wentworth's motive in asking.

'Pray,' said Captain Wentworth, immediately, 'can you tell us the name of the gentleman who is just gone away?'

'Yes, Sir, a Mr Elliot; a gentleman of large fortune,—came in last night from Sidmouth,—dare say you heard the carriage, Sir, while you were at dinner; and going on to Crewkherne, in his way to Bath and London.'

'Elliot!'—Many had looked on each other, and many had repeated the name, before all this had been got through, even by the smart rapidity of the waiter.

'Bless me!' cried Mary; 'it must be our cousin;—it must be our Mr Elliot, indeed!—Charles, Anne must not it? In mourning, you see, just as our Mr Elliot must be. How very extraordinary! In the very same inn with us! Anne, must not it be our Mr Elliot; my father's next heir? Pray Sir,' (turning to the waiter), 'did not you hear,—did not his servant say whether he belonged to the Kellynch family?'

'No, ma'am,—he did not mention no particular family; but he said his master was a very rich gentleman, and would be a baronight some day.' (*P* 126)

The key words: *fortune, carriage, heir, rich gentleman,* and '*baronight*'. The information given in each of these passages is similar. Wealth, property, and social position are closely linked with one another. It is significant that as the action unfolds much of this information proves to be misleading if not totally incorrect. Not all of the characters have such 'merits'.

Jane Fairfax was an orphan, the only child of Mrs Bates's youngest daughter.

The marriage of Lieut. Fairfax, of the —— regiment of infantry, and Miss Jane Bates, had had its day of fame and pleasure, hope and interest; but nothing now remained of it, save the melancholy remembrance of him dying in action abroad—of his widow sinking under consumption and grief soon afterwards—and this girl.

By birth she belonged to Highbury: and when at three years old, on losing her mother, she became the property, the charge, the consolation, the fondling of her grandmother and aunt, there had seemed every probability of her being permanently fixed there; of her being taught only what very limited means could command, and growing up with no advantages of connection or improvement to be engrafted on what nature had given her in a pleasing person, good understanding, and warm-hearted, well-meaning relations.

But the compassionate feelings of a friend of her father gave a change to her destiny. This was Colonel Campbell, who had very highly regarded Fairfax, as an excellent officer and most deserving young man; and farther, had been indebted to him for such attentions during a severe camp-fever, as he believed had saved his life. These were claims he did not learn to overlook, though some years passed away from the death of poor Fairfax, before his own return to England put any thing in his power. (*E* 177)

In this passage the key words are: *limited means, connection, improvement,* and perhaps the secondary meanings or associations of *deserving, indebted,* and *claims.* Like Fanny Price, Jane Fairfax's destiny depends on the generosity of others. Colonel Campbell's intervention on her behalf improves her prospects appreciably. Fanny and Jane's situations illustrate the fact that the fate of young women in Jane Austen's world is even more dependent than that of the young men on money and social connections, for unlike their male counterparts they do not have the opportunity of trying to make their own way by joining the navy or going into the church. When Fanny turns down Henry Crawford's proposal of marriage, Sir Thomas's response is one of incomprehension. He cannot understand how Fanny can reject all the wealth and security which this alliance would mean. He sends Fanny for a visit to her mother in the hope that, when Fanny is confronted with the impoverished circumstances in which Mrs Price lives, she will come to her senses. If Colonel Campbell had not taken an interest in Jane Fairfax, her claims would hardly have been superior to Fanny's. Both of them are at the lower end of the middle-class social scale and Darcy and Mr Rushworth are at the upper. This statement indicates nothing about the quality of their minds or their morals, but it specifies the first criterion by which they are likely to be judged by those who have not yet come to know them as individuals. Their 'eligibility' is determined in much the same manner as that of the gentlemen, though it may not be spoken of so openly.

Most of Jane Austen's characters fall somewhere between the extremes of the social scale represented by Darcy and Jane Fairfax, being neither as wealthy as the former nor as poor as the latter. However, no matter what their economic situation, nearly all of the characters are acutely aware of their own material circumstances and very much interested in those of others, which is not to suggest that everyone would ascribe the same importance to material values. Some, like Mrs Price and Mrs Smith, are resigned to their situation; others, such as Mr Wickham and Mr Elliot, try to improve it; and still others, for example, Emma or Mr Rushworth, take a little too much pride in the superiority of their situation. It is significant that in the passage from *Persuasion* cited in the preceding paragraph, Mary Musgrove assumes that the waiter has informed himself about his guest, Mr Elliot, and, as it turns out, he has. One's circumstances and, especially, the circumstances of others are a frequent topic of conversation and speculation. This interest in materialistic matters— money, property, eligibility, and status (defined in terms of wealth)—carries over into the language and the thoughts of several of the characters in situations where it would not necessarily be expected.

It was as much as Emma could bear, without being impolite. The idea of her being indebted to Mrs Elton for what was called an *introduction.* . . . (*E* 278)

Mrs Weston was exceedingly disappointed—much more disappointed, in fact, than her husband, though her dependence on seeing the young man had been so much more sober: but a sanguine temper, though forever expecting more good than occurs, does not always pay for its hopes by any proportionate depression. (*E* 162)

It would be going only to multiply trouble to the others, and increase his own distress. . . . (*P* 137)

Lady Russell was now perfectly decided in her opinion of Mr Elliot. She was as much convinced of his meaning to gain Anne. . . . (*P* 171)

I have intentionally chosen unremarkable examples in order to make a point. Such words as *indebted, pay, multiply, increase, gain,* and dozens of similar words used in similar ways are so much a part of the English idiom that they may be passed over unnoticed, though they are all in fact lexical items in the semantic field of material values. In Jane Austen this is true even where the meaning of a word in context has little or nothing to do with material or mercantile matters. The word evokes a second meaning even where this meaning is not appropriate in context. Schorer has gone so far as to claim that Jane Austen's consistent use of certain words, phrases, and 'buried metaphors' constitute the 'analogical matrix' of her novels. He argues that in *Persuasion* a superficial morality is imposed on the harsh economic realities implied in the metaphorical structure which in fact determines the novel's values.[61] This interpretation is untenable. The characters' habits of evaluating, assessing, calculating, and reckoning with the world do not reflect the real ethical structure of *Persuasion* or any of the other novels; however, they do represent—and to this extent Schorer is correct—a pattern of associations which taken together signify a serious threat to the ethical structure the author is upholding. But to designate this pattern as a 'metaphorical substructure', as Schorer does, is to overstate the case. As with the symbolism in *Mansfield Park*, the pattern is suggestive, but it first becomes significant when considered in the light of the behaviour of various individuals. The second meaning of a word would not necessarily be evoked when it occurs in a text. This association depends upon the thematic structure of the novel. It is doubtful that Jane Austen's contemporaries immediately thought of all four usages of *sensible* whenever it occurred. In other words, the pattern does not stand for something else; it confirms what the reader comes to suspect about certain characters' habitual manner of viewing the world.

The pattern of associations evoked by the words in the semantic field of material values occurs not only when such obviously related topics as 'eligibility', marriage, or a profession are brought up, and not only incidentally as in the vocabulary of Emma or Lady Russell, but also—and most prominently—in the language of those characters who appear incapable of thinking or speaking in terms which do not reflect their preoccupation with the material values and the material objects of their small universe. In this context, a distinction needs to be made between such characters as Willoughby, Mr Elliot and Wickham on the one hand, and Mrs Allen, Mary Crawford, Mr Collins, Mrs Elton and Mrs Norris on the other. All these individuals give materialistic values the highest priority; however, the gentlemen in the first group have learned to hide their obsession behind a façade of impeccably good manners—at least until their true motives and attitudes are exposed. Wherever material values outweigh all other considerations, it is a sign of weakness. It may indicate an individual's naïveté, foolishness, egotism, capacity for self-deception, or a more general lack of moral sensibility and responsibility. Mrs Allen in *Northanger Abbey* and Mary Crawford in *Mansfield Park* illustrate an innocent and a not-so-innocent materialistic orientation.

In one respect she was admirably fitted to introduce a young lady into public, being as fond of going every where and seeing every thing herself as any young lady could be. Dress was her passion. She had a most harmless delight in being fine; and our heroine's entrée into life could not take place till after three or four days had been spent in learning what was mostly worn, and her chaperon was provided with a dress of the newest fashion. (*NA* 43)

They were interrupted by Mrs Allen:—'My dear Catherine,' said she, 'do take this pin out of my sleeve; I am afraid it has torn a hole already; I shall be quite sorry if it has, for this is my favourite gown, though it cost but nine shillings a yard.'

'That is exactly what I should have guessed it, madam,' said Mr Tilney, looking at the muslin.

'Do you understand muslins, sir?'

'Particularly well; I always buy my own cravats, and am allowed to be an excellent judge; and my sister has often trusted me in the choice of a gown. I bought one for her the other day, and it was pronounced to be a prodigious bargain by every lady who saw it. I gave but five shillings a yard for it, and a true Indian muslin.'

Mrs Allen was quite struck by his genius. 'Men commonly take so little notice of those things,' said she: 'I can never get Mr Allen to know one of my gowns from another. You must be a great comfort to your sister, sir.' (*NA* 49–50)

At almost any given moment in the story, it is to be expected that Mrs Allen is thinking about clothes. This preoccupation makes her oblivious to almost everything else which is happening around her. Fortunately, very little happens, so that she is of very little danger to herself or to her charge, although she seems to think less of Catherine than of the 'clogs' Mrs Allen suspects she has forgotten at an inn on their way to Bath (*NA* 42). Mrs Allen belongs to a group of older women in Jane Austen's fiction, a group which includes Mrs Dashwood, Mrs Weston, Mrs Bennet, Mrs Jennings, Mrs Norris, and Lady Bertram, who are at least theoretically in charge of looking after some young woman's well-being. Despite many significant differences in their personalities—ranging from Lady Bertram's indolence to Mrs Bennet's boistrous silliness—they have in common the characteristic of being totally ineffective as moral guides to the younger generation. Placing Mrs Allen in this group suggests that the reader should assign a more serious function to Mrs Allen's appearance in the narrative than the author probably intended. Mrs Allen's weaknesses invite comparisons of her with similar characters in the other novels; however, considering the burlesque nature of the part of *Northanger Abbey* in which she appears, it is more in keeping with the general tenor of the narrative to view her as a figure of fun. Her materialistic concerns are culpable, and are the object of the author's irony, but they do not pose—or even imply—a threat to the ethical structure of the society in which she lives. By contrast, Mary Crawford's material interests amount to considerably more than just a foolish preoccupation with clothes. Some excerpts from a long conversation Mary has with Fanny reveal her materialistic orientation.[62]

'For as to secrecy, Henry is quite the hero of an old romance, and glories in his chains. You should come to London, to know how to estimate your conquest. . . .'

L

'You must have seen that he was trying to please you, by every attention in his power. Was not he devoted to you at the ball? And then before the ball, the necklace! Oh! you received it just as it was meant. You were as conscious as heart could desire. I remember it perfectly.'

'Do you mean then that your brother knew of the necklace beforehand? Oh! Miss Crawford, *that* was not fair.'

'. . . He has now and then been a sad flirt, and cared very little for the havock he might be making in young ladies affections. I have often scolded him for it, but it is his only fault; and there is this to be said, that very few young ladies have any affections worth caring for. And then, Fanny, the glory of fixing one who has been shot at by so many; of having it in one's power to pay off the debts of one's sex! Oh, I am sure it is not in a woman's nature to refuse such a triumph.'

'. . . I cannot imagine Henry ever to have been happier,' continued Mary, presently, 'that when he had succeeded in getting your brother's commission.'

She had made a sure push at Fanny's feelings here. (*MP* 356–358)

The general direction of Mary's remarks is obvious enough: Fanny should not even entertain the idea of rejecting Henry Crawford's proposal. Even more revealing are the language and the arguments Mary uses. She reminds Fanny of the necklace Fanny received as a gift, and explains the circumstances relating to it. Had Fanny known these circumstances at the time, she would have considered the gift improper and refused to accept it. Mary cannot or will not comprehend Fanny's attitude on this point. In the course of the conversation, Mary comes finally to what must appear to her the clinching argument, namely, what Henry has done for Fanny's brother, and Fanny is in fact deeply moved by this reminder of her indebtedness to Henry. Whereas the matter of the necklace or the knowledge of Henry's popularity among the young ladies of London can only reinforce an opinion which Fanny has already formed of Mary's brother, Henry's intervention on William's behalf generates a feeling of gratitude. Mary is convinced that Fanny only stands to gain by such a match. Personal feelings or moral values do not enter into her thinking. She is quite consciously trying to

manipulate Fanny without taking into consideration or even
fully understanding the reasons for Fanny's hesitancy.

A materialistic vocabulary is used to characterize a number
of characters other than Mrs Allen and Mary Crawford.
Mrs Norris's materialistic attitudes are in the end detrimental
to no one so much as herself. Her acquisitive and miserly
nature determines the range of her conversation and the extent
of her interest in others. Her feelings towards Fanny can
only be negative, for she cannot directly or indirectly share
in the material possessions of someone who has none.

'It is amazing,' said she, 'how much young people cost their
friends, what with bringing them up and putting them out in the
world! They little think how much it comes to, or what their
parents, or their uncles or aunts pay for them in the course of a
year. Now, here are my sister Price's children;—take them all
together, I dare say nobody would believe what a sum they cost
Sir Thomas every year, to say nothing of what *I* do for them.'
(*MP* 308)

The Grants showing a disposition to be friendly and sociable,
gave great satisfaction in the main among their new acquaintance.
They had their faults, and Mrs Norris soon found them out. The
Dr was very fond of eating, and would have a good dinner every
day; and Mrs Grant, instead of contriving to gratify him at little
expense, gave her cook as high wages as they did at Mansfield
Park, and was scarcely ever seen in her offices. Mrs Norris could
not speak with any temper of such grievances, nor of the quantity
of butter and eggs that were regularly consumed in the house.
'Nobody loved plenty and hospitality more than herself—
nobody more hateful of pitiful doings—the parsonage she believed had never been wanting in comforts of any sort, had never
borne a bad character in *her time*, but this was a way of going on
that she could not understand. A fine lady in a country parsonage
was quite out of place. *Her* storeroom she thought might have
been good enough for Mrs Grant to go into. Enquire where she
would, she could not find out that Mrs Grant had ever had more
than five thousand pounds. (*MP* 65)

Whether she is preoccupied with herself, or, more commonly,
busying herself with other people's affairs, Mrs Norris

seldom wanders far from her favourite topics of money and social rank. 'Money' rather than 'wealth' is the appropriate word in this context, for it comes closer to suggesting the vulgar manner in which Mrs Norris discusses the subject. A few lines before the first passage cited above, Mrs Norris brags about 'something rather considerable' which she has given to Fanny's brother. According to a family tradition, Jane Austen is supposed to have explained that Mrs Norris's gift in fact amounted to no more than one pound; but, at this point in the narrative, the reader hardly needs such supplementary information to recognize that Mrs Norris's 'generosity' is not likely to go beyond very narrow limits.[63] The key words in these passages are *cost, pay, sum, expense, wages, quantity, consumed, plenty, hospitality, comforts, storeroom,* and *five thousand pounds.* The reader is given no reason to assume that Mrs Norris is capable of thinking in any categories other than those suggested by such words. For her there is only one scale of values. Considering his social status—or lack of it—one pound is more than enough for William Price; and, to summarize another of Mrs Norris's opinions, the life style of the Grants is obviously too extravagant for someone in their social position.

Material values are also the basis of much of the hypocrisy in Jane Austen's fiction, whether it is of the petty, self-deluding kind exemplified by Mr Collins or the more thoroughgoing type characteristic of Mrs Elton. The author renders the fundamentally materialistic orientation of Mrs Norris, Mary Crawford, and Mrs Allen not only through the particular words which they choose, but also through their behaviour and the subject matter of their conversations. Such consistency need not be the case, as can be seen in the portrayal of Mr Collins.

'My reasons for marrying are, first, that I think it a right thing for every clergyman in easy circumstances (like myself) to set the example of matrimony in his parish. Secondly, that I am convinced it will add very greatly to my happiness; and thirdly—which perhaps I ought to have mentioned earlier, that it is the particular advice and recommendation of the very noble lady whom I have the honour of calling patroness. Twice has she condescended to give me her opinion (unasked too!) on this subject; and it was but the very Saturday night before I left Hunsford—between our pools at quadrille, while Mrs Jenkinson was arranging Miss de Bourgh's foot-stool, that she said, "Mr Collins, you must marry. A clergyman like you must marry.— Chuse properly, chuse a gentlewoman for *my* sake; and for your *own*, let her be an active, useful sort of person, not brought up high, but able to make a small income go a good way. This is my advice. Find such a woman as soon as you can, bring her to Hunsford, and I will visit her." Allow me, by the way to observe, my fair cousin, that I do not reckon the notice and kindness of Lady Catherine de Bourgh as among the least of the advantages in my power to offer. You will find her manners beyond any thing I can describe; and your wit and vivacity I think must be acceptable to her, especially when tempered with the silence and respect which her rank will inevitably excite. Thus much for my general intention in favour of matrimony; it remains to be told why my views were directed to Longbourn instead of my own neighbourhood, where I assure you there are many amiable young women. But the fact is, that being, as I am, to inherit this estate after the death of your honoured father, (who, however, may live many years longer), I could not satisfy myself without re-solving to chuse a wife from among his daughters, that the loss to them might be as little as possible, when the melancholy event takes place—which, however, as I have already said, may not be for several years. This has been my motive, my fair cousin, and I flatter myself it will not sink me in your esteem. And now nothing remains for me but to assure you of the violence of my affection. To fortune I am perfectly indifferent, and shall make no demand of that nature on your father, since I am well aware that it could not be complied with; and that one thousand pounds in the 4 per cents. which will not be yours till after your mother's decease, is all that you may ever be entitled to. On that head, therefore, I shall be uniformly silent; and you may assure yourself that no ungenerous reproach shall ever pass my lips when we are married.' (*PP* 147–148)

This has to be one of the most impersonal proposals in literature. Upon his arrival in Longbourn, Mr Collins quickly succeeds in making himself disagreeable. Elizabeth's father is able to amuse himself by observing Mr Collins's ridiculous behaviour, and her mother can occupy her thoughts in trying to decide which of the daughters Mr Collins will select; however, for Elizabeth the situation is more than a little awkward. For a number of reasons, she finds Mr Collins repugnant. The most significant are at least implicit in his proposal; the form contradicts the content and the content in itself is sufficiently damning. It all turns about its very egotistical author, whose style sounds like an unsuccessful imitation of Samuel Johnson's most conspicuous mannerisms in *The Rambler* (1749–1752) or in *Rasselas* (1759). The heavy reliance on parallel structures and the repeated references to himself and to Lady Catherine—in whom he seems to discover his own identity—are, however, less disquieting than Mr Collins's total incapacity to express a sincere emotion. His motives are obvious enough, but whatever he may feel is obscured by the hollow rhetoric of his 'most animated language'. In Elizabeth's view, more damning than all the rest is his conception of marriage as a matter of economics. In fact it is not at all certain that Mr Collins realizes that the matrimonial state might be anything more than a convenient financial arrangement, satisfactory to all of the parties concerned, to his 'patroness' in particular. His proposal is filled with references to material possessions and to the calculating and planning which accompany them: *easy circumstances, rank, small income, inherit, estate, loss, fortune, demand,* and *one thousand pounds.* Evidently, Mr Collins has given considerable thought to his proposal. He lists his arguments: 'first', 'secondly', 'thirdly', but his arguments fail to persuade. In all his calculations and speculations, he succeeds only in revealing his own hypocrisy, insensibility, and foolishness. The most extraordinary thing about Mr Collins is his apparent capacity to take his own insincere rhetoric seriously. He does not seem to be completely aware of his hypocrisy, a fact which presumably can be attributed to his stupidity. Mrs Elton has much in common with Mr Collins. For both of them, life appears to be an opportunity for convincing others of one's own merits. Essentially everything either one of them says needs to be reinterpreted in terms of the real world. Any denial must be read as an affirmation, and any assertion is as highly questionable; however,

Mrs Elton is more than just a female variation of Elizabeth Bennet's first suitor.

'I do not ask whether you are musical, Mrs Elton. Upon these occasions, a lady's character generally precedes her; and Highbury has long known that you are a superior performer.'

'Oh! no, indeed; I must protest against any such idea. A superior performer!—very far from it, I assure you. Consider from how partial a quarter your information came. I am doatingly fond of music—passionately fond;—and my friends say I am not entirely devoid of taste; but as to any thing else, upon my honour my performance is *mediocre* to the last degree. You, Miss Woodhouse, I well know play delightfully. I assure you it has been the greatest satisfaction, comfort, and delight to me, to hear what a musical society I am got into. I absolutely cannot do without music. It is a necessary of life to me; and having always been used to a very musical society, both at Maple Grove and in Bath, it would have been a most serious sacrifice. I honestly said as much to Mr E. when he was speaking of my future home, and expressing his fears lest the retirement of it should be disagreeable; and the inferiority of the house too—knowing what I had been accustomed to—of course he was not wholly without apprehension. When he was speaking of it in that way, I honestly said that *the world* I could give up—parties, balls, plays—for I had no fear of retirement. Blessed with so many resources within myself, the world was not necessary to *me*. I could do very well without it. To those who had no resources it was a different thing; but my resources made me quite independent. And as to smaller-sized rooms than I had been used to, I really could not give it a thought. I hoped I was perfectly equal to any sacrifice of that description. Certainly I had been accustomed to every luxury at Maple Grove; but I did assure him that two carriages were not necessary to my happiness, nor were spacious apartments. "But," said I, "to be quite honest, I do not think I can live without something of a musical society. I conditioned for nothing else; but without music, life would be a blank to me."' (*E* 278–279)

In contrast to Mr Collins, there are probably no moments in Mrs Elton's life when she is not affecting a pose. The key to her personality is the word *resources*, which she uses here and on many other occasions. Perhaps no one has ever had fewer and presumed to have more. Her capacity for self-deception is nearly equal to the degree to which she imagines she is deceiving others. Her inner *resources* are simply non-existent. This same word *resources* also suggests her attitude towards other people, places, and things. All are at least implicitly thought of in materialistic terms and assigned an appropriate value. For example, her marriage to Mr Elton represents a personal commitment on her part to a specific social status, which has a net worth. She is willing to accept the 'inferiority' of this position in society and the house which goes along with it, because she will be able to continue talking about what she has had in the past. It is not really so bad not having 'two carriages' if you can continue to remind everyone of what it was like to have had them. Mrs Elton's social and material ambitions cause her to behave in a vulgar, condescending, and hypocritical manner.

From what has already been said, it is evident that Jane Austen's novels are among other things about the economics of marriage, the problems and material advantages of a profession, the question of 'eligibility' as it relates to young women as well as to young men, and the foolish and often dangerous consequences for anyone who allows material concerns to prevail over all others. Jane Austen's position concerning the economic realities of her world is much less ambiguous than some critics have argued. She is neither rejecting the society in which these realities are manifest in nearly every aspect of life—whether it is a yard of muslin, two carriages, a living, or a marriage contract; nor is she ignoring the existence of these economic facts of life. What she does do is to assume and demonstrate through the examples of such characters as Elinor, Fanny, Knightley, and Anne that there is a real alternative to the conduct of such characters as Willoughby, Wickham, Mrs Norris, the Crawfords, Mr Collins and Mrs Elton. In her world and in her view, material objects and material values have their place, but it is not and should not be at the top of one's list of priorities. All of Jane Austen's admirable characters either have or acquire in the course of the narrative the ability to discriminate properly among material, social, and moral values. This is a prerequisite to coming to terms with those elements and those forces which threaten to undermine the ethical structure of the society. The individual who fails to make the necessary discriminations runs the risk of failing completely. In the end Mrs Norris is ostracized from the society which meant everything to her. Additional themes are developed out of the conflicts which arise between moral and social values.

A second semantic field includes all of those words relating to *social values*. These words constitute a set of assumptions governing the behaviour of the middle-class in Regency England. The nineteenth century in general viewed Jane Austen's work as *novels of manners*, seeing in them the forerunners of the novels of the 'silver-fork school', which became popular in the third decade of the nineteenth century.[64] This line of interpretation ignores or at least under-values the moral seriousness of Jane Austen's fiction, but it rightly draws attention to the author's practice of using manners to render character. This approach to character portrayal cuts two ways. On the one hand, character is revealed through the individual's behaviour in social situations; and on the other hand through the individual's ability to judge the propriety of the conduct of others. In both respects a distinction must be made between moral and social values—a distinction which some of the characters fail to make in regard to their own conduct or in their evaluation of the propriety of other's behaviour. Wherever a conflict arises, moral values should prevail. Each of the heroines is faced repeatedly with the challenge of having to choose between such alternatives. The crucial decisions tend to isolate the heroine even from those closest to her. The implications of these difficult decisions and their possible consequences are less obvious to the heroine than to the reader, and not even such clear-sighted figures as Elinor or Anne are as certain about their judgement as they would like to be. The happy resolution of these conflicts reintegrates the heroine into society; in the interim, she has gained more insight into herself, her situation, and the verities which shape the world in which she lives. Usually, the reader gains similar insights long before the heroine does. He is guided by the subtle and exact distinctions the author makes in her choice of vocabulary to discriminate and evaluate character. She assigns a specific value to such words as *polite, amiable, civil, ease, open, gallant*, and *reserved*.[65] In looking more closely at this semantic field, it becomes apparent that these along with the other words in this field can be ordered according to a scale of values, indicating degrees of acceptability in respect to the social conventions of Jane Austen's fictional world. These conventions are defined through the precise and consistent reference given each of these words in context. Additional nuances of meaning are achieved by collocating these words or through an adverbial or adjectival modifier. The relative position of a word on this scale of acceptability is in some instances obvious even out of context. *Polite* and *amiable* rank near the top while *gallant* and *reserved* occur much further down on the scale. Much more revealing, however, are the finer distinctions made in context.

Knightley's definition of *amiable* and his distinction between the English word and its French cognate have already been mentioned (cf. *E* 166).[66] *Amiable* has taken on a more generalized and slightly condescending meaning since Knightley defined it for Emma.[67] The following passages illustrate that Knightley's definition is also the author's. Marianne is not as impressed as her sister by Edward Ferrars. Her criteria for judging a gentleman's manner are not Elinor's; nevertheless, she does not want to hurt her sister's feelings.

'Do not be offended, Elinor, if my praise of him is not in every thing equal to your sense of his merits. I have hot had so many opportunities of estimating the minuter propensities of his mind, his inclinations and tastes as you have; but I have the highest opinion in the world of his goodness and sense. I think him every thing that is worthy and amiable.' (*SS* 53)

The collocation of *amiable* with *goodness, sense* and *worthy* is consistent with Knightley's definition. Similarly, when Mary Crawford takes her leave of Fanny, her remarks are intended as a generous compliment: 'good-bye, my dear, my amiable, my excellent Fanny. . . .' (*MP* 359). And, in *Persuasion*, Charles Hayter is placed in the category in which Emma thought Frank Churchill belonged. 'Charles Hayter was the eldest of all the cousins, and a very amiable, pleasing young man. . . .' (*P* 97). On Jane Austen's scale of values *amiable* ranks a little below *polite*, which signifies the quintessence of good manners. Not even Mary Crawford in all of her insincerity and inclination to hyperbole ascribes this degree of perfection to Fanny. Somewhat further down on the scale of values is the word *civility*.

Civility is used to signify a correct but reserved manner. The word implies an absence of any kind of emotional involvement and a certain air of disinterestedness. Jane Austen uses *candour* to designate those qualities which are here lacking. She almost never gives *candour* the sense which is common today.[68] It is one of the most admirable qualities which an individual may have. It goes beyond good manners. It signifies a sincere interest and empathy with other individuals. Its absence may have serious consequences, as in Willoughby's treatment of Marianne or in Emma's behaviour towards Miss Bates at Box Hill. *Candour* is closely related to such words as *delicacy* and *sensibility*. It is not the opposite of *civility*, but it is a great deal more.

Mr Shepherd, a civil, cautious lawyer, who, whatever might be his hold or his views on Sir Walter, would rather have the *disagreeable* prompted by any body else, excused himself from offering the slightest hint, and only begged leave to recommend an implicit deference to the excellent judgment of Lady Russell,— from whose known good sense he fully expected to have just such resolute measures advised, as he meant to see finally adopted. (*P* 42)

Mr Shepherd's manner is conditioned by the difficult gentleman whose affairs he is trying to put in order; nevertheless, the word *civil* signals to the reader that Mr Shepherd should not be viewed uncritically. In *Sense and Sensibility*, John Dashwood unexpectedly meets his half-sisters, Elinor and Marianne, in London. He feels obliged to pay them a call.

His visit was duly paid. . . . His manners to *them*, though calm, were perfectly kind; to Mrs Jennings most attentively civil; and on Colonel Brandon's coming in soon after himself, he eyed him with a curiosity which seemed to say, that he only wanted to know him to be rich, to be equally civil to *him*. (*SS* 230)

The reader has been well acquainted with John Dashwood's character since the second chapter, where the conversation Dashwood has with his wife concerning some possible support for his stepmother and half-sisters places him and his wife. As a consequence, this later episode only confirms the impression that John Dashwood is an egotistical and materialistic gentleman. The phrase 'perfectly kind' used to describe his attitude towards his sisters anticipates Elizabeth Bennet's intentionally ambiguous description of Darcy's manner: 'Mr Darcy is all politeness' (*PP* 73).[69] In the light of what follows, the narrator's comment can only be read negatively. The emphasis throughout is on Dashwood's inability to relate to others. If it happens that Colonel Brandon merits his attention, Dashwood is willing to exert himself and make an effort to be courteous. The conditions Dashwood mentally imposes on this possibility as well as the self-imposed limit generally manifest in his behaviour towards the others and reflected in the extent he might be willing to go to establish a relationship with Colonel Brandon, indicate Dashwood's incapacity to be genuinely polite. The word *civil* is used repeatedly in this sense. It may reflect on the one using the word as well as on the one being described. When Mr Collins refers to the 'civility' of Mr Darcy's manner towards him, this may be an accurate description of Darcy's manner, but it may also be understood as an indication of Mr Collins's need to define his own social position in relation to that of his superiors. Similarly, in *Sense and Sensibility*, when Sir John and Lady Middleton receive a visit from the Steele sisters, their impression of the new arrivals reveals more about them than about Anne and Lucy Steele.

The young ladies arrived, their appearance was by no means ungenteel or unfashionable. Their dress was very smart, their manners very civil, they were delighted with the house, and in raptures with the furniture, and they happened to be so doatingly fond of children that Lady Middleton's good opinion was engaged in their favour before they had been an hour at the Park. (*SS* 141–142)

The Middletons' estimate of their guests' manners as 'civil' —not to mention 'very civil'—is more than a little inaccurate, as the behaviour of the young ladies in the ensuing scene soon demonstrates. Additional shades of meaning and, as in this instance, irony are achieved by collocating *civil* with various modifiers. As a social value, it can be upgraded or downgraded. In response to Mrs Bennet's concerned inquiry about the care of her daughter Jane will receive after falling ill while visiting the Bingleys, Miss Bingley replies:

'You may depend upon it, Madame,' said Miss Bingley, with cold civility, 'that Miss Bennet shall receive every possible attention while she remains with us.' (*PP* 87)

Catherine Morland, determined to become better acquainted with Miss Tilney, seeks her out in the Pump Room.

Miss Tilney met her with great civility, returned her advances with equal good will, and they continued talking together as long as both parties remained in the room. (*NA* 91)

Presumably, only her general lack of insight into human nature prevents Mrs Bennet from realizing how close Miss Bingley comes to being outright rude. Considerably more perceptive than Mrs Bennet, Darcy perceives a similar rudeness in Miss Bingley's manner towards Elizabeth. His observation is also one of the early indications of his growing interest in Elizabeth. 'She attracted him more than he liked— and Miss Bingley was uncivil to *her*, . . .' (*PP* 104). Miss Tilney's manners differ markedly from Miss Bingley's. Although Miss Tilney and Catherine do not yet know one another very well, Miss Tilney makes an effort to be more than just *civil*, suggesting that there is a strong inclination on both sides to establish a real friendship. *Civil* is not necessarily a negative attribute. In some social situations, it may be the appropriate response; however, most often this word is used to signal a character weakness, an incapacity to become genuinely interested in others. Out of context, Mr Shepherd's *civility* might be explained as the necessary consequence of his business relationship with Sir Walter Elliot, but in context it becomes evident that Mr Shepherd's *civility* has more complex motives. Or, to cite a second illustration, Mr Woodhouse is described as being 'universally civil' (*E* 39). As the story develops, it becomes obvious that this is one of several indications of Mr Woodhouse's self-centredness. The description *universally civil* need not be negative. It could signify a 'minimum of politeness' towards everyone. However, in the case of Emma's father, it is only one sign among many of Mr Woodhouse's incapacity to get beyond himself and relate to others.

Gallantry ranks below *civility* on the author's scale of values. It just borders on acceptability; therefore, it is hardly surprising that it tends to be associated with characters such as Wickham, Mr Elton, and Mr Collins.

This gallantry was not much to the taste of some of his hearers, but Mrs Bennet, who quarrelled with no compliments, answered most readily. (*PP* 109)

She was not the better pleased with his gallatry, from the idea it suggested of something more. (*PP* 130)

These two passages refer to Mr Collins, who cannot even be properly *gallant*. He behaves in a manner inappropriate to the situation. Elizabeth suspects his motives; predictably, her mother does not suspect anything. *Gallantry* signifies superficially good manners which are intended as a kind of flattery of those to whom they are addressed. Mr Collins misjudges his audience. Mr Elton and, especially, Wickham are much more skilful in the art of flattery and in making a good impression, though Mr Elton is also given at times to misinterpreting the impression he is making.

He had seen them go by and had purposely followed them; other little gallatries and allusions had been dropt, but nothing serious. (*E* 114)

Mr Wickham began to speak on more general topics, Meryton, the neighbourhood, the society, appearing highly pleased with all that he had yet seen, and in speaking of the latter especially, with gentle but very intelligible gallantry. (*PP* 122)

In the first of these passages Emma is trying to discover some evidence in Mr Elton's manner of his affection for Harriet Smith. She is disappointed to observe so little feeling and interest directed at her friend, and is oblivious to the fact that she herself is the real object of Mr Elton's *gallantries*. Wickham is very refined in his conversation with Elizabeth. In reality, he wants to relate how he has been ill-judged and mistreated by Darcy, but he first evokes Elizabeth's interest and sympathy by making a point of being *pleasing* and *gallant. Gallantry* refers to a superficial minimum of good manners. With this in mind, the reader along with Anne must assume that the heroine no longer has reason to hope when Louisa observes:

'Captain Wentworth is not very gallant by you, Anne, though he was attentive to me. Henrietta asked him what he thought of you, when they were away; and he said, "You were so altered he should not have known you again." ' (*P* 85)

For the reader the impression made by this remark is corrected immediately with a brief inside view of what Wentworth actually thought when Henrietta asked her question, but it gives Anne more cause than ever to feel uncertain about the future.

The exactness with which *amiable, civil,* and *gallant* are used is characteristic of Jane Austen's method of specifying degrees of politeness. However, in this context a further important point needs to be made. Whenever a new character is introduced, the reader soon learns something about his or her manners. How much is learned depends upon the character's significance for the development of the action. As a rule, minor characters are placed immediately. Major characters are also placed, but this placing, since it is usually dependent upon the heroine's subjective impressions, is subject to change. The following three passages from *Persuasion* illustrate how a minor character is fixed for the rest of the narrative.

The Musgroves like their houses, were in a state of alteration, perhaps of improvement. The father and mother were in the old English style, and the young people in the new. Mr and Mrs

Musgrove were a very good sort of people; friendly and hospitable, not much educated, and not at all elegant. Their children had more modern minds and manners. There was a numerous family; but the only two grown up, excepting Charles, were Henrietta and Louisa, young ladies of nineteen and twenty, who had brought from a school at Exeter all the usual stock of accomplishments, and were now, like thousands of other young ladies, living to be fashionable, happy, and merry. Their dress had every advantage, their faces rather pretty, their spirits extremely good, their manners unembarassed and pleasant; they were of consequence at home, and favourites abroad. (*P* 67)

Mrs Croft, though neither tall nor fat, had a squareness, uprightness, and vigour of form, which gave importance to her person. She had bright dark eyes, good teeth, and altogether an agreeable face; though her reddened and weatherbeaten complexion, the consequence of her having been almost as much at sea as her husband, made her seem to have lived some years longer in the world than her real eight and thirty. Her manners were open, easy, and decided, like one who had no distrust of herself, and no doubts of what to do; without any approach to coarseness, however, or any want of good humour. (*P* 74–75)

Captain Harville, though not equalling Captain Wentworth in manners, was a perfect gentleman, unaffected, warm, and obliging. Mrs Harville a degree less polished than her husband, seemed however to have the same good feelings; and nothing could be more pleasant than their desire of considering the whole party as friends of their own, because the friends of Captain Wentworth, or more kindly hospitable than their entreaties for their all promising to dine with them. (*P* 119)

From these introductions the reader learns enough about each of these characters to understand their behaviour as the narrative unfolds. Moreover, sufficient information is given for the reader to be able to anticipate how they are likely to act or react in the situations which develop in the course of the narrative. For example, Louisa and Henrietta have those personal qualities presumably of interest to a young man like Captain Wentworth, who is looking for a wife; and it is more than probable that they will respond readily to such an interest if it is forthcoming. The Harvilles have a generosity of spirit which suggests that they would do everything in their power to help in the event of an emergency. Louisa's accident very quickly puts their generosity to the test. Although the reader has not anticipated this incident, he is hardly surprised by the Harvilles' response to it. In placing these characters, Jane Austen uses the key words *unaffected, warm, obliging, good feelings, open, easy, decided, unembarrassed, pleasant, friendly, hospitable,* and, in a negative sense, *elegant.* Most of these words occur in groups of two or three, which reinforces the weight of the individual words and further specifies their meaning. The collocation of *open, easy,* and *decided,* for example, supports the image of Mrs Croft as a woman who has sufficient self-confidence and experience to feel comfortable in whatever social situation she might find herself. The subsequent behaviour of each of these characters confirms the reader's perception of them when they are first introduced.

The words in the semantic field of social values are used to characterize an individual's public behaviour. Although the technique of presentation varies from novel to novel, it is axiomatic in Jane Austen's fiction that manners mirror morals; however, in making this generalization, it needs to be kept in mind that for long stretches of the narrative a character may successfully affect a pose and assume a manner before he is exposed. The care taken by the author to define an individual's manners suggests the importance of public behaviour as in index of a character's sense of moral values. Some individuals give themselves away as soon as they begin to speak, e.g., Mrs Bennet, Lucy Steele, Mrs Jennings and Mrs Norris. With others, however, such as Wickham or Mr Elliot, a façade of impeccable manners prevents the immediate detection of their true motives. With still others the question of exposure is more complex. From the beginning, Knightley finds Frank Churchill's behaviour suspect, but Emma discovers little in Knightley's argument to convince her. She ignores a great deal before finally comprehending the truth. The first half of *Pride and Prejudice* turns on Elizabeth's false assessment of Darcy's manner. By contrast, her

M

sister Jane never fully subscribes to Elizabeth's critical view of Darcy's pride. Whereas Edmund Bertram remains blind to Mary Crawford's hypocrisy until her brother Henry 'elopes' with Maria, already at Sotherton Fanny senses that Mary is a threat not only to her own interest in Edmund but also to those values which Edmund has committed himself to uphold. Social values are manifest in human interaction. The priority these values are given by a particular character may not be immediately apparent, but the individual's attitude towards social conventions and the moral principles implicit in this attitude is exposed sooner or later to the harsh critical light of the society in which he lives. How he is judged partly depends upon his position in this society. More is expected of individuals like Darcy, Emma, Lady Catherine, Sir Walter Elliot and Sir Thomas Bertram than of characters such as Robert Martin or William Price. This point is made explicit in the scene between Knightley and Emma, where he remonstrates with her for her ill-considered treatment of Miss Bates (cf. *E* 367–368).[70] Ideally, everyone should adhere to the social conventions, but in addition to this, those who enjoy the privileges of wealth and rank have social and moral obligations to their 'inferiors'. Under Knightley's guidance, Emma may yet learn this lesson. Through the actions he undertakes on behalf of Elizabeth's family, Darcy overcomes his own prejudice. With the possible exception of Sir Thomas Bertram, the other 'superior' personages in Jane Austen's novels do not appear to take any cognizance of these responsibilities.

A third semantic field includes all of the words relating to *moral values*. The abstract words used to specify these values are made concrete as the plot develops. The convention of using abstract nouns to designate moral values Jane Austen inherits from her eighteenth-century predecessors, in particular, the essayists:[71] however, in adapting this convention for her own purposes, the author transforms these abstractions into substantive moral issues which shape the course of events.[72] In turning to an examination of the moral values, I am actually returning to a topic which has been touched on already in several contexts in the present study. This is almost inevitable, since these values are at the very centre of Jane Austen's fiction.

Whately was the first to comment on the moral purport of her work. He recognized in it a new kind of fiction, and saw in the author's accurate portrait of life a potential for effective moral instruction, which was missing from most novels because of their lack of verisimilitude.[73] Whately's emphasis on the moral implications of Jane Austen's novels was not immediately taken up by anyone. In part this was due to the relatively modest amount of critical interest of any kind in Jane Austen until the publication of the *Memoir* in 1870, which presented to the world the biography of an author of whom almost nothing had been known previously.[74] In part it stemmed from a failure to appreciate the moral significance of Jane Austen's fictional response to middle-class life in a country village and to certain contemporary intellectual and literary tendencies. During the interim between Scott's and Whately's reviews and the publication of the *Memoir*, 'the criticism of Jane Austen is remarkable only for its missionary zeal, not for its perceptions. The critics were enthusiastic, but weighed down by their sense that Jane Austen was out of fashion, little known, and unjustly undervalued. Few of them were capable of escaping from the formulations of Scott and Whately; fewer still were able to communicate their personal experience of reading the novels.'[75] There are a few scattered comments which indicate or, at least, hint at an awareness of the author's didactic intent, but nothing more substantial. Perhaps Mark Twain's violent antipathy is the most interesting. He claimed that he felt an 'animal repugnance' in reading Jane Austen, which presumably can be attributed to his suspicion of a puritanism in her novels.[76] But the lack of critical interest in the moral aspect of her novels persists long after the publication of the *Memoir*. A significant change in this critical view is distinguishable in Lord David Cecil's lecture on Jane Austen in 1935, which observes that her novels are based on an unerring perception of moral quality.[77] However, it is not until Trilling's seminal study of *Mansfield Park* that we have a close and systematic examination of Jane Austen's moral themes.[78] He is the first to fully appreciate the moral dimensions of Jane Austen's fiction and to recognize the significance of a proper understanding of *Mansfield Park* for an understanding of all the novels. Trilling's essay has since been followed by numerous studies of the moral implications of character and conduct in Jane Austen's fiction.[79] The moral themes have been variously named, e.g., 'art and nature', 'individual freedom and society', 'nature and nurture', and 'prudence and love', but it seems more useful to adopt Jane Austen's own terminology for her moral concepts. In considering these concepts, it is important to keep in mind the fact that Jane Austen's moral universe is founded on Christian principle.

It is unlikely that Jane Austen ever indulged in the atheistic speculations associated with such eighteenth-century figures as Holbach or Diderot; on the other hand, she was not inclined to accept matters of religion unquestioningly; and, in fact, her correspondence suggests a keen interest in issues which were the subject of much debate among theologians at the time.[80] Nevertheless, to speak of her religion is to refer to something which is implied rather than stated.[81] Unlike Dickens, Jane Austen almost never allows religious issues to obtrude into her narrative.[82] Whately writes: 'Miss Austin [sic] has the merit (in our judgment most essential) of being evidently a Christian writer: a merit which is much more enhanced . . . by her religion being not at all obtrusive.'[83] Her religion is inobtrusive because it is undifferentiated for the most part from the social and moral aspects of her narratives: there is a 'secularization of spirituality' which imbues even the most trivial incident with religious significance.[84] In *Mansfield Park*, for instance, Mary Crawford indulges in a kind of blasphemy in deceiving Fanny about the chain for the *cross*. The *cross* is a symbol of some of those things which Fanny holds to be most precious. Appropriately, it is Edmund and not the deceitful Crawfords who gives Fanny the chain best suited to the *cross*. The whole incident, Fanny's embarrassment and the ensuing confusion are trivial; yet they serve to reveal some of the deeper layers of the personalities of those involved (cf. *MP* 265–277). Or, to take a second example, in *Sense and*

Sensibility, Marianne fails to make any examination at all of her own conduct. She demonstrates none of the Christian's understanding of the sinfulness of her own heart; and she shows a notable lack of Christian charity towards Colonel Brandon, Mrs Jennings, and the Middletons. Elinor alone exercises the self-examination prescribed for the Christian, by questioning the state of her heart in relation to Edward, and, even more, her complex and disagreeable feelings about Lucy.[85] This religious dimension of Jane Austen's fiction has usually been neglected, with the result that the author's system of moral values has been misinterpreted. Trilling's influential view that the morality of any novel must derive from a sympathetic treatment of individual human beings overlooks the fact that in Jane Austen the individual must learn to take a critical view of himself and others and to subjugate his own individualistic impulses to a set of established values based on a Christian ethic.[86] It is these religious assumptions underlying the moral conflicts which constitute a major challenge to the modern critic. The author's assumptions are not likely to be shared by the modern reader, nor are they so readily apparent as Jane Austen may have anticipated. Her distrust of too much individual freedom and her misgivings concerning the subjective consciousness are indices of her conservative ethical stance. It is within this ethical context that the words she chooses to designate moral values need to be considered. Her frame of reference may not be ours, but it is implicit in all of the texts. An examination of some of the words in the semantic field of moral values should illustrate how these values are realized and how they function in context.

It was noted above that a few key words occur in both the semantic field of social values and in the one for moral values.[87] The most important are *manners, propriety, decorum, elegance,* and *principle.* The two perspectives—moral and social—from which character and behaviour may be viewed coalesce in these key words. Ideally, social and moral values should be in harmony, and blend with one another as they do in these words, but, much more often than not, the individual fails to achieve the ideals signified by *propriety (decorum)* and *elegance*, and manifest in one's *manners (temper, address)* and understanding of *principle*.[88] There are three possible reasons for failure: an inability to discriminate properly between conflicting values, an inability to comprehend the significance of these values, or a conscious rejection of them. In other words, there are degrees of failure, or, viewed the other way around, there are degrees of success, measured according to the standard of social values on the one hand, and according to the standard of moral values on the other. These two frames of reference need to be kept in mind if the reader is to make the proper discriminations between, for example, an *elegant manner* and an *elegant mind*. Out of context, the first of these two epithets is ambiguous. It might denote a high degree of politeness, a seemingly effortless adherence to social convention with a certain grace and charm; or it might mean about the same as an *elegance of mind*, that is, a very admirable moral quality, a manifestation of one's *principle* and one's regard for others. The two sets of *principles* by which character and conduct are judged are contained in the word *propriety*, which is used in two closely related senses: either it signifies 'conformity with good manners or polite usage', or it designates 'fitness, appropriateness, suitability . . . and conformity with principle.'[89] These two frames of reference enable the reader along with the heroine to discern gradations of moral quality in character and behaviour. For most of the heroines, this is a skill which they learn in the course of the narrative.

No other words in Jane Austen have attracted so much critical interest as *sense* and *sensibility*.[90] Used in the title of her first published novel, *sense* and *sensibility* refer to moral qualities which are at issue in varying degrees in all of the novels. They specify the limits of possible positive responses in human interaction within the moral frame of reference: at one extreme *sense* and at the other extreme *sensibility*. However, this dichotomy is a little misleading. The concepts are not in opposition; they are related to one another in a complex manner. Neither of them is necessarily a negative moral quality, though an excess of *sensibility* may have very negative consequences. But these generalizations have little meaning

before the concepts have been defined. This is not unprob-
lematical, for *sense* and *sensibility* have taken on new meanings
since the end of the eighteenth century, and even at the
time Jane Austen was writing several usages were current:

'The citations in the *OED* of *sense*, *sensibile* and *sensibility* as
used during Jane Austen's lifetime show that these words were
related to each other in a continuum, without precise demarcation.
Each has meanings connecting to sense experience; to intensities
of sensation; and to a proper apprehension of the world. A man
has sense, presumably, because his estimate of the world is
founded on the information of his senses. Sensibility is allied to
emotion and is, therefore, at a greater distance from the senses;
consequently it leads to a less precise understanding of the world.
Nevertheless, sensibility is also a sharp and full response to the
sense and is productive of an insight that the man may be emotional
or matter-of-fact. He may be sensible of responses from within
or sensible of the world without.'[91]

These distinctions need to be placed in their historical
perspective. In the seventeenth century, philosophers became
preoccupied with the question of whether or not man is a
wholly self-centred and self-seeking being. Hobbes argued
that he was, and this also seemed a possible consequence of
Locke's theory of the *tabula rasa*.[92] These speculations led
in the eighteenth century to a consideration of the problem
of how the sensations in a man's mind were related to the
people and the world outside it; and, since these sensations
involved feelings as well as the intellect, great attention was
paid to the process of emotional identification of sympathy.[93]
Lord Shaftesbury and Francis Hutcheson led a group of
philosophers who argued 'that man was naturally *benevolent*;
that he had an innate *moral sense*, in the meaning of a specific
ethical faculty, and that this faculty, spontaneously led the
individual to satisfy his impulses of sympathetic good will
through his personal relationships.'[94] These outgoing impulses included the sensations of imagination and aesthetic
pleasure; 'these also were unselfish feelings, and as a result
an intense love both of nature and art somehow became indi-
cators of the individual's moral superiority in general.'[95]
One of the literary consequences of this attitude was the

Sentimental novel—a favourite target of Jane Austen's satire in the *Juvenilia* as well as a subject for more serious treatment in her novels.[96] Sentimental fiction set out to portray intense emotional reactions to situations, reactions which demonstrated the depth of a character's *sensibility*. Jane Austen found this kind of fictional response to human experience wholly unacceptable. Her own use of *sensibility* together with her use of *sense* and *sensible* reveals what place, in her opinion, natural impulses should have in human interaction. Her youthful responses to the spate of novels which followed Henry Mackenzie's *The Man of Feeling* (1771) focus on the excesses of the genre.[97] Her more mature work deals with the assumptions underlying a 'sentimental' view of man. It is doubtful that Jane Austen would have ascribed to the view implicit in Sentimental fiction that man is *naturally benevolent*; more likely, she would have described *benevolence* as an example of 'learned behaviour' if the term had been current.

Some examples should illustrate the range and exactness with which Jane Austen uses the words *sense, sensible*, and *sensibility*. At first glance, *sensibility* appears to be a negative characteristic. Mary Bennet, Catherine Morland, and Marianne Dashwood are all objects of the author's irony because of their *sensibility*.[98] However, what is actually being criticized is an excess of *sensibility*, an attitude which causes each of them to misdirect her energies, misinterpret her situation, and misjudge herself and others. It is an attitude which has been learned from books. Marianne prides herself on her powers of perception, her independence, and her ability to make judgements, but in reality her *sensibility* generally prevents her from demonstrating any of these things. Elinor suggests to her sister that it was not a very good idea for Marianne to have gone alone with Willoughby to Allenham. Marianne replies angrily that she has never spent a pleasanter morning in all her life. Elinor points out that pleasantness of employment does not always evince its *propriety*. Marianne disagrees: 'If there had been any real impropriety in what I did, I should have been sensible of it at the time, for we always know when we are acting wrong, and with such a conviction

I could have had no pleasure' (*SS* 97–98). Of course, the point is that Marianne is not at all 'sensible' of the implications of her conduct. She interprets any restraint which might be imposed on her behaviour as an unnatural and unjust restriction of her right to act according to the dictates of her emotions. When Willoughby suddenly leaves Devonshire, it is supposedly just for a short time; nevertheless, Marianne's response to the situation is extreme. She cannot eat or sleep and is constantly in tears. In her opinion, anything less would have placed in question the intensity of her affection for Willoughby. Marianne's attitude represents a *false sensibility*, a conviction that natural impulses are a reliable guide to behaviour.

By contrast, Knightley obviously has something else in mind when he says of Jane Fairfax, 'Her sensibilities, I suspect are strong—and her temper excellent in its powers of forbearance, patience, self-controul' (*E* 290). Here *sensibility* is seen as a virtue. As it is manifest in Knightley, Jane Fairfax, Henry Tilney, Fanny Price, Jane Bennet, and Anne Elliot, *sensibility* is a 'heightened perception of feelings in a complex social moment and it is accompanied by a moral response, an increase in life.'[99] It is in this sense that Elinor in contrast to her sister has a *true sensibility*. Edmund perceives quite early that his little cousin has a 'great sensibility of her situation' (*MP* 53). When Henry Tilney meets Catherine's mother, he is very aware of the awkwardness of the situation in light of General Tilney's treatment of Catherine. 'With a look of much respect, he immediately rose, and being introduced to her by her daughter as "Mr Henry Tilney," with the embarrassment of real sensibility began to apologize for his appearance there, . . .' (*NA* 238). A *real* or *true sensibility* differs from a *false sensibility* in that the former is tempered by at least a modicum of *sense*, that is, natural impulses are governed by a perception of their moral implications.

A number of characters demonstrate neither a *true* nor *false sensibility*: Mr Collins, Lady Russell, Harriet Smith, Mary Musgrove, and Mrs Allen, to mention only a few of the possible examples. The author is on occasion quite explicit on this point. 'Mr Collins was not a sensible man' (*PP* 114).

Or, in a reference to Harriet Smith, 'she is not a sensible girl, nor a girl of any information' (*E* 87).

A *real sensibility* involves the intellect as well as the emotions. A character who is not *sensible* lacks perception. He makes errors of *judgment*,[100] lacks *understanding*, and fails to evince such admirable qualities as *benevolence*, *candour*, or *elegance*. Anne Elliot is a woman of 'strong sensibility' (*P* 165), which enables her to recognize this quality or its absence in others. Upon learning of Louisa's engagement to Captain Benwick, she reflects that 'if the woman who had been sensible of Captain Wentworth's merits could be allowed to prefer another man, there was nothing in the engagement to excite wonder' (*P* 178).[101] Elizabeth Bennet is less mature than Anne, but equally perceptive even where her prejudice inclines her not to be. 'In spite of her deeply rooted dislike, she could not be insensible to the compliment of such a man's affections, and though her intentions did not vary for one instant, she was at first sorry for the pain he was to receive' (*PP* 221).[102] In responding to Darcy's first proposal, Elizabeth's feelings are more ambiguous than she is willing to admit at the time. She is too clever to be simply impressed and flattered by Darcy's social position; therefore, her consciousness that his interest is a compliment to herself must have another source. What this might be she is not capable of admitting even to herself for the time being. As with other key words in Jane Austen, the use of *sensible* may reflect more on the speaker than on the one being described. Still very much in love with Mary Crawford, Edmund observes, 'good-humoured, unaffected girls, will not do for a man who has been used to sensible women. They are two distinct orders of being. You and Miss Crawford have made me too nice' (*MP* 351).[103] In linking Fanny and Mary together in this observation, Edmund reveals the extent to which he has been blinded by his infatuation. Whatever *sensibility* Mary may have, it is not of the same order as Fanny's.

Sense is the counterweight to *sensibility*. Its usage is less complex, for there is no distinction between the true and the false. *Sense* is understood to mean common sense or reason; however, it is never assumed that the rational faculty can operate independent of the emotions. They are interdependent, but, as demonstrated repeatedly, emotions should be governed by reason and not the reverse. *Sense* is one of the most admirable virtues an individual may have. In context this abstraction is given substance. For instance, in arguing with Emma as to whether or not Robert Martin would be a suitable husband for Harriet, Knightley points out that 'Robert Martin's manners have sense, sincerity, and good humour to recommend them; and his mind has more true gentility than Harriet Smith could understand' (*E* 91)[104] Here 'sense' is joined with other attributions to suggest an understanding of human nature and a generosity of spirit which places Robert Martin higher on the social and moral scale than many who have inherited their rank but failed to gain any insight or understanding of their moral responsibilities to others as well as to themselves. In other words, 'true gentility' is not a question of birth but of moral understanding. Elinor feels that it is better not to confide in her mother or Marianne what she has learned of Lucy Steele's engagement to Edward: 'From their counsel, or their conversation she knew she could receive no assistance, their tenderness and sorrow must add to her distress, while her self-command would neither receive encouragement from their example nor from their praise. She was stronger alone, and her own good sense so well supported her, that her firmness was unshaken, her appearance of cheerfulness as invariable, as with regrets so poignant and so fresh, it was possible for them to be' (*SS* 159). Here, in effect, Jane Austen sets down what it means to control one's emotions with common sense. Elinor's emotional shock is even greater than her sister's, for there is no series of events foreshadowing Lucy's revelations. Without warning, Elinor is confronted with what at first seems like an incomprehensible fact: Edward intends to marry Lucy Steele. When Henry Crawford arrives completely unexpected in Portsmouth to visit Fanny, she too has the strength to bear up under a challenging situation. 'Good sense, like hers, will always act when called upon' (*MP* 392). Although she lacks the self-confidence of Elinor or Anne, Fanny shares with them a proper understanding of moral values and a fortitude to hold to them even under considerable pressure. Despite the fact that in this instance she is taken by surprise and caught off guard emotionally, Fanny does not mistake Henry's addresses as a compliment to herself. Sir Thomas and Edmund view Henry's attraction to Fanny in this light, but Fanny can see in Henry's infatuation only a threat to her own moral integrity. Throughout the course of the action, Fanny has to rely on her reason, which is based on her understanding of 'serious' matters, whenever, as in this situation, there is no other moral support to be found.[105] This attitude isolates Fanny throughout most of the narrative, but in the end she is shown to have been right in her judgement.

Closely related to the concepts of *sense* and *sensibility* are such words as *benevolence, candour, judgment, understanding,* and *elegance*. The meanings of these words overlap. All of them signify a rather high degree of *sense* and *sensibility*, that is, the powers of moral perception. *Elegance* like *sensibility* cuts both ways; in other words, there is a *true* and a *false elegance*. The latter is very close to the modern usage of the term.[106] *False elegance* refers to outward appearances and superficial manners as manifest in the conduct of Lady Middleton, Mr Elton, Lady Catherine, and Wickham. But a *true elegance* originates in an inner beauty of the mind. It is a refined sense of propriety, or, to quote from Johnson's dictionary, 'the beauty of propriety'.[107]

The contrast between *true* and *false elegance* is one of the major themes in *Emma*.[108] The heroine fancies herself a great connoisseur of *elegance*, and imagines that she herself is the embodiment of *true elegance*. More than a little taken aback by the presumption of Mr Elton to make her a proposal of marriage, Emma reflects, 'Perhaps it was not fair to expect him to feel how very much he was her inferior in talent, and all the elegances of mind. The very want of such equality might prevent his perception of it; but he must know that in fortune and consequence she was greatly his superior' (*E* 154). Emma assumes that the proper object for Mr Elton's affections is her protégée Harriet Smith. She sees in Harriet an *elegance* which is non-existent, allowing her preconception of what Harriet should be like to interfere with the objective facts. This is brought out most tangibly in the scene where Emma has just finished a drawing of Harriet. Knightley suggests discreetly that the image is not entirely like the original. ' "You have made her too tall, Emma," said Knightley. Emma knew she had, but she would not own it' (*E* 75). Even Mrs Weston, who has always indulged Emma, recognizes that Emma has heightened her subject's beauty, but Emma refuses to accept these criticisms, though she knows they are justified. *Elegance* is also a key word in Emma's relations with Jane Fairfax. Jane comes closer than anyone else in the novel to demonstrating the *true elegance* Emma supposedly so much admires, and from the first Emma is conscious of Jane's *elegance*; nevertheless, Emma prefers to slight Jane in favour of Harriet. When she is introduced, Jane is described as being very *elegant*, and this epithet accompanies her throughout the rest of the novel. It is emphasized that Emma is not blind to this quality in Jane. Upon meeting her after an absence of two years, Emma is struck by her manners and appearance: 'Jane Fairfax was very elegant, remarkably elegant' (*E* 180). Knightley suggests that Emma's disinclination to become more intimate with the young lady who would be a more suitable companion than Harriet stems from Emma's awareness that Jane is the accomplished young woman which she wanted to be herself (cf. *E* 180). In making this point, however, Knightley is not suggesting that Jane is perfect. He realizes that her *elegance* is marred by a *reserve* and a lack of *openness*; her motives are unknown to him and to everyone else except for Frank Churchill until the final chapters of the novel. Soon after her arrival on the scene, Mrs Elton takes the notice of Jane Fairfax which Emma should have taken. This marks the beginning of a rivalry between Mrs Elton and the heroine, which, as it develops, shows both of them to be a little too proud of their 'superiority' in the small community of Highbury to have any *true elegance*. Even before Emma has had an opportunity to become really acquainted with Mrs Elton, she suspects that there is no *elegance* in her manner, that she has *ease* but not *elegance*.[109] Upon closer acquaintance, Emma discovers that Mrs Elton does not even have the less admirable quality of *ease*. Emma makes her opinion known to Knightley and Mrs Weston: '. . . dear Mrs Elton, who wants to be wiser and wittier than all the world! I wonder how she speaks of the Coles—what she calls them! How can she find any appellation for them, deep enough in familiar vulgarity? She calls you, Knightley—what can she do for Mr Cole? And so I am not surprized that Jane Fairfax accepts her civilities and consents to be with her' (*E* 289). Emma is not unperceptive. Where there is little or no contradiction between her prejudices and the facts, she sees as clearly as Elinor or Anne, but, more often, her perceptions are blurred—if not completely distorted—by her inability to discriminate between reason and rationalization. Just as Mr Bennet forms an opinion of Mr Collins before his arrival at Longbourn, Emma also forms her opinions in advance. Mrs Elton's behaviour confirms Emma's expectations, but more commonly this is not the case. Emma's mixed feelings towards Jane can be partly explained as an example of the heroine's unwillingness to admit evidence which is inconsistent with her preconceptions. In this instance Emma's motives are rather complex, but she demonstrates a similar inflexibility in her attitudes towards some of the other characters as well. Once she has hit upon an idea and made it her own, she is intransigent. For example, she has grave difficulties in reconciling the image she has fixed in her mind of Frank Churchill with the gentleman of that name, who after many delays finally comes to Highbury. She is extremely slow to comprehend his true character, though her suspicions are aroused quite early. She wonders whether he may not show an indifference to rank and society which amounts to an 'inelegance of mind' (*E* 210), but, for the time being, she does not let this influence her opinion of him.

The use of *elegance* as a key word is not restricted to *Emma*. Elegance is an important moral value and index of character in all of the novels. In *Sense and Sensibility*, it occurs as a rule in the negative, that is, in the description of characters who do not have this quality. Neither Lucy Steele nor her sister have *elegance*.[110] Mrs Palmer also lacks this quality, though she is a friendly and good-humoured individual. 'The openness and heartiness of her manner, more than atoned for that want of recollection and elegance, which made her often deficient in the forms of politeness' (*SS* 300). Willoughby maintains a façade of *elegance*, a *false elegance* which is accepted as genuine by Marianne and her mother until his conduct forces them to re-examine their judgement of his character.

Had he been even old, ugly, and vulgar, the gratitude of Mrs Dashwood would have been secured by any act of attention to her child; but the influence of youth, beauty, and elegance, gave an interest to the action which came home to her feelings. (*SS* 75)

'He is a good sort of fellow, I believe, as ever lived,' repeated Sir John, 'I remember last Christmas at a little hop at the park, he danced from eight o'clock till four, without once sitting down.'
'Did he indeed,' cried Marianne with sparkling eyes, 'and with elegance and spirit?' (*SS* 77)

Willoughby has the outward trappings of *elegance*, an observable, *agreeable* manner, which makes him appear at *ease* and *pleasing* in society; however, to someone more perceptive than Mrs Dashwood or her daughter Marianne, Willoughby's apparent *elegance* is less perfect than he himself may suppose. Elinor is disturbed from the beginning by Willoughby's propensity 'of saying too much what he thought on every occasion, without attention to persons or circumstances. In hastily forming and giving his opinion of other people, in sacrificing general politeness to the enjoyment and undivided attention where his heart was engaged, and in slighting too easily the forms of worldly propriety' (*SS* 80). Willoughby's disregard of social convention excludes the possibility of his being *elegant* even in the narrower sense of 'polite'. Only those already very much prejudiced in his favour could overlook his faults. Elinor tries to reason with her sister; however, at this point in the narrative, Elinor and Marianne are as close to being diametrically opposed in their thinking as they ever will be. Elinor's misgivings fall on deaf ears. In *Persuasion* neither Mary Musgrove nor her husband has *elegance*. 'Charles Musgrove was civil and agreeable; in sense and temper he was undoubtedly superior to his wife; . . . a more equal match might have greatly improved him; . . . a woman of real understanding might have given more consequence to his character, and more usefulness, rationality, and elegance to his habits and pursuits' (*P* 70). As it happens, Charles Musgrove is interested in little else besides hunting. The description is particularly revealing for an understanding of the author's scale of values. Charles Musgrove is not an immoral character, nor does he threaten to undermine the moral fabric of society. He is just very limited. A potential has not been realized. He needed the influence of a real (moral) *understanding*, a rationality (i.e. *sense*) and a (*true*) *elegance*. A similar point is made concerning Lucy Steele. A potential, a promise of future accomplishment has been lost because of an inadequate education and unfortunate influences (cf. *SS* 149). Of all the characters in Jane Austen, it is Anne Elliot who realizes what Emma aspires to and Jane Fairfax approaches: a *true elegance* of mind.

But Anne, with an elegance of mind and sweetness of character, which must have placed her high with any people of real understanding, was nobody with either father or sister. (*P* 37)

Anne always contemplated them as some of the happiest creatures of her acquaintance; but still, saved as we all are by some comfortable feeling of superiority from wishing for the possibility of exchange, she would not have given up her more elegant and cultivated mind for all of their enjoyments; and envied them nothing but that seemingly perfect good understanding and agreement together, that good-humoured mutual affection, of which she had known so little herself with either of her sisters.' (*P* 67–68)

Anne is in one respect like Fanny Price. Each of these heroines is isolated by her superior *understanding* of the situations in which she finds herself. Neither of them has anyone to whom she can turn and confide her thoughts and feelings about what she observes and experiences. Although they are both unerring in their moral judgements, Anne is unwavering whereas Fanny is unsure. Fanny may have the potential of achieving an *elegance* of mind, but she has yet to reach this stage in her development. Sir Thomas seems half-conscious of this potential when he sees 'with pleasure the general elegance of her appearance and her being in remarkably good looks' (*MP* 278). Sir Thomas, of course, is thinking in terms of externals, the surface of character and conduct visible to everyone, but, as so often in *Mansfield Park*, the surface is suggestive of what is not visible to the participants in the action.

Jane Fairfax's lack of *openness*, her *reserve*, prevents her from being *candid*, that is, from demonstrating a sympathy and sensitivity—Jane Austen would write 'sensibility'—to another's thoughts and feelings.[111] Very few characters have *candour*. Jane Bennet is exceptional, for she seems to have been born with it; whereas, it is something her sister Elizabeth still has to learn. Jane is very hesitant to criticize anyone, assuming the best until the opposite is proven: 'her mild and steady candour always pleaded for allowances, and urged the possibility of mistakes' (*PP* 176). Jane's *candour* enables her at times to be more perceptive than her sister. As the narrative unfolds it becomes apparent that Elizabeth is more likely than Jane to err in her assessment of character. Jane pleads, for example, for a suspension of judgement when Elizabeth finds confirmation of her opinion of Darcy in Wickham's revelations. It is not that Elizabeth does not understand the nature of *candour*, but that throughout much of the narrative her prejudice prevents her from demonstrating it in her own behaviour. Near the beginning of the novel, she defines this virtue. Speaking to Jane, she says, 'Affectation of candour is common enough;—one meets it every where. But to be candid without ostentation or design—to take the good of every body's character and make it still better, and say nothing of the bad—belongs to you alone' (*PP* 62). Elizabeth is of course correct in suggesting that the affectation of *candour* is only too common. Wickham, Mrs Jennings, Mrs Norris, and Mr Elliot are some obvious examples in Jane Austen's fiction. Willoughby and Marianne show a conspicuous lack of interest in Colonel Brandon only because he is neither lively nor young, that is, because he is not like them. An intense discussion develops between Marianne and

Willoughby on the one side and Elinor on the other. Marianne's sister feels compelled to remonstrate with both of them. 'I may venture to say that *his* observations have stretched much farther than your candour. But why should you dislike him?' (*SS* 82). *Candour* knows no pride of place; it is a virtue which may be found in those with modest social claims as well as in those whose station in life is much higher. Knightley informs Emma that Miss Bates's response to Emma's cruel remarks at Box Hill was 'candour and generosity' (*E* 368).[112] *Candour*, *elegance*, and the proper balance of *sense* and *sensibility* are the seldom achieved ideals in Jane Austen's novels, and the standards by which character and conduct are measured. Many of the characters have at least something of these virtues, though their moral *understanding*, their powers of discrimination, and their sense of *propriety* leave much to be desired.

Perhaps the single most striking feature of the system of moral values in Jane Austen's fiction is the emphasis on the individual's commitment to his fellow human beings. The individual has a *duty*, a moral obligation to others; wherever conduct reveals a neglect or disregard of this *duty*, the individual's behaviour is placed in a critical light. Moral behaviour is in most instances social behaviour; that is, an individual's moral character is manifest in his conduct in social situations. His *manners* may readily give him away, or, for some time at least, he may succeed in passing off a *false candour* or *elegance* for the genuine moral quality; however, sooner or later, his neglect of *duty* is exposed. All of the serious moral failings are evinced in anti-social behaviour. As soon as an individual withdraws from the dictates of society's norms—whether his motive is love, material gain, or freedom, he becomes a risk not only to himself but also to the moral underpinnings of the society in which he lives. Marianne's rejection of social convention and the consequences of her anti-social attitude illustrate the inherent dangers of such behaviour.

But anti-social behaviour takes many forms in Jane Austen's fiction. When the Crawfords advocate various 'improvements', they are also challenging the principles upon which the society is based. Whatever its form, anti-social behaviour always reflects the assertion of the individual's will over the demands of *propriety*. In some cases such behaviour may appear relatively harmless. Mary Musgrove's absorption in herself—her concern about the state of her health and about her lack of companionship—is certainly less culpable than Willoughby's egotistical behaviour; however, both of them show a neglect of *duty*, Mary Musgrove to her family, and Willoughby to Marianne and to Colonel Brandon's relation Eliza. When it is far too late for it to make any difference any more, Sir Thomas Bertram and Mr Bennet realize that they have failed to take the interest in the up- bringing and affairs of their children which was necessary. Some individuals remain oblivious to the fact that they neglect anything of importance. The problem lies in their interpretation of what is important. For Sir Walter Elliot and his daughter Elizabeth, one's rank and one's good looks are not to be undervalued; for Mrs Allen, it is having on the right gown; for Mrs Norris, it is managing with less today than she spent yesterday; for Mrs Bennet, it is getting her daughters married and news. With their distorted sense of values and extremely narrow range of interests, these characters evoke our laughter. The same can hardly be said of such characters as Wickham, Willoughby, Mr Elliot, General Tilney, or the Crawfords. Their faults are too grave to be taken lightly. The moral implications of their conduct focus attention on Jane Austen's serious themes. There are of course also individuals who are not so negligent of their moral responsibilities to others.

If there are few who approach perfection, there are a num- ber who manifest—at least to a degree—such admirable qualities as *benevolence*, *understanding*, *candour*, and *elegance*. In their relations with others they are likely to be *agreeable*, at *ease*, *amiable*, *pleasing*, or something more. It would be a mistake to equate these two groups of words. The words taken from the semantic field of social values are often also appropriate as a description of the outward manner of several individuals who in other respects are not admirable at all. There are orders of merit in the moral and social spheres. In the novels one is often taken as a sign for the other. When Lady Russell praises Mr Elliot's impeccable *manners*, little does she realize that she is judging no more than the surface. Lady Russell is blinded perhaps by her pride in rank, but in any event she lacks the moral perceptiveness to judge character and conduct properly. This is the task which confronts all the heroines again and again. Some of them have a great deal to learn before they can judge properly; others only have to put their moral *understanding* and clear-sightedness to the test. The author provides the reader with key words to guide him in his assessment of the heroines' judgements.

V

The Distance between the Real and Technical Points of View

The Challenge to the Reader

In concluding this study of the *real* and *technical points of view* in Jane Austen's fiction, it is necessary to consider a little more closely how these perspectives are related to one another. As was noted in the Introduction, the author is situated by the text: the language as well as the technical means of presentation place the author in relation to the imaginative world which has been created. In other words, the language and the means of presentation serve as a complex link, on the one hand, between the author and an external reality, and, on the other, between the author and the reader. The process of creating the text involves a series of choices which represent the author's conscious or unconscious attempt to impose a fictional world upon the reader. The author commits herself or himself to a particular subject matter and a means of presenting it. These commitments imply a set of norms and values which define the frame of reference within which the reader experiences the text. At the outset Jane Austen commits herself to the portrayal of middle-class life in Regency England. Each of her novels focuses on some of the moral conflicts with which the individual might be confronted in this milieu. In each instance, the action climaxes with the heroine having gained in insight and understanding of herself and others and having increased her ability to discriminate among conflicting values.

The novels present character, conduct, and the system of values by which these are judged. The means of presentation are of two kinds: on the one hand, the author's narrative strategies, and on the other, her choices of words, characters, events, and the moral assumptions governing the course of the action. Chapters I and II examined *irony* as the structuring principle in Jane Austen's fiction, and the various means she uses to achieve an ironic perspective on the characters and events portrayed. The reader is at one, or, more often, two removes from these events. They are presented more or less from the heroine's angle of vision, usually filtered through the ironic lens of the narrator. The reader's relative closeness to the heroine's perspective depends upon the heroine and the reliability of her judgements; the degree of Elinor Dashwood's reliability is, for example, of a completely different order from that of Emma Woodhouse. Inside views are one of the means used to control the distance between the reader and the heroine. The function and significance of these inside views differ considerably from one novel to the next. But the control of distance is not limited to the reader's relation to the heroine. Until near the end of all of the novels, experience is mediated through a narrator, who provides the reader with a knowledge superior to that of any of the participants in the action. From his position of superior knowledge, the reader recognizes, for example, that in most of the dramatic scenes one of the characters takes advantage of his own superior knowledge to direct the course of the conversation. In brief, then, *irony* originates in the varying degrees of knowledge and understanding of character, conduct, and society's system of norms and values. The reader's superiority is clearly defined. In the course of the narrative, his knowledge gradually reaches the point at which it is equal to the narrator's and, by implication, to the author's.

Jane Austen's attitude towards characters, the conduct and the values she portrays has been the subject of some misinterpretations of her novels. Of course, it is not a question of her knowledge of the characters, their behaviour, and their values, but of her attitude towards this subject matter. Chapters III and IV bring together the most important evidence for an understanding of this attitude: her apprehension, comprehension, and interpretation of the imaginative world she has created. The basis of the various misreadings of her texts is a failure to understand the function of *irony*. She does not reject the values of the society she portrays. All the evidence argues against such a line of interpretation. Although her novels are by choice not explicitly didactic, they are nevertheless an affirmation of those values upon which this society is based. The primary function of *irony* in the novels is to guide the reader, usually along with the heroine, in learning to perceive and discriminate among grades of moral quality. This is true of both the structural ironies (the ironies of the plot) and the local ironies (the ironic perspectives of the inside views and dramatic scenes). The object of the author's *irony* is not the system of norms and values, but the human foibles, moral weakness, and neglect of duty which represent increasingly serious degrees of failure to accept and properly distinguish moral and social values.

Furthermore, the reader is assisted in his judgement of character by the key words drawn from three interrelated semantic fields, and used to signify material, social, and moral values. The material values need to be viewed somewhat apart from other values, for they are in themselves never the basis of positive action. At best, they represent a secondary, supporting argument in favour of a positive action. Darcy's wealth enhances the correctness of Elizabeth's decision to marry him, but it is not—and should not be—her primary consideration. More often, however, material values are the basis of negative action, in which the individual rejects or disregards other values, acting according to a false sense of priorities.

Moral and social values are much more closely related to one another. It is no accident that certain key words occur in both semantic fields; often the disregard of social convention has moral consequences. But even more common is a conflict or contradiction between moral and social values. A contradiction occurs wherever an individual's behaviour does not reflect his moral views. A conflict arises whenever social values are given priority or when the moral implications of a situation are not clear. For example, the implications of Darcy's behaviour, Captain Wentworth's relations to Louisa and her sister, or Frank Churchill's flirtation with Emma are not readily apparent. Jane Austen gives weight and significance to her key words by collocating them, by placing them in particular contexts, and by associating them with particular individuals whose character and conduct the reader comes to know. There is a reciprocal relationship between portrayals of character and conduct, which exemplify the meaning of key words, and these key words, which place character and conduct according to the author's scale of values.

Jane Austen's method can perhaps best be illustrated with one final example. In a letter to her sister Cassandra dated shortly after the manuscript of *Pride and Prejudice* was finished for the publisher, Jane Austen writes that she is now working on something quite different, a novel on the subject of 'ordination'.[1] No one has ever challenged the idea that *Mansfield Park* is very unlike its predecessor, but to what extent is it about 'ordination'? Critics have been inclined to dismiss this remark of the author's as an idea which has little relevance for our understanding of the novel as we know it. Up to a point such an attitude seems valid. *Ordination* does not have the place in *Mansfield Park* that *pride* and *prejudice* have in its predecessor, but it could in fact be considered the focal point about which the action turns. Assuming that this is the case, the action might be summarized as follows:

A young man about ready to go into orders comes back from the university to his home Mansfield Park, the symbol of those traditional values which he has learned to cherish and respect. While he is home and in the absence of his father, who is the guardian of Mansfield Park and all that it represents, the young man is exposed to temptation. Two young people have come recently into the neighbourhood and brought with them from London ideas quite different from those of the future clergyman. At first these differences are not apparent, and the young man becomes quickly enamoured of the young lady. That they do not always think along the same lines becomes evident during a visit at another estate, where they have a look at a chapel which is no longer used, but by this time, the young man is so much in love that he finds excuses for her behaviour, and a few minutes later they are walking alone together in a nearby park. But the testing of this young man's moral integrity does not end here. Soon he finds himself involved in the production of a play in which he will play the role of the young lady's lover, which of course by this time involves no role-playing at all. He knows this is wrong. The whole business of the play is a serious mistake, but he cannot resist the temptation. The course of events from the arrival of the young man up to this crisis and beyond is presented from the perspective of the only individual who has the moral understanding to appreciate the significance of what is happening. She is also in love with the young man, and far more deserving of his love than the young lady from London, but she has little reason to hope until it is almost too late. The young man hesitates until an act by the young lady's brother opens the future clergyman's eyes to the truth.

The point of this summary is to emphasize the central significance of the theme of *ordination*. Much of the action and all of the principals can be viewed in relation to the decisive step Edmund Bertram is about to take. The romance which holds centre stage until the final pages of the novel is not the relationship between Fanny and Edmund but the one between Mary Crawford and the future clergyman. Edmund is not only tempted, but is also forced to articulate his ideas, to justify his position, and to consider compromise. The extent to which he loses his sense of perspective is suggested by the pressure he tries to exert on Fanny to marry Mary's brother. This approach to *Mansfield Park*, of course, accounts for only half of the novel. The other half is Fanny's 'story'. But it indicates that the author's comment to her sister concerning the subject of the novel should not be disregarded, and it illustrates the fact that, while the author is not explicit, she nevertheless takes great care to lead the reader to the perception of moral quality. All of the strategies and vocabulary employed to structure the reader's experience guide him to a recognition of Fanny's moral superiority. Her marriage to Edmund functions as a coda to a narrative in which the values that both of them hold most dear are first challenged and then affirmed. In the first half of the novel, Fanny is the passive observer, while Edmund becomes more and more deeply involved in circumstances which threaten his moral integrity. In the second half of the novel, it is Fanny who is compelled to examine her conscience, and to consider the well-meant advice given her by those whose opinion she values most. Fanny remains firm and Edmund recovers his sense of values.

Nowhere does Jane Austen come closer to being openly didactic than in *Mansfield Park*, but even here she is far from being explicit. She demands the reader's active participation in the narrative.

'*It is a truth universally acknowledged, that a single man in possession of a good fortune, must be in want of a wife*': the opening sentence of *Pride and Prejudice* cannot really be understood out of context. It represents a challenge, and it becomes comprehensible only in the light of what follows. Similarly, if less obviously, the heroines' perception of character and conduct constitutes a challenge to the reader to make his own evaluations in the light of his knowledge of the course of events, the moral frame of reference, and the additional perspective afforded him by the narrator. Whatever the historical individual named 'Jane Austen' may have been like, the author, as she is known through her novels, takes great care to make *nice* distinctions, and she expects her reader to learn to be equally perspicacious in assessing her characters and their conduct.

Notes

INTRODUCTION

1 Virginia Woolf, 'Jane Austen', *Jane Austen: A Collection of Critical Essays*, ed., Ian Watt (Englewood Cliffs, N.J., 1963), 15–24, quotation from 15. This comment originally appeared in a review: 'Jane Austen at Sixty', *Nation* XXXIV (15 Dec. 1923), 433.

2 F. R. Leavis, *The Great Tradition: George Eliot, Henry James, Joseph Conrad* (Harmondsworth, 1967, org., 1948), 16–19.

3 Henry James, 'The Lesson of Balzac,' *Atlantic Monthly* (August 1905), reprinted in: Henry James, *The Future of the Novel: Essays on the Art of Fiction*, ed., Leon Edel (New York, 1956), 97–124, quotation from 100–101.

4 Cf. R. W. Chapman, *Jane Austen: A Critical Bibliography* (2nd edn, Oxford, 1955); Barry Roth and Joel Weinsheimer, *An Annotated Bibliography of Jane Austen Studies 1952–1972* (Charlottesville, 1973); and Avrom Fleishman, 'The State of the Art: Recent Jane Austen Criticism,' *Modern Language Quarterly* 37 (1976), 281–289.

5 Although reference is made below to much of the scholarship on Jane Austen, the following major studies should be mentioned at the outset: A. C. Bradley, 'Jane Austen,' *Essays and Studies by Members of the English Association* 11 (Oxford, 1911), 7–36; Mary Lascelles, *Jane Austen and her Art* (London, 1963, org., 1939); Howard S. Babb, *Jane Austen's Novels: The Fabric of Dialogue* (Columbus, 1962); A. Walton Litz, *Jane Austen: A Study of her Artistic Development* (New York, 1965); Kenneth L. Moler, *Jane Austen's Art of Allusion* (Lincoln, 1968); Lloyd W. Brown, *Bits of Ivory: Narrative Techniques in Jane Austen's Fiction* (Baton Rouge, 1973); Marilyn Butler, *Jane Austen and the War of Ideas* (Oxford, 1975).

6   John Odmark, 'The Aesthetics of Reception' (unpub. MS, 1980).

7   Cf. Michael Riffaterre, 'Criteria for Style Analysis,' *Word* 15 (1959), 154–174; Stanley E. Fish, 'Literature in the Reader: Affective Stylistics,' *New Literary History* 2 (1970), 123–162; Samuel R. Levin, 'Internal and External Deviation in Poetry,' *Word* 21 (1965), 225–237.

8   Cf. Wayne C. Booth, *The Rhetoric of Fiction* (Chicago, 1961); Wolfgang Iser, *Der implizite Leser: Kommunikationsformen des Romans von Bunyan bis Beckett* (Munich, 1972); W. Iser, *Der Akt des Lesens* (Munich, 1976); John Preston, *The Created Self: The Reader's Role in Eighteenth-Century Fiction* (London, 1970).

9   Cf. Jan Mukařovský, 'The Place of the Aesthetic Function among the other Functions' in: J. Mukařovský, *Structure, Sign, Function*, trans., John Burbank and Peter Steiner (New Haven, 1978), 31–48.

10 Cf. Jan Mukařovský, 'Two Studies of Poetic Designation,' in: J. Mukařovský, *The Word and Verbal Art*, trans., John Burbank and Peter Steiner (New Haven, 1977), 65–80; Roman Ingarden, *Das literarische Kunstwerk* (2nd edn, Tübingen, 1960); R. Ingarden, *Studia z estetyki III* (Warsaw, 1970); John Odmark, 'Ingarden and the *Concretization* of the Literary Text,' *Proceedings of the Ninth Congress of the International Comparative Literature Association* (Innsbruck, forthcoming).

11 John Odmark, 'Style, Meaning and the Concept of Literary Competence,' *Proceedings of the Twelfth International Congress of Linguists* (Innsbruck, 1978), 666–668.

12 Cf. Manfred Naumann's concept *Rezeptionsvorgabe* ('structured prefigurement'): M. Naumann et al., *Gesellschaft—Literatur—Lesen: Literaturrezeption in theoretischer Sicht* (Berlin, 1973); for a critique of this concept: Hans Robert Jauss, 'Zur Fortsetzung des Dialogs zwischen "bürgerlicher" und "materialistischer" Rezeptionsästhetik,' *Rezeptionsästhetik*, ed., Rainer Warning (Munich, 1975), 343–352; and Wolfgang Iser, 'Im Lichte der Kritik,' in: Warning: 1975, 325–342.

13 On the concept of *open spaces* see: Umberto Eco, *The Role of the Reader* (Bloomington, 1979); 'places of indeterminacy' is a translation of Ingarden's concept *Unbestimmtheitsstellen*: Ingarden: 1960, cf. Henryk Markiewicz,

'Places of Indeterminacy in a Literary Work,' *Roman Ingarden and Contemporary Polish Aesthetics*, eds., Piotr Graff and Sław Krzemień-Ojak (Warsaw, 1975), 159–171.

14 V. Woolf: 1963, 19, cf. Iser: 1972.

15 Wolfgang Iser, *The Act of Reading : A Theory of Aesthetic Response* (Baltimore, 1978), 178 [translation of Iser: 1976].

16 Percy Lubbock, *The Craft of Fiction* (London, 1954, org. 1921), 251.

17 René Wellek and Austin Warren, *Theory of Literature* (3rd edn, New York, 1962), 222.

18 See: Henry James, 'Preface to *The Ambassadors*,' *The Art of the Novel*, ed., R. B. Blackmur (London, 1962), 307–326; cf. James's remark: 'The author makes his reader very much as he makes his characters.' in: 'The Novels of George Eliot,' *Atlantic Monthly* (October 1866), 485.

19 Mark Schorer, 'Technique as Discovery,' *20th Century Literary Criticism*, ed., David Lodge (London, 1972), 387–400, quotation from 387.

20 See, e.g., Seymour Chatman, *Story and Discourse : Narrative Structure in Fiction and Film* (Ithaca, 1978), 196–262; Robert Weimann, *Structure and Society in Literary History : Studies in the History and Theory of Historical Criticism* (Charlottesville, 1976), 234–266; Manfred Markus, *Moderne Erzählperspektive in den Werken des Gawain-Autors* (Nürnberg, 1971); Franz K. Stanzel, *Typische Formen des Romans* (Göttingen, 1964); Kristen Morrison, 'James's and Lubbock's Differing Points of View,' *Nineteenth Century Fiction* 16 (1961), 245–246.

21 See: Preston: 1970; and Iser: 1972; cf. Erwin Wolff, 'Der intendierte Leser,' *Poetica* 4 (1971), 141ff.

22 Weimann: 1976, 234–266.

23 Roland Barthes suggests that such objectivity is possible in *Le Degré zéro de l'écriture* (Paris, 1953), esp., 105–111.

24 This assumption is central to Booth: 1961.

25 In Jane Austen's novels there is always a dramatized narrator; however, in more recent fiction, this is not necessarily the case, for example, in Ernest Hemingway's 'The Killers' (cf. Chatman: 1978, 146–195).

26 Cf. Roger Fowler, *Linguistics and the Novel* (London, 1977), 75ff.

CHAPTER I : IRONY AND THE SHAPING OF THE NOVEL

1   *Irony* is perhaps the most frequently used term in Jane
    Austen criticism. It has taken a wide range of not always
    very carefully defined meanings. It may refer to structural
    features (cf. Philip Stevick, *The Chapter in Fiction : Theories
    of Narrative Division* (Syracuse, 1970); and the references
    below in n. 4); but more commonly the term is used to
    refer to the content. 'Jane Austen's novels posit a central
    irony between social status, a kind of appearance, and love,
    a kind of reality, between egoism and altruism,' (Albert
    Cook, 'Modes of Irony: Jane Austen and Stendhal,' *The
    Meaning of Fiction* (Detroit, 1960), 38–47). Or, to para-
    phrase a second critic, Jane Austen is a comic writer, focus-
    ing on inconsistencies and incongruities and using both to
    raise a smile and to offer a serious criticism of people and
    society (Norman Sherry, *Jane Austen* (London, 1966)).
    Similarly, Jane Austen's conceptual terms (as in the titles
    Sense and Sensibility, Pride and Prejudice, and *Persuasion*)
    comprehend the ambiguous usages which juxtapose mul-
    tiple, even contradictory meanings, which are rooted in the
    philosophical assumptions of the novelist's background
    and which go far to explain the novels' ironies (Brown: 1973).
2   D. W. Harding, 'Regulated Hatred: An Aspect of the Work
    of Jane Austen,' *Scrutiny* VIII (1940), 346–362, reprinted
    in Watt: 1963, 166–179; Marvin Mudrick, *Jane Austen:
    Irony as Defense and Discovery* (Princeton, 1952).
3   Mudrick also views irony as informing all of the novels;
    however, despite a chapter entitled 'Irony as Form', he
    deals with irony primarily in terms of content, which leads
    him to some questionable conclusions. For a critique of
    Mudrick's views see: Frederick M. Link, 'Jane Austen,
    Mr Mudrick and Critical Monism,' *Boston University
    Studies in English* 3 (1957); W. A. Craik, *Jane Austen:
    The Six Novels* (New York, 1965); and Litz: 1965.
4   Booth's criticism represents an important breakthrough in
    the analysis of Jane Austen's irony. (See: Booth: 1961,
    244–266, and passim; W. C. Booth, *A Rhetoric of Irony*
    (Chicago, 1974), 129–134, 197–200, and passim; and W. C.
    Booth, '*The Rhetoric of Fiction* and the Poetics of Fictions,'
    Towards a Poetics of Fiction, ed., Mark Spilka (Bloomington,
    1977), 77–89.) Prior to Booth, irony as a structural pheno-

menon receives only the most superficial treatment, e.g., Andrew Wright's discussion of 'ironic devices' in *Jane Austen's Novels : A Study in Structure* (New York, 1953); or Margaret Shenfield's study of point of view in which she misses the essence of the problem : Jane Austen's method is 'wholly composed of irony : by showing an individual's picture of himself (which is always quite false) and, at the same time, hinting at the tone of character of the individual, she is able to give a very clear picture of isolation.' ('Jane Austen's Point of View,' *Quarterly Review* 296 (1958), 298–306).

5 Cf. Weimann: 1976, 238.

6 *Northanger Abbey* was written during 1798–1799. In an 'Advertisment by the Authoress,' written in 1816–1817, the novel is said to have been finished in 1803, and intended for immediate publication. In other words, it antedates the first version of *Sense and Sensibility*—entitled 'Elinor and Marianne'—written in epistolary form about 1795, and the original version of *Pride and Prejudice*—entitled 'First Impressions'—composed from October 1796 to August 1797. *Sense and Sensibility* and *Pride and Prejudice* were repeatedly reworked before finally appearing in 1811 and 1813 respectively. *Northanger Abbey* was first published posthumously December 1817 (1818).

7 Douglas Bush, *Jane Austen* (London, 1975), 70.

8 All references to *Northanger Abbey* (*NA*) are to the Penguin edition edited by Anne Ehrenpreis (Harmondsworth, 1972).

9 Cf. Karl Heinz Göller, *Romance und Novel : Die Anfänge des englischen Romans* (Regensburg, 1972), 233–236.

10 Cf. Lascelles: 1963, 60.

11 Alan D. McKillop, 'Critical Realism in *Northanger Abbey*,' in Watt: 1963, 52–61, quotation from 60.

12 Cf. Butler: 1975, 173.

13 Cf. Lionel Trilling, 'Mansfield Park,' *The Opposing Self* (New York, 1959), 206–230.

14 Cf. McKillop in Watt: 1963, 52–61.

15 Litz, for example, argues that the author fails to completely free herself from the antithetical structure and stereotyped characters of the early, epistolary form of the novel; see: Litz: 1965.

16 The relationship between the two concepts of *sense* and *sensibility* is considered in some detail below: 166–172.

17   For an analysis of the complex geometry of the plot's structure see Tony Tanner's 'Introduction' to the Penguin edition of *Sense and Sensibility* (Harmondsworth, 1969), 7–34, esp., 9–13.

18   All references to *Sense and Sensibility* (*SS*) are to the Penguin edition edited by Tony Tanner (Harmondsworth, 1969).

19   See, for example, the introductions of John Dashwood, Mrs Jennings, and Edward Ferrars, 41, 69, and 49, respectively (cf. Craik: 1965, 34–35).

20   Nardin disagrees with this interpretation, arguing that Elinor is the object of much more irony than has been generally recognized (see: Jane Nardin, *Those Elegant Decorums : The Concept of Propriety in Jane Austen's Novels* (Albany, 1973), 24–46.

21   Cf. Nardin: 1973; Tanner: 1969; and Ian Watt, 'On *Sense and Sensibility*,' in Watt: 1963, 41–51.

22   Cf. Bush: 1975, 87.

23   At the time, for example, Elinor underestimates how seriously Marianne has been affected by Willoughby's sudden departure.

24   Mudrick's comment on this development: 'Marianne, the life and center of the novel, has been betrayed; and not by Willoughby' (Mudrick: 1952, 93).

25   Another obviously contrived development is the arrival of the servant with the report that Mr Ferrars and Lucy Steele are married. For further examples see: Bush: 1975, 79–83.

26   See: 1–2.

27   This of course would not be the case if Mudrick's interpretation were accepted.

28   Cf. Nardin: 1973, 47–61.

29   Trilling: 1959, 206–230.

30   Cf. Butler: 1975, 220–223.

31   All references to *Mansfield Park* (*MP*) are to the Penguin edition edited by Tony Tanner (Harmondsworth, 1966).

32   Duckworth views Jane Austen's conception of the 'estate' and her idea of 'improvement' as offering a basis for the thematic unity of all her fiction. See: Alistair M. Duckworth, *The Improvement of the Estate : A Study of Jane Austen's Novels* (Baltimore, 1971).

33   Cf. Trilling: 1959, 206–230; see also Butler and Lodge, who agree with Trilling on the significance of this episode, but

disagree on its interpretation (Butler: 1975, 232; and David Lodge, *Language of Fiction* (New York, 1966), 94–113).

34   All references to *Emma* (*E*) are to the Penguin edition edited by Ronald Blythe (Harmondsworth, 1966).

35   See: R. W. Chapman, *Jane Austen: Facts and Problems* (Oxford, 1948), 60–69.

36   Cf. Craik: 1965, 169ff.

37   Mudrick: 1952, 222.

38   Babb: 1967, 239.

39   Babb's italics (Babb: 1967, 239). All references to *Persuasion* are to the Penguin edition [title: *Persuasion* with *A Memoir of Jane Austen*] (*P*), ed., D. W. Harding (Harmondsworth, 1965).

40   For a discussion of this scene, see: 115–117.

41   Cf. Bush: 1975, 169.

42   The system of norms and values governing the course of the action, and reflecting the author's attitude towards her fictional world, is examined in detail in Chapter IV.

CHAPTER II: PUTTING THE READER IN HIS PLACE

1   Cf. Harding: 1963. For a criticism of Harding's interpretation, see: Nardin: 1973, 2 and passim.

2   Ian Watt, *The Rise of the Novel* (Berkeley, 1957), 297.

3   E. M. Forster, *Aspects of the Novel* (New York, 1954, org., 1927), 74.

4   All references to *Pride and Prejudice* (*PP*) are to the Penguin edition edited by Tony Tanner (Harmondsworth, 1972).

5   See: 1.

6   See: *NA* 61.

7   Cf. Butler: 1975, 173–175.

8   Catherine has five important conversations about the Gothic novel: with Isabella Thorpe (quoted in part above); with John Thorpe (69–70); with Eleanor and Henry Tilney (121–125); with Henry Tilney on their way to the abbey (164–167); and with Henry Tilney again (196–200).

9   Jane Austen's choice of name for Isabella's friend seems to be an intentional allusion to Richardson's Pamela Andrews and to the kind of literature Catherine and Isabella should be reading. The author's own interest in Richardson was stressed by her first biographer: 'Her knowledge of Richardson's works was such as no one is likely again to acquire.'

J. E. Austen-Leigh, *A Memoir of Jane Austen* (Harmonds-worth, 1965), 331 [see: Chapter I, n. 39].

10   Cf. *NA* 62.

11   For a recent well-argued attempt to resolve these problems, see: Katrin Ristkok Burlin, ' "The Pen of the Contriver": the Four Fictions of *Northanger Abbey*' in *Jane Austen: Bicentenary Essays*, ed., John Halperin (Cambridge, 1975), 89–111.

12   See: Chapter I, n. 6.

13   For a discussion of *implicit parallel* and *explicit parallel*, see: W. K. Wimsatt, *The Prose Style of Samuel Johnson* (Hamden, Conn., 1972, org., 1941), 15–20.

14   Cf. the discussion of the passage from *Persuasion*, 35–38.

15   See Chapter I for a discussion of this problem: 2ff.

16   Bush: 1975, 83.

17   Wright and Lascelles are two of the most influential critics to point out inconsistencies in the portrayal of Darcy's character (cf. Wright: 1953, 122–127; and Lascelles: 1963, 22).

18   Reuben Brower was the first to make this point in 'Light and Bright and Sparkling: Irony and Fiction in *Pride and Prejudice*,' included in his book: *The Fields of Light* (New York, 1951), 164–181, reprinted in Watt: 1963, 62–75. Also see Babb: 1962, 113–144.

19   Cf. Bush: 1975, 90. Also see: Lascelles: 1963, 9; Butler: 1975, 168–170; and Frank W. Bradbrook, *Jane Austen and her Predecessors* (Cambridge, 1966), 168–170.

20   The ambiguities in *Emma*, for example, arise for the most part not from mutual misunderstandings, but from the heroine's errors in judgement.

21   The most important example of an inside view in *Pride and Prejudice* occurs in Chapter 52 where Elizabeth examines her own feelings after receiving a letter from Darcy.

22   Cf. 12–24.

23   Cf. Bush: 1975, 151.

24   My italics.

25   Cf. Karl Kroeber, *Styles in Fictional Structure: The Art of Jane Austen, Charlotte Brontë, George Eliot* (Princeton, 1971), 81.

CHAPTER III: JANE AUSTEN'S SENSE OF ENDING

1   Two critics who place more emphasis on the similarities than I would are: Lloyd W. Brown, 'The Comic Conclusion in Jane Austen's Novels,' *PMLA* 84 (1969), 1582–1587; and Richard E. Morahan, 'Jane Austen's Endings' (the third chapter of his dissertation) *DAI* 32: 3318A–3319A.

2   Virginia Woolf was one of the first to recognize this fact (see: Woolf: 1963).

3   For the relevant passages from *Mysteries of Udolpho*, see: R. W. Chapman's edition of *Northanger Abbey* in Vol. V of *The Novels of Jane Austen* (3rd edn, London, 1969), 306–312. Also see: Karl Kroeber, 'Subverting a Hypocrite Lecteur,' *Jane Austen Today*, ed., Joel Weinsheimer (Athens, 1975), 33–45.

4   Cf. Brown: 1973, 224.

5   See: Litz: 1965, 102 (cf. Brower: 1963; and Dorothy van Ghent, *The English Novel: Form and Function* (New York, 1961, org., 1953), 99–111).

6   For a discussion of this usage, see: 7–10.

7   Cf. 7–10.

8   Cf. *PP* 374–380; and *E* 412–420.

9   Brower: 1963.

10 Cf. 12–13.

11 Cf. 24–25.

12 See: 74–82.

13 This statement is a little misleading. In *Pride and Prejudice*, Jane Austen records Mr Collins's proposal to Elizabeth (*PP* 147–148, cf. 206–209); however, the function of Mr Collins's speech is to reveal his foolishness; whereas, the function of Wentworth's letter is to unite him finally with Anne.

14 Cf. Cecil S. Emden, 'The Composition of *Northanger Abbey*,' *Review of English Studies* XIX (1968), 279–287.

15 Cf. 48–50.

16 Maria Edgeworth offers this explanation in 'The Advertisement' to *Belinda*. C. L. Thomson was the first to make this point (see: *Jane Austen: A Survey* (London, 1929), 45–46).

17 For Isabella's 'list' see: *NA* 61 (cited in Chapter II, 48–50).

18 Quoted from Anne Ehrenpreis' 'Introduction' to the Penguin edition of *Persuasion*, 21.

19 Jane Austen is not objecting here to the kind of overt

moralizing characteristic of such works as Elizabeth Inchbald's *A Simple Story* (1791), Jane West's *The Advantages of Education* (1793), or Hannah More's *Coelebs in Search of a Wife* (1808), though her own example represents an alternative to such explicit didacticism.

20   Lady Sarah Pennington, *An Unfortunate Mother's Advice to Her Absent Daughters* (1761), reprinted in the appendix to Bradbrook: 1966, 143–154, quotation from 145.

21   Anne Radcliffe is the best representative of one of the main streams of Gothic romance; Matthew Gregory Lewis' *Ambrosio, or The Monk* (1796) represents another. The latter is distinguished by its lack of moral delicacy and a disinterest in offering rational explanations for the extraordinary and fantastic phenomena in the stories.

22   See Catherine's speculations concerning the 'black veil': *NA* 60 (cf. 48–50).

23   Cf. 48–50.

24   Lionel Stevenson, *The English Novel : A Panorama* (Boston, 1960), 176.

25   Butler: 1975, 23.

26   In this regard, *Mansfield Park* is an exception. A proposal does not mark the climax, but the resolution of other problems which open the way to a proposal of marriage. The proposal itself is only mentioned in passing (see: *MP* 454).

CHAPTER IV : ORDERING ONE'S PRIORITIES

1   Cf. Butler : 1975, 1.

2   In an unsigned review in *North British Review* 52 (April 1870), 129–152, reprinted in *Jane Austen : The Critical Heritage*, ed., B. C. Southam (London, 1968), 241–265, the Shakespearean scholar Richard Simpson was the first to suggest that Jane Austen was very critical of the society she portrays in her novels. This line of interpretation has been taken up and variously argued by Reginald Farrer, 'Jane Austen,' *Quarterly Review* CCXXVIII (1917), 1–30; Harding: 1963, and 'Jane Austen and Moral Judgment,' *From Blake to Byron* (Harmondsworth, 1957), 51–59; Geoffrey Gorer, 'The Myth in Jane Austen,' *American Imago* II (1941), 197–204; Leonard Woolf, 'The Economic Determination of Jane Austen,' *New Statesman and Nation* n.s. 24 (18 July 1942); David Daiches, 'Jane Austen, Karl

Marx and the Aristocratic Dance,' *American Scholar* 17 (1948), 289–296; Mark Schorer, 'Fiction and the "Analogical Matrix",' *Critiques and Essays on Modern Fiction*, ed., John W. Aldridge (New York, 1952), 83–98, 'The Humiliation of Emma Woodhouse,' in Watt: 1963, 98–111, 'Jane Austen,' the introduction to Schorer's edition of *Pride and Prejudice* (New York, 1959); and Kingsley Amis, 'What Became of Jane Austen?' in Watt: 1963, 141–144. Duckworth refers to Harding, Mudrick (1952), Schorer, Gorer, and Amis as 'subversives' (Duckworth: 1971, 6 and passim). Along with Butler (1975), Trilling (1959, 'Emma,' *Encounter* 8 (1957), 49–59, 'Why We Read Jane Austen,' *TLS* 3860 (5 March 1976), 250–252), and a number of other critics, Duckworth objects to the view of Jane Austen implicitly shared by these 'subversives', namely, that she is rejecting the values upon which the society she portrays is based. This also seems to me an untenable interpretation, and in the course of this chapter I will go into this point in detail.

3 Cf. R. W. Chapman, 'Miss Austen's English,' in Chapman's edition of *Sense and Sensibility* (3rd edn, London, 1965), 388–421; and K. C. Phillips, *Jane Austen's English* (London, 1970).

4 Cf. Gilbert Ryle, 'Jane Austen and the Moralists,' *Oxford Review* I (1966), 5–18.

5 Cf. Avrom Fleishman, *A Reading of Mansfield Park: An Essay in Critical Synthesis* (Minneapolis, 1967). The significance of Burke's ideas for an interpretation of *Mansfield Park* is pursued further by Duckworth: 1971, esp., 45–48; and also touched on by Brown: 1973.

6 Basil Willey, for example, has noted the affinities between Jane Austen and the early eighteenth century. See: *The Eighteenth Century Background: Studies on the Idea of Nature in the Thought of the Period* (London, 1940), 109.

7 Schorer: 1952, 1959, 1963; Duckworth: 1971; and Butler: 1975.

8 *Jane Austen's Letters to her Sister Cassandra and Others*, ed., R. W. Chapman (2nd edn, Oxford, 1952), 443.

9 Chapman: 1948, 35.

10 Cf. H. W. Garrod, 'Jane Austen: A Depreciation,' *Essays by Divers Hands* (London, 1928), 21–40.

11 Jane Austen's eldest brother, James, who attended Oxford,

seems to have been an important influence on his sister's education, directing her reading and forming her taste (cf. Chapman: 1948, 12).

12   Jane Austen appears to have little in common with such women as Mme de Châtelet (1706–1749), Voltaire's companion for many years, or Mme de Staël (1766–1817), whom Jane Austen declined to meet (cf. Chapman: 1948, 132).

13   Garrod, Forster and Nicolson all found Jane Austen's correspondence disappointing and trivial. Garrod, who made use of an earlier edition of the letters, wrote: 'Her letters may be described as a desert of trivialities punctuated by occasional cases of clever malice' (1928). Cf. E. M. Forster, 'Miss Austen and Jane Austen,' *TLS* (10 November 1932), 821–822, reprinted together with two other Jane Austen reviews in *Abinger Harvest* (New York, 1936), 140–156; and Harold Nicolson, untitled review, *New Statesman and Nation* (26 Nov. 1932), 659. Chapman's response to this criticism is in Chapman: 1948, 90–120. Also see: R. W. Chapman, 'Jane Austen: A Reply to Mr Garrod,' *Essays by Divers Hands* (London, 1931); and Robert Alan Donovan, 'The Mind of Jane Austen,' in Weinsheimer: 1975, 109–127.

14   There are in fact a number of literary references scattered through the letters, though nothing more substantial than a passing comment. See: Chapman's appendix 'Authors, Books, Plays' in his edition of the letters (2nd edn, Jane Austen: 1952).

15   This is the central thesis of Litz: 1965.

16   Lodge: 1966, 113.

17   Cf. Horst Geckeler, *Strukturelle Semantik und Wortfeldtheorie* (Munich, 1971), 97–100.

18   Louis Hjelmslev, *Prolegomena to a Theory of Language*, trans., Francis J. Whitfield (2nd edn, Madison, 1963), 45.

19   The aim of this research is the construction of an operationally and materially adequate model for the specification of semantic fields, if not for the specification of the structural relations of the vocabulary as a whole. The formal criteria and the problematics relating to the construction of such a model need not be gone into for present purposes, since it is the fundamental assumptions rather than the analytical tools of Semantic Field Theory which are relevant to the analysis of the literary text. Therefore, in what follows

I only touch on the various directions in which Semantic Field Theory has developed and the internecine controversies that have been a part of this research. For an account of the origins and development of Semantic Field Theory, see: Suzanne Öhman, *Wortinhalt und Weltbild: Vergleichende und methodologische Studien zu Bedeutungslehre und Wortfeldtheorie* (Stockholm, 1951), 72–89; Stephen Ullmann, *The Principles of Semantics* (2nd edn, Oxford, 1957), 152–170; S. Ullmann, *Semantics: An Introduction to the Science of Meaning* (Oxford, 1962), 238–248; Els Oksaar, *Semantische Studien im Sinnbereich der Schnelligkeit* (Stockholm, 1958), 13–20; Pierre Guiraud, *La sémantique* (3rd edn, Paris, 1962), 68–86; Geckeler: 1971; and John Lyons, *Semantics* (Cambridge, 1977), I, 250–269.

20 Trier first set forth his theory in *Der Deutsche Wortschatz im Sinnbezirk des Verstandes. Die Geschichte eines sprachlichen Feldes, I: Von den Anfängen bis zum Beginn des 13. Jh.* (Heidelberg, 1931). Trier's theoretical position has been most actively supported by L. Weisgerber. See, e.g., *Grundzüge der inhaltbezogenen Grammatik* (3rd edn, Düsseldorf, 1962) and *Die sprachliche Gestaltung der Welt* (3rd edn, Düsseldorf, 1962).

21 See: Geckeler: 1971, 84–100.

22 'La notion de champ linguistique, défine par Trier, constitue la grand révolution de la sémantique moderne.' Guiraud: 1962, 73.

23 Cf. Walter Porzig, 'Wesenhafte Bedeutungsbeziehungen,' *Beiträge zur deutschen Sprache und Literatur* 58 (1934), 70–97.

24 Cf. Öhman: 1951, 82; and Helmut Gipper, 'Der Inhalt des Wortes und die Gliederung des Wortschatz,' *Duden Grammatik der deutschen Gegenwartssprache* (3rd edn, Mannheim, 1973), 415–473.

25 Cf. Walter Porzig, *Das Wunder der Sprache* (5th edn, Bern, 1971), 117–135.

26 A. Jolles, 'Antike Bedeutungsfelder,' *Beiträge zur deutschen Sprache und Literatur* 58 (1934), 97–109.

27 G. Ipsen, 'Der neue Sprachbegriff,' *Zeitschrift für Deutschkunde* 46 (1932), 1–18.

28 Charles Bally, 'L'Arbitraire du signe,' *Le Français Moderne* 8 (1940), 193–206.

29 Ullmann: 1962, 245.

30 The field of a word is formed by an intricate network of associations, some based on similarity, others on contiguity, some arising between the senses, others between names, others again between both. As a consequence, some of the associations are bound to be subjective, though the most central ones will be largely the same for most speakers (Ullmann: 1962, 240).

31 On the relationship between language and the system of culture in which it functions, see: Yu. M. Lotman and B. A. Uspensky, 'On the Semiotic Mechanism of Culture,' *New Literary History* IX (1978) 2, 211–232; and, in the same issue of *NLH*, Yu. M. Lotman and A. M. Piatigorsky, 'Text and Function,' 233–244.

32 The usual translation is of course 'associative field', but 'semantic field' is less cumbersome, though Bally would have termed what Trier and Porzig investigate the 'champ sémantique'.

33 Cf. Dell H. Hymes, 'Phonological Aspects of Style: Some English Sonnets,' *Style in Language*, ed., Thomas A. Sebeok (Cambridge, Mass., 1960), 109–131.

34 See below: 228–235.

35 This is a paraphrase of Lyons's restatement of Firth's view of *meaning*. Lyons: 1977, II, 607; cf. J. R. Firth, *Papers in Linguistics, 1934–1951* (London, 1957), 225.

36 There is of course a second context, namely, the one defined by the coordinates author-text-reader.

37 Whereas Trier and his followers are concerned with the lexical meaning of a word within the system of language; Matoré, like Bally, is interested in the context of language use. Georges Matoré published an example of how his theory might be applied two years before he brought out a description of the method itself. See: *Le Vocabulaire et la Société sous Louis-Philippe* (Geneva, 1951); and *La Méthode en lexicologie: Domaine français* (2nd edn, Paris, 1972; org., 1953).

38 Matoré: 1972, 65.

39 Matoré: 1972, 68.

40 Cf. Phillips: 1970, 17.

41 Austen: 1952, 142.

42 Austen: 1952, 139.

43 Leonard has noted that from 1750 to 1800 more than two hundred titles on grammar, rhetoric, etc. were published; whereas, in the first half of the century, fewer than fifty were

brought out. See: S. A. Leonard, *The Doctrine of Correctness in English Usage 1700–1800* (New York, 1962), 12.

44 In the following examples, the italics are mine.

45 In the following examples, the italics are mine.

46 The reasons behind Elizabeth's rejection are more complex than she is willing to admit at the time. Her refusal to allow herself to be tempted by Darcy's material wealth stems in part from her pride.

47 Austen: 1952, 483.

48 For further comment on this 'dangerous age', see: 34–35.

49 The search for correspondences between Jane Austen's life and fiction—a diversion which was already enjoyed in her lifetime by those who knew her—is of considerably less interest than it might be with an author such as James Joyce. Whatever correspondences may exist, have been so transformed as to make a knowledge of their origin impossible to prove and of negligible critical interest. Cf. Austen-Leigh: 1965, 373–376; and Chapman: 1948, 125–129.

50 Cf. Raymond Williams, *The Country and the City* (New York, 1973), 112–119.

51 This is the line of interpretation taken, for example, by Schorer (1952, 1959, 1963); also see the other references given in n. 2 of this chapter.

52 Cf. Duckworth: 1971, 27–30.

53 Russian translations of Jane Austen's novels began appearing in the Soviet Union in 1967. For a criticism of the first of these translations [*Gordost' i predubeždenie* (*Pride and Prejudice*) (Moscow, 1967)], see: Andrew Wright, 'Jane Austen Abroad,' in Halperin: 1975, 298–317, esp., 309–311.

54 The phrase 'Marxist before Marx' occurs in Daiches: 1948, 294; the opinion expressed takes on various forms in the criticism of L. Woolf: 1942; Schorer: 1952, 1959, 1963; Williams: 1973; van Ghent: 1961; and Arnold Kettle, *An Introduction to the English Novel* (New York, 1960, org., 1951).

55 Butler: 1975, 2.

56 Harold J. Harris develops this point in 'A Note on Snobbishness in *Emma*,' *Ball State Teachers College Forum* 5 (1964), 55–57.

57 Cf. Schorer: 1952.

58 Cecil: 1935, 33.

59   Cf. Williams: 1973, 113–114.

60   Two of Jane Austen's brothers, Charles and Francis, became admirals in the navy, and two other brothers, James and Henry, followed their father's example and went into the clergy.

61   Schorer: 1952; cf. Schorer: 1959, 1963; and van Ghent: 1961. Schorer's interpretation (and by implication that of van Ghent, who follows Schorer) has been challenged by Babb and Duckworth, among others. Babb points out that Schorer sees metaphors for finance, banking, etc. where they do not necessarily exist. See: Babb: 1962, 239; and Duckworth: 1971, 29–31.

62   Cf. Mary Crawford's comments in the scene at Sotherton, discussed in the first chapter: 29–35.

63   This information is recorded by Jane Austen's nephew in his biography of the author. Jane Austen 'took a kind of parental interest in the beings whom she had created, and did not dismiss them from her thoughts when she had finished her last chapter.' Austen-Leigh: 1965, 375–376.

64   There are some significant exceptions to this generalization, most notably, Whately and Simpson's critical assessments of the author (see: Richard Whately's unsigned review of *Northanger Abbey* and *Persuasion, Quarterly Review* XXIV (1821), 352–376, reprinted in Southam: 1968, 87–105; and Simpson: 1968 [1870]), but among Jane Austen's nineteenth-century readers the view seems to have been wide-spread. In the course of the nineteenth century, the implied comparison with such novels as Robert Plumer Ward's *Tremaine, or the Man of Refinement* (1825), Thomas Henry Lister's *Granby* (1826), Benjamin Disraeli's *Vivian Grey* (1826), and Edward Bulwer-Lytton's *Pelham, or the Adventures of a Gentleman* loses its relevance (cf. M. W. Rosa, *The Silver Fork School* (New York, 1936)), but this line of interpretation persists. As late as 1915, Léonie Villard takes this view in *Jane Austen: sa Vie, son Oeuvre* (Lyon, 1915).

65   This list is suggestive, not exhaustive, though the most important words in this field are given. A few words have been omitted, because their place in the semantic field of moral values is at least as significant as it is in this field: *elegance, propriety, manners,* and *decorum.* The two inter-related meanings of these words will be dealt with below:

Jane Nardin is wrong when she claims that the word *elegance* refers only to social conventions (Nardin: 1973, 12). The moral and social significance of this word are treated on 165–180. Nardin's study of *propriety* in Jane Austen's fiction is of general relevance to the present examination of the vocabulary used to designate social and moral values.

66 See: 131.

67 Cf. Phillips: 1970, 25.

68 Jane Austen's use of *candour* has received considerable attention in the secondary literature; see, e.g., Phillips, Page, and Tave. Chapman began the discussion by pointing out that Jane Austen never uses the word in its modern sense (cf. Chapman's appendix 'Miss Austen's English' in his edition of *Sense and Sensibility* (3rd edn, Oxford, 1965), 388–421). This is not quite correct. Exceptions have been noted (cf. Phillips: 1970, 27; and Norman Page, *The Language of Jane Austen* (Oxford, 1972). Tave discusses *true* and *false candour*; the latter refers to the affectation of *candour* (Stuart M. Tave, *Some Words of Jane Austen* (Chicago, 1973), 86–89.

69 For a discussion of this scene, see: 65–66.

70 Cf. discussion of this scene in Chapter II, 81–82.

71 Cf. Lascelles' observation: 'To us Jane Austen appears like one who inherits a prosperous and well-ordered estate—the heritage of a prose style in which neither generalization nor abstraction need signify vagueness, because there was a close enough agreement as to the scope and significance of such terms' (Lascelles: 1963, 107).

72 Babb carries this point a little further when he writes that in Jane Austen abstract 'concepts are the real actors. She often handles these groups of nouns as if they need only step on the stage in order to convince the audience, but we must never doubt their power on that account. For conceptual terms of this sort gain a kind of life of their own in that they seem to universalize whatever aspects of experience they name, treating them less as parts of a single configuration—the way the individual would encounter them in reality—than as absolutes. . . . Any page of the novels will witness the supreme role these terms play: enunciating the general principles that underlie the individual variety, they embody enduring values' (Babb: 1962, 9).

73 Cf. the comments on Whately and Jane Austen's reception

on 163–164. The notion of a new development in fiction Whately takes over from Walter Scott's unsigned review of *Emma* in the *Quarterly Review* XIV (October 1815), 188–201, reprinted in Southam: 1968, 58–69. See: Whately: 1968 [1821].

74 In the decade prior to the appearance of the *Memoir*, Tennyson 'spoke of Jane Austen... as next to Shakespeare!' and went on to thank 'God Almighty that he knew nothing of Jane Austen, and that there were no letters preserved either of Shakespeare's or of Jane Austen's, that they had not been ripped open like pigs' (cited in Watt: 1963, 6). The most important immediate critical response to the biography of Jane Austen was Richard Simpson's (1968 [1870]); for others see: Southam: 1968, 215–240.

75 B. C. Southam, 'Introduction,' in Southam: 1968, 1–33, quotation from 21.

76 Mark Twain's various vituperative remarks on Jane Austen are discussed by Sydney J. Krause in *Mark Twain as Critic* (Baltimore, 1967), esp., 103, 123, and 269. Also see: Watt: 1963, 6–7.

77 Cecil: 1935.

78 Trilling: 1959. Cf. Trilling: 1957, 1976, and 'A Portrait of Western Man,' *Listener* (11 June 1953), 969–971.

79 Among the more important the following should be mentioned: Schorer: 1963; W. R. Martin, 'Sensibility and Sense: a Reading of *Persuasion*,' *English Studies in Africa* 3 (1960), 119–130; Dawes Chillman, 'Miss Morland's Mind,' *South Dakota Review* 1 (December 1963); Ian Watt, 'On *Sense and Sensibility*,' in Watt: 1963, 41–51; Everett Zimmerman, 'Pride and Prejudice in *Pride and Prejudice*,' *Nineteenth-Century Fiction* 23 (1968), 64–73; Ann Banfield, 'The Moral Landscape in *Mansfield Park*,' *ARIEL: A Review of International English Literature* 2 (October 1971), 30–44; Joel Weinsheimer, 'Chance and the Hierarchy of Marriages in *Pride and Prejudice*,' *Journal of English Literary History* 39 (1972), 404–419; K. K. Collins, 'Mrs Smith and the Morality of *Persuasion*,' *Nineteenth-Century Fiction* 30 (1975), 383–397; and Susan Morgan, 'Polite Lies: The Veiled Heroine of *Sense and Sensibility*,' *Nineteenth-Century Fiction* 31 (1976), 188–205.

80 Page and Lerner have come to conclusions which differ from mine (cf. Page: 1972, 88–89; and Laurence Lerner,

    The Truth-tellers: Jane Austen, George Eliot, D. H. Lawrence (New York, 1967), esp., 23–28).

81 Cf. A. E. H. Tucker, 'Religion in Jane Austen's Novels,' *Theology* 55 (1952), 260–265.

82 The one obvious exception is the question of Edmund's ordination in *Mansfield Park*.

83 Whately: 1968, 95.

84 This translation from Hegel occurs in Trilling: 1959, 128.

85 Butler makes this point (1975, 189).

86 Cf. Butler: 1975, 292–299.

87 See: 213.

88 The words in parentheses are approximate synonyms.

89 The definitions are from the *O.E.D.* as cited in Nardin: 1973, 13.

90 Cf. William Empson, *The Structure of Complex Words* (London, 1977, org., 1951), 250–269; C. S. Lewis, *Studies in Words* (2nd edn, Cambridge, 1967), 133–164; Susie I. Tucker, *Protean Shape: A Study in Eighteenth-Century Vocabulary* (London, 1967), 249–251; and Phillips: 1970, 37–40. Also see the treatment of these concepts in the studies of *Sense and Sensibility* by Watt: 1963, 41–51; Tave: 1973, 74–115; and Everett Zimmerman, 'Admiring Pope no more than is proper: *Sense and Sensibility*,' in Halperin: 1975, 112–122.

91 Zimmerman: 1975, 113. Cf. Lewis: 1967, 163–164.

92 Here and in what follows I am summarizing a point made in Watt: 1963, 44–45.

93 Cf. R. S. Crane, 'Suggestions Towards a Genealogy of the "Man of Feeling",' *A Journal of English Literary History* 1 (1934), 205–230, reprinted in *Henry Fielding und der englische Roman des 18. Jahrhunderts*, ed., Wolfgang Iser (Darmstadt, 1972), 319–347.

94 Watt: 1963, 44 (my italics).

95 Watt: 1963, 44 (my italics).

96 Another consequence was manifest in Rousseau's work, but there is no evidence that Jane Austen read him, though some parallels have been noted between her fiction and *Julie, ou la Nouvelle Héloïse* (1761) (cf. Bradbrook: 1966, 121).

97 For her use of *sense* and *sensibility* in the *Juvenilia*, see: Tave: 1973, 74–76.

98 Henry Crawford's name could be added to the list, for he

too demonstrates a *false sensibility*; however, Jane Austen focuses on other aspects of his character, and does not make this particular weakness an object of her irony. In discussing Henry's character with Fanny, Edmund says, 'Crawford's *feelings*, I am ready to acknowledge, have hitherto been too much his guides' (*MP* 347).

99   Tave: 1973, 76–77.

100   Lodge discusses the significance of the word *judgment* and the words formally related to *judgment* (*judge, judicious*, etc.) in Lodge: 1966, 104–107.

101   The context of this quotation is cited on: 37.

102   The development of the relationship between Elizabeth and Darcy is dealt with in Chapter II, 93–99.

103   Edmund's use of 'nice' recalls Henry Tilney's definition (cf. 184–185).

104   For a discussion of Emma's reaction, see: 30–31.

105   Jane Austen sometimes uses the word 'serious' in the sense of 'religious'. Cf. 'She has never been taught to think on serious subjects' (*PP* 300); and Edmund's remarks in the chapel, cited in Chapter I, 15–17.

106   Cf. Page: 1970, 66.

107   The definition is from Johnson's dictionary as cited in Tave: 1973, 222.

108   Cf. Kettle: 1960, 96; and Tave: 1973, 222–228.

109   *E* 273. Context cited on: 131.

110   *SS* 237. Context cited on: 131.

111   Cf. the comments on *candour* in n. 68 of this chapter.

112   The context of this phrase is cited in Chapter II, 80.

112   The context of this phrase is cited in Chapter II, 80. Also see: 162.

CHAPTER V: THE DISTANCE BETWEEN THE REAL AND TECHNICAL
POINTS OF VIEW

1   Austen: 1952, 298.

Bibliography

TEXTS

E   Jane Austen, *Emma*, ed., Ronald Blythe (Harmonds-
    worth, 1966)
        *Jane Austen's Letters to her Sister Cassandra and
    Others*, ed., R. W. Chapman (2nd edn, Oxford, 1952)
MP   *Mansfield Park*, ed., Tony Tanner (Harmonds-
    worth, 1966)
NA   *Northanger Abbey*, ed., Anne Henry Ehrenpreis
    (Harmondsworth, 1972)
P   *Persuasion* with *A Memoir of Jane Austen* (by J. E.
    Austen-Leigh), ed., D. W. Harding (Harmonds-
    worth, 1965)
PP   *Pride and Prejudice*, ed., Tony Tanner (Har-
    mondsworth, 1972)
SS   *Sense and Sensibility*, ed., Tony Tanner (Har-
    mondsworth, 1969)
        The Novels of Jane Austen, ed., R. W. Chapman,
    5 vols (3rd edn, London, 1965)

WORKS REFERRED TO IN THE TEXT

Aldridge, John W., ed., *Critiques and Essays on Modern Fiction 1920–1951* (New York, 1952)
Amis, Kingsley, 'What Became of Jane Austen?' in Watt:
1963, 141–143
Austen-Leigh, J. E., *A Memoir of Jane Austen* (Harmondsworth, 1965)
Babb, Howard S., *Jane Austen's Novels: The Fabric of Dialogue* (Columbus, 1962)

Bally, Charles, 'L'Arbitraire du signe,' *Le Français Moderne*
8 (1940), 193–206

Banfield, Ann, 'The Moral Landscape of *Mansfield Park*,'
ARIEL: A Review of International English Literature 2
(October 1971), 30–44

Barthes, Roland, *Le Degré zéro de l'écriture* (Paris, 1953)

Booth, Wayne C., *The Rhetoric of Fiction* (Chicago, 1961)
'*The Rhetoric of Fiction* and the Poetics of Fiction,'
in Spilka: 1977, 77–89
A Rhetoric of Irony (Chicago, 1974)

Bradbrook, Frank W., *Jane Austen and her Predecessors*
(Cambridge, 1966)

Bradley, A. C., 'Jane Austen,' *Essays and Studies by Members
of the English Association* 11 (Oxford, 1911), 7–36

Brower, Reuben A., 'Light and Bright and Sparkling: Irony
and Fiction in *Pride and Prejudice*,' in Watt: 1963, 62–75

Brown, Lloyd W., *Bits of Ivory: Narrative Techniques in
Jane Austen's Fiction* (Baton Rouge, 1973)
'The Comic Conclusion in Jane Austen's Novels,'
PMLA 84 (1969), 1582–1587

Burlin, Katrin Ristkok, '"The Pen of the Contriver": The
Four Fictions of *Northanger Abbey*,' in Halperin: 1975,
89–111

Bush, Douglas, *Jane Austen* (London, 1975)

Butler, Marilyn, *Jane Austen and the War of Ideas* (Oxford,
1975)

Cecil, Lord David, *Jane Austen: The Leslie Stephen Lecture*
(Cambridge, 1935)

Chapman, R. W., *Jane Austen: A Critical Bibliography*
(2nd edn, Oxford, 1955)
'Jane Austen: A Reply to Mr Garrod,' *Essays by Diverse
Hands* (London, 1931)
Jane Austen: Facts and Problems (Oxford, 1948)

Chatman, Seymour, *Story and Discourse: Narrative Structures in Fiction and Film* (Ithaca, 1978)

Chillman, Dawes, 'Miss Morland's Mind,' *South Dakota
Review* 1 December 1963) 37–47

Collins, K. K., 'Mrs Smith and the Morality of *Persuasion*,'
Nineteenth-Century Fiction 30 (1975), 383–397

Cook, Albert, *The Meaning of Fiction* (Detroit, 1960)

Craik, W. A., *Jane Austen: The Six Novels* (New York, 1965)

Crane, R. S., 'Suggestions Toward a Genealogy of the "Man of Feeling",' in Iser: 1972, 319–347

Daiches, David, 'Jane Austen, Karl Marx and the Aristocratic Dance,' *American Scholar* 17 (1948), 289–296

Donovan, Robert Alan, 'The Mind of Jane Austen,' in Weinsheimer: 1975, 109–127

Duckworth, Alistair M., *The Improvement of the Estate: A Study of Jane Austen's Novels* (Baltimore, 1971)

Eco, Umberto, *The Role of the Reader* (Bloomington, 1979)

Emden, Cecil S., 'The Composition of *Northanger Abbey*,' *Review of English Studies* XIX (August 1968), 279–287

Empson, William, *The Structure of Complex Words* (3rd edn, London, 1977; org., 1951)

Farrer, Reginald, 'Jane Austen,' *Quarterly Review* CCXXVIII (1917), 1–30

Firth, J. R., *Papers in Linguistics, 1934–1951* (London, 1957)

Fish, Stanley E., 'Literature in the Reader: Affective Stylistics,' *New Literary History* 2 (1970), 123–162

Fleishman, Avrom, *A Reading of Mansfield Park: An Essay in Critical Synthesis* (Minneapolis, 1967)

'The State of the Art: Recent Jane Austen Criticism,' *Modern Language Quarterly* 37 (1976), 281–289

Forster, E. M., *Abinger Harvest* (New York, 1936)

Aspects of the Novel (New York, 1954)

Fowler, Roger, *Linguistics and the Novel* (London, 1977)

Garrod, H. W., 'Jane Austen: A Depreciation,' *Essays by Diverse Hands* (London, 1928), 21–40

Geckeler, Horst, *Strukturelle Semantik und Wortfeldtheorie* (Munich, 1971)

Gipper, Helmut, 'Der Inhalt des Wortes und die Gliederung des Wortschatz,' *Duden Grammatik der deutschen Gegenwartssprache* (3rd edn, Mannheim, 1973), 415–473

Göller, Karl Heinz, *Romance und Novel* (Regensburg, 1972)

Gorer, Geoffrey, 'The Myth in Jane Austen,' *American Imago* II (1941), 197–204

Guiraud, Pierre, *La sémantique* (3rd edn, Paris, 1962)

Halperin, John, ed., *Jane Austen: Bicentenary Essays* (Cambridge, 1975)

Harding, D. W., 'Jane Austen and Moral Judgement,' *From Blake to Byron*, ed., Boris Ford (Harmondsworth, 1957), 51–57

    'Regulated Hatred: An Aspect of the Work of Jane Austen,' in Watt: 1963, 166–179

Harris, Harold J. 'A note on Snobbishness in *Emma*,' *Ball State Teachers College Forum* 5 (1964), 55–57

Hjelmslev, Louis, *Prolegomena to a Theory of Language*, trans., Francis J. Whitfield (2nd edn, Madison, 1963)

Hymes, Dell H., 'Phonological Aspects of Style: Some English Sonnets,' *Style in Language*, ed., Thomas A. Sebeok (Cambridge, Mass., 1960), 109–131

Ingarden, Roman, *Das literarische Kunstwerk* (2nd edn, Tübingen, 1960)

    Studia z estetyki III (Warsaw, 1970)

Ipsen, G., 'Der neue Sprachbegriff,' *Zeitschrift für Deutschkunde* 46 (1932), 1–18

Iser, Wolfgang, *Der Akt des Lesens* (Munich, 1976), English translation: *The Act of Reading: A Theory of Aesthetic Response* (Baltimore, 1978)

    ed., *Henry Fielding und der englische Roman des 18. Jahrhunderts* (Darmstadt, 1972)

    Der implizite Leser: Kommunikationsformen des Romans von Bunyan bis Beckett (Munich, 1972)

    'Im Lichte der Kritik,' in Warning: 1975, 325–342

James, Henry, *The Art of the Novel*, ed., R. B. Blackmur (London, 1962)

    The Future of the Novel: Essays on the Art of Fiction, ed., Leon Edel (New York, 1956)

    'The Novels of George Eliot,' *Atlantic Monthly* (October 1866), 485

Jauss, Hans Robert, 'Zur Fortsetzung des Dialogs zwischen "bürgerlicher" und "materialistischer" Rezeptionsästhetik,' in Warning: 1975, 343–352

Jolles, A., 'Antike Bedeutungsfelder,' *Beiträge zur deutschen Sprache und Literatur* 58 (1934), 97–109

Kettle, Arnold, *An Introduction to the English Novel* (New York, 1960), 2 vols

Krause, Sydney J., *Mark Twain as Critic* (Baltimore, 1967)

Kroeber, Karl, *Styles in Fictional Structure: The Art of Jane Austen, Charlotte Brontë, George Eliot* (Princeton, 1971)

    'Subverting a Hypocrite Lecteur,' in Weinsheimer: 1975, 33–45

Lascelles, Mary, *Jane Austen and her Art* (London, 1963)

Leavis, F. R., *The Great Tradition: George Eliot, Henry James, Joseph Conrad* (Harmondsworth, 1967)

Leonard, S. A., *The Doctrine of Correctness in English Usage 1700–1800* (New York, 1962)

Lerner, Laurence, *The Truthtellers: Jane Austen, George Eliot, D. H. Lawrence* (New York, 1967)

Levin, Samuel R., 'Internal and External Deviation in Poetry,' *Word* 21 (1965), 225–237

Lewis, C. S., *Studies in Words* (2nd edn, Cambridge, 1967)

Link, Frederick M., 'Jane Austen, Mr Mudrick and Critical Monism,' *Boston University Studies in English* 3 (1957)

Litz, A. Walton, *Jane Austen: A Study of her Artistic Development* (New York, 1965)

    '*Persuasion*: Forms of Estrangement,' in Halperin: 1975, 221–232

Lodge, David, *Language of Fiction: Essays in Criticism and Verbal Analysis of the English Novel* (New York, 1966)

Lotman, Yu. M. and A. M. Piatigorsky, 'Text and Function,' *New Literary History* IX (1978), 2, 233–244

Lotman, Yu. M. and B. A. Uspensky, 'On the Semiotic Mechanism of Culture,' *New Literary History* IX (1978), 2, 211–232

Lubbock, Percy, *The Craft of Fiction* (London, 1954; org., 1921)

Lyons, John, *Semantics* (Cambridge, 1977), 2 vols

Markiewicz, 'Places of Indeterminacy in a Literary Work,' *Roman Ingarden and Contemporary Polish Aesthetics*, eds, Piotr Graff and Sław Krzemień-Ojak (Warsaw, 1975), 159–171

Markus, Manfred, *Moderne Erzählperspektive in den Werken des Gawain-Autors* (Nürnberg, 1971)

Martin, W. R., 'Sensibility and Sense: A Reading of *Persuasion*,' *English Studies in Africa* 3 (1960), 113–130

Matoré, Georges, *La Méthode en lexicologie: Domaine français* (2nd edn, Paris, 1972; org., 1953)
    Le Vocabulaire et la Société sous Louis-Philippe (Geneva, 1951)

McKillop, Alan D., 'Critical Realism in *Northanger Abbey*,' in Watt: 1963, 52–61

Moler, Kenneth L., *Jane Austen's Art of Allusion* (Lincoln, 1968)

Morahan, Richard Edward, 'Jane Austen's Endings,' (Chapter III of his dissertation) *DAI* 32: 3318A–3319A (Rutgers)

Morgen, Susan, 'Polite Lies: The Veiled Heroine of *Sense and Sensibility*,' *Nineteenth-Century Fiction* 31 (1976), 188–205

Morrison, Kristen, 'James's and Lubbock's Differing Points of View,' *Nineteenth-Century Fiction* 16 (1961), 245–256

Mudrick, Marvin, *Jane Austen: Irony as Defense and Discovery* (Princeton, 1952)

Mukařovský, Jan, *Structure, Sign, Function*, trans., John Burbank and Peter Steiner (New Haven, 1978)
    The Word and Verbal Art, trans., John Burbank and Peter Steiner (New Haven, 1977)

Nardin, Jane, *Those Elegant Decorums: The Concept of Propriety in Jane Austen's Novels* (Albany, 1973)

Naumann, Manfred, et al., *Gesellschaft—Literatur—Lesen: Literaturrezeption in theoretischer Sicht* (Berlin, 1973)

Nicolson, Harold, Untitled review of R. W. Chapman's edition of Jane Austen's correspondence, *New Statesman and Nation* (26 November 1932), 629

Odmark, John, 'The Aesthetics of Reception' (unpub. MS, 1980)
    'Ingarden and the *Concretization* of the Literary Text,' *Proceedings of the Ninth Congress of the International Comparative Literature Association* (Innsbruck, forthcoming)
    'Style, Meaning and the Concept of Literary Compe-

tence,' *Proceedings of the Twelfth International Congress of Linguists* (Innsbruck, 1978), 666–668

Öhman, Suzanne, *Wortinhalt und Weltbild: Vergleichende und methodologische Studien zu Bedeutungslehre und Wortfeldtheorie* (Stockholm, 1951)

Oksaar, Els, *Semantische Studien im Sinnbereich der Schnelligkeit* (Stockholm, 1958)

Page, Norman, *The Language of Jane Austen* (Oxford, 1972)

Phillips, K. C., *Jane Austen's English* (London, 1970)

Porzig, Walter, 'Wesenhafte Bedeutungsbeziehungen,' *Beiträge zur deutschen Sprache und Literatur* 58 (1934), 70–97
  Das Wunder der Sprache (5th edn, Bern, 1971)

Preston, John, *The Created Self: The Reader's Role in Eighteenth-Century Fiction* (London, 1970)

Riffaterre, Michael, 'Criteria for Style Analysis,' *Word* 15 (1959), 154–174

Rosa, M. W., *The Silver Fork School* (New York, 1936)

Roth, Barry and Joel Weinsheimer, *An Annotated Bibliography of Jane Austen Studies 1952–1972* (Charlottesville, 1973)

Ryle, Gilbert, 'Jane Austen and the Moralists,' *Oxford Review* 1 (1966), 5–18

Schorer, Mark, 'Fiction and the "Analogical Matrix",' in Aldridge: 1952, 83–98
  'The Humiliation of Emma Woodhouse,' in Watt: 1963, 98–111
  'Jane Austen,' the introduction to Schorer's edition of *Pride and Prejudice* (New York, 1959)
  'Technique as Discovery,' *20th Century Literary Criticism*, ed., David Lodge (London, 1972), 387–400

Scott, Walter, Unsigned review of *Emma*, in Southam: 1968, 58–63

Shenfield, Margaret, 'Jane Austen's Point of View,' *Quarterly Review* 296 (1958), 238–306

Sherry, Norman, *Jane Austen* (London, 1966)

Simpson, Richard, Unsigned review of the *Memoir*, in Southam: 1968, 241–265

Southam, B. C., ed., *Jane Austen: The Critical Heritage* (London, 1968)

Spilka, Mark, ed., *Towards a Poetics of Fiction* (Bloomington, 1977)

Stanzel, Franz K., *Typische Formen des Romans* (Göttingen, 1964)

Stevenson, Lionel, *The English Novel: A Panorama* (Boston, 1960)

Stevick, Phillip, *The Chapter in Fiction: Theories of Narrative Division* (Syracuse, 1970)

Tave, Stuart M., *Some Words of Jane Austen* (Chicago, 1973)

Thomson, C. L., *Jane Austen: A Survey* (London, 1923)

Trier, Jost, *Der deutsche Wortschatz im Sinnbereich des Verstandes: Die Geschichte eines sprachlichen Feldes I: Von den Anfängen bis zum Beginn des 13. Jh.* (Heidelberg, 1931)

Trilling, Lionel, 'Emma,' *Encounter* 8 (1957), 43–59
  The Opposing Self (New York, 1959)
  'A Portrait of Western Man,' *Listener* (11 June 1953), 969–971
  'Why We Read Jane Austen,' *TLS* (5 March 1976), 250–252

Tucker, A. E. H., 'Religion in Jane Austen's Novels,' *Theology* 55 (1952), 260–265

Tucker, Susie, *Protean Shape: A Study in Eighteenth-Century Vocabulary* (London, 1967)

Ullmann, Stephen, *The Principles of Semantics* (2nd edn, Oxford, 1957)
  Semantics: An Introduction to the Science of Meaning (Oxford, 1962)

van Ghent, Dorothy, *The English Novel: Form and Function* (New York, 1961; org., 1953)

Villard, Léonie, *Jane Austen: Sa vie et son oeuvre* (Lyon, 1915)

Warning, Rainer, ed., *Rezeptionsästhetik* (Munich, 1975)

Watt, Ian, ed., *Jane Austen: A Collection of Critical Essays* (Englewood Cliffs, N.J., 1963)
  'On *Sense and Sensibility*,' in Watt: 1963, 41–51
  The Rise of the Novel (Berkeley, 1957)

Weimann, Robert, *Structure and Society in Literary History: Studies in the History and Theory of Historical Criticism* (Charlottesville, 1976)

Weinsheimer, Joel, 'Chance and the Hierarchy of Marriages in *Pride and Prejudice*,' *Journal of English Literary History* 39 (1972), 404–413
  ed., *Jane Austen Today* (Athens, Georgia, 1975)
Weisgerber, L., *Grundzüge der inhaltbezogenen Grammatik* (3rd edn, Düsseldorf, 1962)
  Die sprachliche Gestaltung der Welt (3rd edn, Düsseldorf, 1962)
Wellek, René and Austin Warren, *Theory of Literature* (3rd edn, New York, 1962)
Whately, Richard, Unsigned review of *Northanger Abbey* and *Persuasion*, in Southam: 1968, 87–105
Willey, Basil, *The Eighteenth Century Background: Studies on the Idea of Nature in the Thought of the Period* (London, 1940)
Williams, Raymond, *The Country and the City* (New York, 1973)
Wimsatt, W. K., *The Prose Style of Samuel Johnson* (Hamden, Conn., 1972)
Wolff, Erwin, 'Der intendierte Leser,' *Poetica* 4 (1971), 141ff.
Woolf, Leonard, 'The Economic Determination of Jane Austen,' *New Statesman and Nation* n.s. 24 (18 July 1942)
Woolf, Virginia, 'Jane Austen,' in Watt: 1963, 15–24
Wright, Andrew, 'Jane Austen Abroad,' in Halperin: 1975, 298–317
  Jane Austen's Novels: A Study in Structure (New York, 1953)
Zimmerman, Everett, 'Admiring Pope no more than is proper: *Sense and Sensibility*,' in Halperin: 1975, 112–122
  'Pride and Prejudice in *Pride and Prejudice*,' *Nineteenth-Century Fiction* 23 (1968), 64–73

Index of Fictional Characters

General Index